You Ask, God Answers

You Ask, God Answers

Vital Questions on Salvation

Erwin R. Gane

5685 Parsons Road, Wildersville, Tennessee 38388

Orion Publishing, Wildersville, TN 38388.

Copy edited by Paulette Hodges
Design and layout by Michael Prewitt

Printed in the United States of America.

ISBN 0-9659327-3-7

Dedicated to . . .

. . . my beloved wife Winsome, who for long years has patiently and lovingly encouraged me to speak and write the truths of God's Word. Not only did she read the manuscript for this book, offering helpful suggestions, but, more importantly, her life has consistently demonstrated the love and tender concern of the Lord Jesus Christ for every individual within the orbit of her influence.

Contents

Preface

Many Christians cherish religious ideas because they have been traditionally believed. It is not especially important to these people whether their views are supported by the Bible. As long as the church of which they are members accepts and promotes certain religious beliefs, they feel secure in espousing them. The authority for their ideas comes from popular, generally accepted belief. Often these traditional beliefs are directly or indirectly promoted by radio and television programs.

Some Christians cannot imagine that their denomination, whether Catholic or Protestant, could possibly be mistaken on any doctrinal issue. They regard the teachings of the church as authoritative because of the supposed knowledge, insight, inspiration, or infallibility of their religious leaders.

Many non-Christians embrace philosophies of life and afterlife based on the cultural, educational, and religious influences to which they have been exposed. If pressed for evidence supporting their particular ideas, they may appeal to great philosophical thinkers, or they may simply admit that they are guided by their own predilections in regard to ultimate reality.

This book is written for both Christians and non-Christians. It is addressed to the average reader not the scholar. Even so, I have endeavored to provide scholarly support for the beliefs this book promotes. The basic premise is that the Bible and the Bible only should be the rule for religious faith and practice. If the teachings of the Bible conflict with those of popular belief or traditional understanding, the Bible should be accepted and commonly-held teachings rejected or modified. If Christians would accept this principle, there would be hope of their coming together on the basis of a commonly accepted source of religious authority. If non-Christians would recognize that the Judeo-Christian Scriptures are the most authoritative source of religious truth, they would have the means of testing and modifying their philosophical ideas in accordance with genuine spiritual reality.

Why is Bible teaching so important and authoritative? Because it is God's revelation of Himself as the Creator and Ruler of the universe. The Bible depicts cosmic reality. It explains simply and authoritatively where we came from, why we are here, and where we are going. Why should you believe the Bible? Because it provides evidence that its ultimate Author is God. No other literature, no other religious book contains such internal evidence of inspiration as does the Bible. The only way to discover this evidence is to study the Bible for yourself. Give God a chance! Read, listen to His Word, allow Him to speak to you. Examine the prophetic evidence the Bible contains, and absorb the spiritual truths it reveals.

Where does the premise that the Bible only is the true source of faith and practice lead us? What religious concepts emerge from an objective, unbiased study of the biblical evidence? What popular religious ideas are exploded by the teachings of Scripture? The purpose of this book is not to facilitate your effort to explore your spiritual feelings. The purpose rather is to explore the objective spiritual realities revealed in the Bible, which then can become the basis of genuine, meaningful spiritual experience. If you can put aside your religious and philosophical biases long enough to look objectively at what the Bible really teaches, this book is intended for you.

The questions raised in this book are questions that relate to eternal salvation. Is it really true that people go to heaven when they die? Is it really true that there is only one God who manifests Himself in three Personalities? What is the basis of salvation? Can we have eternal life, even though we are subject to mortality and death? What does God expect of us in this life? Are there some rules that He wants us to obey? If so, what does obedience to these rules have to do with life beyond the grave? How does God decide who should have eternal life and who should not? What about the future? What scenario for future events does the Bible depict?

The ultimate question is that of the Philippian jailer who cried out in distress to the Apostle Paul and his companion, "Sirs, what must I do to be saved?" (Acts 16:30). To answer this question as the Bible does and to enter into the fellowship with God implied in the answer is the secret of true emotional peace and spiritual power in this life and the assurance of eternal life beyond the grave.

Note: Unless otherwise indicated, Bible quotations in this book are from the New Revised Standard Version.

Chapter 1
Do Mary and the Saints Hear and Answer Our Prayers?

Some years ago Oscar Cullmann, the well-known New Testament scholar, wrote a book entitled *Immortality of the Soul Or Resurrection of the Dead? The Witness of the New Testament.*[1] Cullmann argued that the Greek Philosophical concept of the immortality of the soul is incompatible with the New Testament teaching of the resurrection of the dead at the end of human history.

Cullmann wrote that Plato's book *Phaedo* has replaced 1 Corinthians 15. The teaching of the two documents is incompatible, despite attempts to conceal that fact. Cullmann disagrees with those who view the New Testament doctrine of the resurrection as in line with the mythological thought of the time in which the New Testament was written. He opposes the idea that the real truth underlying all New Testament teaching is the immortality of the soul. Cullmann argues, on the contrary, that the real message of the New Testament is the doctrine of the resurrection at the end of time. And this he recognizes to be thoroughly irreconcilable with the Greek concept of the immortality of the soul.

Cullmann wrote: "The question is here raised in its exegetical aspect. If we turn to the Christian aspect, I would venture to remind my critics that when they put in the forefront, as they do, the particular manner in which they *wish* themselves and their loved ones to survive, they are involuntarily giving grounds to the opponents of Christianity who constantly repeat that the faith of Christians is nothing more than the projection of their desires."[2]

Cullmann compared the death of Socrates, as described in Plato's *Phaedo*, with the death of Jesus, described by the Gospel writers.[3] Socrates welcomed death as the release of the immortal soul from the prison-house of the body. Jesus feared death as separation from His Father, and prayed that, if possible, He would not have to face it. Jesus death conquered death, the great enemy of the human race.

"He cannot obtain this victory by simply living on as an immortal soul, thus fundamentally *not* dying. He can conquer death only by actually dying, by betaking Himself to the sphere of death, the destroyer of life, to the sphere of 'nothingness', of abandonment by God. When one wishes to overcome someone else, one must enter his territory. Whoever wants to conquer death must die; he must really cease to live—not simply live on as an immortal soul, but die in body and soul, lose life itself, the most precious good which God has given us. For this reason the Evangelists, who none the less intended to present Jesus as the Son of God, have not tried to soften the terribleness of His thoroughly human death."[4]

The resurrection of Christ, Cullmann emphasized, involved "a new divine act of creation." "And this act of creation calls back to life not just a part of the man, but the whole man—all that God had created and death had annihilated."[5] Socrates and Plato did not think they needed a new act of creation, because the body which is bad should not live again, and the soul which is immortal never did die.

The Greek philosophers had an optimistic view of death. For them death was a liberation of the immortal soul to its natural sphere of existence. But for the New Testament authors death is the result of sin which destroyed God's perfect creation. Only by the resurrection at the end of history will this perfect creation be restored. Only then will believers who have been annihilated and subjected to the "sleep" of death be raised to live with Christ as immortal beings. Believers receive the gift of eternal life when they accept Jesus, and the temporary "sleep" of death does not destroy this gift. But they are not immortal until the second coming of Jesus.

Cullmann's book created a storm of protest from those who believe in the immortality of the soul. It was recognized that, if he were correct, one of the basic tenets of many world religions must be regarded as a myth. Most Christians, Protestant as well as Roman Catholic, accept the doctrine of the immortality of the soul as fundamental Bible teaching. The practical application of this doctrine is regarded as vital to the life of the churches. Mourners of dead loved ones are comforted by the assurance that their dear ones are now in heaven. The Roman Catholic teaching regarding purgatory depends on the doctrine of the immortality of the soul. The souls of the dead who are not yet purified of sin suffer in the fires of purgatory as a preparation for heaven. Thus the church has consistently encouraged Masses, indulgences, and public and private prayers on behalf of souls in purgatory. In fact, the idea that the payment of money to the church could release souls from purgatory was one of the issues that sparked the sixteenth-century Reformation.

It is popularly believed by Roman Catholics and many Protestants that the immortal souls of unbelievers go directly to hell where they will suffer eternal torment. Even though this teaching has turned many away from Christianity and the truth of God's love, it is believed to be squarely based on Scripture.

Appearances of Mary

The Roman Catholic exaltation of Mary and the saints is dependent upon the doctrine of the immortality of the soul. In recent years there has been a proliferation of appearances of Mary in various parts of the world. In their book *Thunder of Justice*, Ted and Maureen Flynn have documented many of these numerous appearances.[6] They assert that these many apparitions and locutions (verbal communications) are a wake-up call to the world which is about to be plunged into unprecedented turmoil. According to the Flynns, heaven granted Satan the twentieth century to do his worst against the Church. As a warning to humanity that the most massive destruction in history is about to occur, they say Mary is appearing in many lands. She offers warning, encouragement, and instruction. But only a remnant of the Church will survive.[7]

Father Stefano Gobbi is said to have received and to be currently receiving "detailed locutions" from Mary, as a result of which there has been established a Marian Movement of Priests with 55,000 members.[8] Ted and Maureen Flynn provide a brief summary of Marian apparitions since the sixteenth century.[9] There have been many more such appearances in the twentieth century than in any previous century. The most impressive of these appearances are those at Medjugorje in the former Yugoslavia. After a first appearance on June 24, 1981, Mary appeared often to six peasant children. In their adult life Mary's messages to them have continued. Mary's messages have been a plea for prayer, fasting, reconciliation with God and neighbor, conversion, and peace.[10] It is estimated that over fifteen million pilgrims have visited Medjugorje in a ten-year period.

When asked by the children what instruction she had for priests, Mary urged that they instruct everyone to pray the rosary. By this means they would overcome all the troubles that Satan is attempting to bring on the Catholic Church.[11]

All six of the children at Medjugorje were shown heaven and purgatory, and four of them were shown hell. They reported that more souls go to purgatory than to heaven or hell. In purgatory there are various levels in which souls exist; some levels are close to heaven and others are close to hell.[12]

The cover of *Newsweek*, August 25, 1997, had a picture of Mary and the caption, "The Meaning of Mary, A Struggle Over Her Role Grows Within the Church." The leading article reports that 40,383 petitions were shipped that week to the pope from a dozen countries, appealing to him to exercise his power of papal infallibility to proclaim that the Virgin Mary is "Co-Redemptrix, Mediatrix of all Graces and Advocate for the People of God."[13] In the past four years, 4,340,429 signatures have been sent to the pope from 157 countries supporting the doctrine.

If the pope makes such an "infallible" declaration, Catholics will be obliged to accept "that Mary participates in the redemption achieved by her son, that all graces that flow from the suffering and death of Jesus Christ are granted only through Mary's intercession with her son, and that all prayers and petitions from the faithful on earth must likewise flow through Mary, who then brings them to the attention of Jesus. This is what theologians call high Mariology, and it seems to contradict the basic New Testament belief that 'there is one God and one mediator between God and man, Christ Jesus' (1 Timothy 2:5). In place of the Holy Trinity, it would appear, there would be a kind of Holy Quartet, with Mary playing the multiple roles of daughter of the Father, mother of the Son and spouse of the Holy Spirit."[14]

Despite strong opposition from Protestant churches and considerable criticism of the proposed new dogma within the Roman Catholic Church, the pope is thought to favor it. "As the patron saint of Poland, Mary has always been especially important to this pope from Wadowice. He also credits her with saving his life during a 1981 assassination attempt. He has referred to her as 'Co-Redemptrix' at least five times, though never as a formal declaration of dogma. He has reflected on her role in more than 50 weekly addresses, often emphasizing her 'cooperation' in redemption."[15]

In the light of the pope's attitude and the strong support within the Roman Catholic Church for the proposed new dogma, it is not difficult to see why Oscar Cullmann's thesis would meet even more bitter opposition today than it did in 1958. If he were correct, and the concept of the immortality of the soul is not taught in the Bible, all this discussion concerning Mary's role as Co-Redemptrix and Mediatrix is totally irrelevant. If the Bible teaches what Cullmann says it teaches, Mary is in her grave waiting to be called forth on the resurrection morning. Mariology would then simply be an untruth despite its acceptance throughout centuries of church history and its enthusiastic propagation today.

But if the idea of the immortality of the soul is unscriptural, how do we explain the apparitions of Mary that have appeared in numerous places around the world? Are they real or imaginary? If they are real, what are they, and where do they come from?

New Age Philosophy

The basic premise of the New Age philosophy is the concept of the immortality of the soul. In his book *Deceived by the New Age,* Will Baron graphically describes how the new age "Master" Djwhal Khul appeared to him as a kingly being bathed in light.[16] This is the spirit being who is said to have dictated verbatim to Alice Bailey the contents of twenty-five volumes of metaphysical information.[17] These books, published between 1919 and 1949 provided a great deal of the doctrinal foundation for the current New Age movement. Djwhal Khul claims that he is a senior member of the Hierarchy of Masters.

"He maintains that he is a human being born more than 350 years ago in Tibet, where he was at one time the abbot of a Tibetan lamasery. He asserts that through the process of meditation and strict spiritual practices, and through the assistance of heavenly beings, he has so evolved his consciousness as to have reached a state of immortality in his current physical body. Hence his claimed ability to have lived for almost four centuries."[18]

Djwahl Khul teaches that the Hierarchy of Masters consists of human beings who have achieved immortality. Their leader, Lord Maitreya, has the title of "the Christ." Jesus and Buddha are senior-ranking members of the Hierarchy of Masters. The Hierarchy are said to be working for "the spiritual evolution of humanity on planet Earth in all its aspects: religious, political, technological, scientific, and cultural."[19]

Khul "emphasizes that Master Jesus is a man who evolved himself over successive incarnations and initiations until he became an immortal 'Son of God,' just as the other masters, such as the Buddha, also became 'Sons of God.'"[20]

The masters are able to assume spirit form or physical form whenever they choose. In spirit form they can visit any part of the planet. And they can appear as visible bodies of light or as physical bodies that can be touched like any human being.

The concept of reincarnation is one of the major tenets of the New Age movement. The idea is based squarely on the doctrine of the immortality of the soul. The doctrines of reincarnation and karma are borrowed from ancient Hindu teaching. The law of karma teaches that a person's good or bad behavior will have to be faced in future existences. Because it is impossible for people to do enough good in one lifetime to pay the debt of their bad deeds, they are obliged to go through as many reincarnations as may be necessary until their good deeds balance out their bad deeds.[21]

Alice Bailey wrote: "The immortality of the human soul, and the innate ability of the spiritual, inner man to work out his own salvation under the Law of Rebirth, in response to the Law of Cause and Effect, are the underlying factors governing all human conduct and all human aspiration. These two laws no man can evade. They condition him at all times until he has achieved the desire and the designed perfection and can manifest on earth as a rightly functioning son of God."[22]

Thus the prime teachings of the New Age movement are the immortality of the soul, reincarnation, and righteousness by human works.

Perhaps the most startling aspect of the New Age movement is its infiltration into the belief and practice of the Christian Church. Will Baron refers to Christian preachers whose biblical teaching is intermingled with New Age concepts.[23] He describes how the New Age center of which he was a member turned to Bible study and identified itself with Christian teaching.[24] Will became a "Christian" preacher.[25] He identified himself with Christian churches and was baptized as a Christian.[26] But the "Christian" teachings he espoused and taught were transformed by New Age concepts, so that their true biblical meaning was destroyed. He endeavored to introduce his Christian friends to New Age meditation techniques, so that their minds, like his, could be controlled and directed by spirit entities.[27] Then he was converted to true Christianity, and he turned away in horror and disgust from the New Age beliefs that had dominated his life.[28]

Will Baron writes: "In essence, I regard the New Age as a counterfeit system of religion devised by Satan to be an attractive alternative to Bible-based Christianity. Its ultimate goal is to lead the churches into a great apostasy in preparation for the appearance of the Antichrist, so that he will be accepted as the Messiah by both *Christians* and New Agers alike."

"As a New Age 'Christian,' I had read those biblical passages that warned against false prophets and teachings. But I never seriously considered that I was involved with them. The deception was possible because I did not believe that the *whole* Bible should be understood just exactly as it is written. Because of this, I was able to compromise and embrace false teachings while knowing that they contradicted plain Scripture."[29]

Appearances of Mary, appearances of New Age masters, appearances in spiritualistic seances of dead loved ones — are these phenomena real? Is it really Mary who is appearing in many place around the world? Are the New Age masters really immortal human beings? Do people's loved ones really appear to them and speak to them, or is there another explanation of these remarkable appearances? What answers to these questions can be found in the Bible?

Death Is a Sleep

In both Old and New Testaments death is represented as a sleep. As sleep is a state of unconsciousness, so is death.

In announcing to Moses that his time had come to die, the Lord said: "Behold, thou shalt sleep with thy fathers" (Deut. 31:16, KJV). The Hebrew verb used in the text is *shakab* that means "to sleep," "to lie down."[30] The same verb is used in Job 7:21, which the King James Version correctly translates, "For now shall I sleep in the dust; and thou shalt seek me in the morning, but I shall not be." Job 14:12 underlines the point: "Mortals lie down and do not rise again; until the heavens are no more, they will not awake or be roused out of their sleep." Emphasizing the resurrection at the end of time, Daniel wrote: "Many of those who sleep in the dust of the earth shall awake, some to everlasting life, and some to shame and everlasting contempt" (Dan. 12:2).

There was a resurrection of certain sleeping saints at the time of Jesus' death and resurrection: "The tombs also were opened, and many bodies of the saints who had fallen asleep were raised. After his resurrection they came out of the tombs and entered the holy city and appeared to many" (Matt. 27:52, 53). Verse 52 uses the Greek word *koimao,* that means "to sleep," "to fall asleep."[31] In describing the death of Lazarus to His disciples, Jesus clearly identified death with sleep. "He told them, 'Our friend Lazarus has fallen asleep, but I am going there to awaken him.' The disciples said to him, 'Lord, if he has fallen asleep, he will be all right.' Jesus, however, had been speaking about his death, but they thought that he was referring merely to sleep. Then Jesus told them plainly, 'Lazarus is dead'" (John 11:11-14). In describing Jairus' daughter who had died, Jesus said, "The child is not dead but sleeping" (Mark 5:39). When Stephen was stoned to death, "he fell asleep" (Acts 7:60, KJV). Referring to the resurrection of the dead at the end of human history, Paul wrote: "We shall not all sleep, but we shall all be changed" (1 Cor. 15:51, KJV).

Never do the Bible writers suggest that part of man sleeps at death while another part goes on living in a conscious state. Never do they even imply that death is not, like sleep, a state of unconsciousness. As Bible writers faced death, they did not expect to be conscious living beings again until, by a divine miracle of recreation, their existence was restored.

Right at the beginning of our study, we are impressed that the doctrine of the immortality of the soul is seriously open to question. We must test our initial impression by searching the Scriptures further.

What Is the *Spirit* in Mankind?

It is popularly believed that there is in humans an immortal, immaterial part that does not sleep when they die. The *spirit* is thought to go on living either in heaven or hell. Does the Bible teach this view?

What were the component parts of man given by God at creation? "And the Lord God formed man of the dust of the ground, and breathed into his nostrils the breath of life; and man became a living soul" (Gen. 2:7, KJV). The breath of life was the life principle or life force that gave life to the body and existence to the individual. When man dies the opposite process takes place. "When their breath departs, they return to the earth; on that very day their plans perish" (Ps. 146:4). "The dust returns to the earth as it was, and the breath returns to God who gave it" (Eccl. 12:7). The word "breath," or "spirit" in these verses is a translation of the Hebrew word *ruach*. The Greek equivalent is *pneuma*. Kittel's *Theological Dictionary of the New Testament* gives the meanings of the Hebrew word for "breath" or "spirit" (*ruach*):

1. "Breath of the Mouth . . . Ps. 33:6."
2. "Breath of Air, Wind. Soft breeze Job 4:15; 41:8."
3. "The Principle which Gives Life to the Body. . . . Gn. 6:17; 7:15."
4. "The Seat of the Emotions, Intellectual Functions and Attitude of Will. . . . 2 K. 19:7; Gn. 41:8; Da. 2:3."
5. "God gives vital force, the spirit of life Isa 42:5; Ez. 37:6 . . . He upholds it Job 10:12 . . . God takes away the spirit of life . . . Ps. 104:29."[32]

Never in Scripture is the *spirit* of a person said to survive the death of the body as an immortal, conscious entity. The breath or spirit is simply the life force implanted by God at creation and shared by every living thing, whether human or animal. "For the fate of humans and the fate of animals is the same; as one dies, so dies the other. They all have the same breath, and humans have no advantage over the animals; for all is vanity. All go to one place; all are from the dust, and all turn to dust again" (Eccl. 3:19, 20). This does not mean that in respect to intellect and the capacity to make moral choices humans have no advantage over the animals. It means that humans and animals have the same life force implanted by God and taken away when they die.

Some Bible interpreters try to use Ecclesiastes 12:7 to prove that the immortal spirits of good people go to heaven when they die. On the contrary, the text is simply referring to the opposite process to that which occurred at creation (Gen. 2:7). If the "spirit" or "breath" spoken of in this verse is a person's immortal soul, then the souls of *all* people, good and bad, must go to heaven when they die. But no one believes that the spirits of evil people go to heaven when they die. The text is not teaching that. It is telling us that the life force that God gives is taken back when a person dies. The doctrine of the immortality of the soul is not even implied.

Both the Old and New Testaments sometimes use the word *spirit* to refer to the mind of man, his capacity to reason, as well as his ability to feel and choose (see Dan. 2:1; 5:12; Matt. 26:41; Rom. 1:9 etc.). Such intellectual and emotional faculties never survive the death of the body. The spirit is not depicted in the Bible as the real self that goes on living after the body has died. In this sense, the spirit is the inner life of man that is totally dependent upon the existence of the body. As we shall see, the dead person has no further reasoning powers, or emotions, or powers of will. Dead persons are totally unconscious. Because the life force has been taken away, they cease to be living persons.

Our study of the breath of life ("spirit") contradicts the teaching that humans have within them an immortal soul that goes on living either in heaven or hell. Now we must look further to see if our conclusions are supported by other things the Bible says about the soul and the state of humans in death.

What is a *Soul?* Is it Immortal?

Did God create an immortal soul for man? Genesis 2:7 says that the body + the breath of life = "a living soul" (KJV). That implies that if the breath of life were withdrawn, the person would be a dead soul. If souls can die, they cannot be regarded as immortal, because immortality is the capacity never to die. What does the Bible teach on this question?

Can a living soul die? "The soul [Hebrew: *nephesh*] that sinneth, it shall die" (Eze. 18:4, KJV). "And every living soul [Greek: *psuche*] died in the sea" (Rev. 16:3, KJV). Writing of the Nazarite, Moses said, "All the days that he separateth himself unto the Lord he shall come at no dead body" (Num 6:6, KJV). The word translated "body" is the Hebrew word *nephesh* that means "soul."

Since souls can die, they are not immortal. When the breath of life is taken from individuals, they cease to be living souls. Now they are dead souls. And dead souls have no consciousness. Jesus said that eventually wicked souls will be destroyed in hell. "Fear him [God] who can destroy both soul and body in hell" (Matt. 10:28). That being so, the doctrine of an ever-burning hell cannot be true. The idea of eternal suffering for lost souls in hell depends on the doctrine of the immortality of the soul. If the soul can die, it is not immortal. And if God plans to destroy wicked mortal souls in hell, they cannot suffer for eternity.

The Hebrew word for *soul* is *nephesh*, and the Greek equivalent is *psuche*. The word *creature* is used to translate the Hebrew *nephesh* in the King James Version of Genesis 1:20, 21, 24, 30; 2:19; 9:10, 12, 15, 16. Animals are spoken of as creatures or souls. God made the animals living souls just as He made humans living souls. He formed the animals from the dust and breathed into their nostrils the breath of life, and they became living souls. Like man, when they die, they are dead souls.

The Bible never teaches the doctrine of the immortality of the soul. It says unequivocally that God "only hath immortality" (1 Tim. 6:16, KJV). In the comparison of God with mankind, only God is immortal. When a human body dies, that is the death of the soul.

Kittel's *Theological Dictionary of the New Testament* comments on the Hebrew word for *soul* (*nephesh*): The soul "has no existence apart from the body. Hence the best translation in many instances is 'person' comprised in corporeal reality. The person can be marked off and counted, Gn. 12:5; 46:18; Jos. 10:28; 11:11. Each individual is a . . . [*nephesh*] and when the texts speak of a single . . . [*nephesh*] for a totality, the totality is viewed as a single person, a 'corporate personality.' Hence . . . [*nephesh*] can denote what is most individual in human nature, namely the ego, and it can become a synonym for the personal pronoun, Gn. 27:25. . . ."[33]

The New Testament Greek word for soul, *psuche*, has meanings similar to those of the Old Testament word *nephesh*. It is often best translated by *life*. A human life is a *soul*. Mark 3:4 translates literally from the Greek: "And he says to them, 'Is it lawful to do good on the Sabbaths or to do harm (evil), to save a soul (life) or to kill?"[34] Mark 8:35 translates literally: "For whoever should wish to save his soul (life) will lose it; and whoever will lose his soul (life) for my sake and the gospel's will save it."[35]

Nowhere in the Scriptures is the *soul* spoken of as a disembodied immortal soul in heaven or hell. The word in both the Hebrew and the Greek may refer to the total personality or to a part of it. Sometimes the reference is to the spiritual self or the intellectual or emotional self. But these aspects of soul are not conceived as entities separate from the physical self. When the body dies so do the other faculties of the soul. What is preserved for believers is God's knowledge of their faithfulness and His undying assurance that they will have eternal life at the second coming of Jesus.

Do the Dead Have Consciousness of Any Kind?

The Bible answer is so simple and direct it is difficult to understand how anyone could have missed it. "The living know that they will die, but the dead know nothing; they have no more reward, and even the memory of them is lost. Their love and their hate and their envy have already perished; never again will they have any share in all that happens under the sun. . . . Whatever your hand finds to do, do with your might; for there is no work or thought or knowledge or wisdom in Sheol [the grave], to which you are going" (Eccl. 9:5, 6, 10).

The dead are not in heaven observing what is happening to their earthly loved ones. "Their children come to honor, and they do not know it; they are brought low, and it goes unnoticed" (Job 14:21).

The dead have no knowledge of God and no capacity to praise Him. "For in death there is no remembrance of you; in Sheol [the grave] who can give you praise?" (Ps. 6:5). "The dead do not praise the Lord, nor do any that go down into silence" (Ps. 115:17).

The Bible's clear teaching is that the dead know nothing and feel nothing. People who die do not go to heaven or hell, where they live on in a state of consciousness. They go to the grave where their bodies disintegrate because the life force has been removed. They are sleeping without any awareness of what is happening on earth or in heaven. They do not praise God because they cannot. If the good were in heaven right after death, wouldn't they praise the Lord? But the Bible says, "The dead do not praise the Lord" (Ps. 115:17).

The parable of the rich man and Lazarus (Luke 16:19-31) is often used as evidence of life in either heaven or hell immediately after death. In fact, the parable is simply designed to teach the danger of covetousness, with no concern to support the doctrine of the immortality of the soul. No one believes that the parable can be taken literally. In fact, if it is interpreted literally, it becomes an absurdity. For example, the beggar went to "Abraham's bosom" (Luke 16:22, KJV). Obviously this is a symbol. Abraham would have needed a very large chest to literally accommodate all the righteous dead. The rich man in hell spoke of Lazarus's finger and his own tongue (verse 24). But immortal soul advocates believe that the souls of the dead are disembodied. In this parable the dead have bodies. Who imagines that it is possible for the good in heaven to converse with the wicked in hell, and vice versa, as they do in this parable? The rich man wanted Lazarus to go to his living brothers and warn them (verses 27, 28). The only way that could happen, according to this story, would be if "one rose from the dead" (verse 31, KJV). That is quite different from the popular idea that dead souls can communicate with the living without a resurrection being necessary.

Jesus was using a popular fable as a sermon illustration. He was not teaching life immediately after death or the doctrine of the immortality of the soul. Josephus, the first-century Jewish historian, tells much the same fable in other words.[36] Jesus was illustrating the danger of covetousness.

The Bible truth of the mortality of the soul and the sleep of the dead takes the fear out of death. For centuries people have been taught that they will go immediately to a painful hell or a miserable purgatory unless they do what is right. The Bible certainly urges us to do right by faith in the Lord Jesus Christ. But it nowhere refers to hell as a place of consciousness for wicked souls after death. If the dead were in hell, suffering for long periods of time until the second coming of the Lord, we would have difficulty understanding how a God of love could bring such protracted suffering. "The dead know nothing" (Eccl. 9:5). Think of the misery the immortal souls of the dead would experience if they were in heaven looking down at the struggles and sufferings of their earthly loved ones. What a mercy it is that they are peacefully sleeping, waiting the call of the Lifegiver!

Where are the Dead?

The Bible clearly explains where the dead are not, as well as where they are. In his great sermon on the Day of Pentecost, the Apostle Peter explained that David's statement in Psalm 16 was a reference to the Messiah, not to David himself (Acts 2:24-33). David is dead and buried, Peter pointed out, and his sepulcher was there for everyone to see. Hence, when David wrote, "Thou wilt not leave my soul in hell, neither wilt thou suffer thine Holy One to see corruption" (verse 27, KJV), he was not referring to himself, but to the Messiah, Jesus Christ, who was crucified, but who has risen from the dead. Then Peter adds, "For David is not ascended into the heavens" (v. 34). Christ rose from the dead and ascended to heaven, but David remained in the grave where he saw corruption. David was a righteous man, a forgiven sinner, but he did not go to heaven when he died. In fact, the Bible nowhere teaches that believers in Christ go to heaven when they die. They sleep peacefully in their graves waiting for the resurrection morning at the second coming of Jesus.

Where are the dead? Job makes that very clear. "If a man die, shall he live again? all the days of my appointed time will I wait, till my change come" (Job 14:14, KJV). "If I wait, the grave is mine house: I have made my bed in the darkness. I have said to corruption, Thou art my father: to the worm, Thou art my mother, and my sister. And where is now my hope? as for my hope, who shall see it? They shall go down to the bars of the pit, when our rest together is in the dust" (Job 17:13-16, KJV). "For I know that my redeemer liveth, and that he shall stand at the latter day upon the earth: And though after my skin worms destroy this body, yet in my flesh shall I see God: Whom I shall see for myself, and mine eyes shall behold, and not another" (Job. 19:25-27, KJV).

Isaiah agreed with Job. "Thy dead men shall live, together with my dead body shall they arise. Awake and sing, ye that dwell in dust: for thy dew is as the dew of herbs, and the earth shall cast out the dead" (Isa. 26:19).

The dead are in the dust of the earth, resting in their graves, waiting for the great change that Jesus promised would come at the end of time. Death need have no fears for us. Since it is a state of unconsciousness, we rest sweetly until the call of the Lifegiver. The Bible truth is that death is a sleep, a state of unconsciousness, and sleep involves no suffering.

Will There Be a Resurrection of the Dead?

The ancient Sadducees denied it. Jesus and the apostles taught it. Jesus explained that there will be a resurrection of the righteous and a resurrection of the unrighteous. "Do not be astonished at this; for the hour is coming when all who are in their graves will hear his voice and will come out — those who have done good, to the resurrection of life, and those who have done evil, to the resurrection of condemnation" (John 5:28, 29; cf. Acts 24:15).

We know from Scripture that the resurrection of the righteous takes place at Jesus' second coming. In comforting the Thessalonian Christians who had lost their loved ones by death, Paul wrote: "For this we declare to you by the word of the Lord, that we who are alive, who are left until the coming of the Lord, will by no means precede those who have died. For the Lord himself, with a cry of command, with the archangel's call and with the sound of God's trumpet, will descend from heaven, and the dead in Christ will rise first. Then we who are alive, who are left, will be caught up in the clouds together with them to meet the Lord in the air; and so we will be with the Lord forever. Therefore encourage one another with these words" (1 Thess. 4:15-18).

The great resurrection chapter of the New Testament is 1 Corinthians, chapter 15. It teaches that everything depends on the resurrection of Christ from the dead. "For if the dead are not raised, then Christ has not been raised. If Christ has not been raised, your faith is futile and you are still in your sins. Then those also who have died in Christ have perished. If for this life only we have hoped in Christ, we are of all people most to be pitied. But in fact Christ has been raised from the dead, the first fruits of those who have died. For since death came through a human being, the resurrection of the dead has also come through a human being; for as all die in Adam, so all will be made alive in Christ. But each in his own order: Christ the first fruits, *then at his coming those who belong to Christ*" (1 Cor. 15:16-23; italics supplied).

It is then that the gift of eternal life is fully realized; it is then that those who died believing are raised from their graves and given immortality along with their living brethren and sisters. "Behold, I shew you a mystery," Paul exclaimed. "We shall not all sleep, but we shall all be changed, in a moment, in the twinkling of an eye, at the last trump: for the trumpet shall sound, and the dead shall be raised incorruptible, and we shall be changed. For this corruptible must put on incorruption, and this mortal must put on immortality. So when this corruptible shall have put on incorruption, and this mortal shall have put on immortality, then shall be brought to pass the saying that is written, Death is swallowed up in victory" (1 Cor. 15:51-54, KJV).

If the saved were immortal already and had been taken to heaven as soon as they died, why would a resurrection be necessary? Of what purpose would it be to have their "immortal souls" linked up with bodies? Nowhere does the Bible teach that idea. The message is delightfully plain that the dead sleep until they are raised at the second coming of Jesus when He will bestow immortality upon them.

The dead are not raised as disembodied spirits. They are raised with perfect, immortal bodies, free from all physical ills and blemishes. At his coming, Jesus "shall change our vile body, that it may be fashioned like unto his glorious body, according to the working whereby he is able even to subdue all things unto himself" (Phil. 3:21, KJV). "If the Spirit of him that raised up Jesus from the dead dwell in you, he that raised up Christ from the dead shall also quicken your mortal bodies by his Spirit that dwelleth in you" (Rom. 8:11, KJV). Living believers are "waiting for the adoption, to wit, the redemption of our body" (verse 23, KJV). Perfect spiritually and with perfect minds and bodies, the raised believers and their living brothers and sisters are taken to receive their eternal reward in the Kingdom of heaven.

Our Lord bestows rewards upon the faithful at His second advent, not at the point at which they die. Good works are not the means of salvation. Salvation is by grace alone (Eph. 2:8-10). Nonetheless, good works are rewarded when Jesus returns. "You will be repaid at the resurrection of the righteous" (Luke 14:14). "When the chief Shepherd shall appear, ye shall receive a crown of glory that fadeth not away" (1 Peter 5:4, KJV). Paul did not expect to receive his eternal crown at death but "at that day" (2 Tim. 4:8, KJV). When is "that day"? The rest of the verse makes it clear: ". . . and not to me only, but unto all them also that love *his appearing*." His appearing is His second advent, when all the righteous will receive their eternal rewards.

The sleep of death comes to an end for the righteous at the second coming of Jesus. What a thrilling day that will be! Mothers and fathers will be reunited with their little ones, husbands with their wives, children with their parents and grandparents, lovers with their sweethearts. It will be a great reunion day. And never again will there be suffering, separation, or death. "And God shall wipe away all tears from their eyes; and there shall be no more death, neither sorrow, nor crying, neither shall there be any more pain: for the former things are passed away" (Rev. 21:4, KJV).

For unbelievers the sleep of death is not broken until the end of the millennium that follows Jesus' second coming. "The rest of the dead did not come to life until the thousand years were ended" (Rev. 20:5). This is the second resurrection, the resurrection of the unrighteous that precedes their second death which is retribution for their rejection of the saving grace of the Lord Jesus Christ (Rev. 20:9. 14).

What Is the Relevance of the Bible Teaching?

The relevance of the Bible teaching on the state of the dead and the resurrection at the second advent of Jesus is that Roman Catholic ideas regarding Mary and the saints as well as New Age philosophies regarding immortal humans are totally false. The only human saints in heaven are the relatively few who have been raised bodily from the grave and those who were taken to heaven without seeing death. For example, the Lord raised Moses from the grave and transported him to heaven (Jude 9; Matt. 17:1-3). Enoch and Elijah were translated without seeing death (Gen. 5:24;

Heb. 11:5; 2 Kings 2:11; Matt. 17:3). There are no examples in Scripture of immortal souls being taken to heaven while their bodies remained in the grave. Nor is there any Bible support for the idea that Mary was taken to heaven at the end of her earthly existence.

Praying to Mary and the saints is futile because, like the rest of the faithful dead, they are sleeping in the grave awaiting the resurrection morning. The Bible says there is only "one mediator between God and men, the man Christ Jesus" (1 Tim. 2:5, KJV). There is no Bible evidence for the view that the immortal souls of the saints in heaven are assistant mediators or that we need mediators between us and the supreme Mediator. The Holy Spirit assists us in making known our requests to God (Rom. 8:26), but the one Mediator is Jesus Christ. Jesus said, "I am the way, and the truth, and the life. No one comes to the Father except through me" (John 14:6). That being so, we cannot approach the Deity through an angel, a redeemed human being in heaven, or an earthly human being. The only One whom the Bible mentions as appearing "in the presence of God on our behalf" (Heb. 9:24) is the Lord Jesus Christ. He is the only One spoken of as the Advocate for sinners in the heavenly sanctuary (1 John 2:1; Heb. 8:1, 2; 9:15; 12:24).

The Bible teaches that it is wrong to pray to an angel or to another human being. The angel before whom John bowed in an act of worship refused to accept such adoration. He said, "You must not do that! I am a fellow servant with you and your comrades who hold the testimony of Jesus. Worship God! For the testimony of Jesus is the spirit of prophecy" (Rev. 19:10). A second attempt by John to worship the angel resulted in a similar response: "You must not do that! I am a fellow servant with you and your comrades the prophets, and with those who keep the words of this book. Worship God!" (Rev. 22:9). It follows that heavenly angels, holy prophets, and humans who obey the will of God are not to be worshiped. Our acts of devotion and our prayers are to be directed solely to the Deity.

The Apostle Peter made it clear to Cornelius that it is wrong to worship a man, even though he happens to be one of Christ's apostles (Acts 10:25, 26). Likewise the Apostle Paul refused to accept acts of worship directed to himself (Acts 14:11-18). Jesus reminded Satan of the divine instruction in this regard: "Worship the Lord your God, and serve only him" (Matt. 4:10).

As supreme Deity (John 5:18; 8:58; Col. 2:9), Jesus accepted people's worship while He was here on earth, and forgave their sins (Matt. 2:11; 14:33; 15:25-28; Luke 5:20-25; John 9:38). After His resurrection, He was worshiped by His followers (Matt. 28:9, 17; Luke 24:52; John 20:28). The New Testament command is that we should bow before Him, acknowledging Him as our Lord (Phil. 2:9-11). It is entirely appropriate to speak directly to Christ in prayer (Acts 7:59; Rev. 22:20). Heavenly beings worship Him (Heb. 1:6; Rev. 5:8, 13, 14), and it is our privilege to worship Him also.

There is no example in Scripture of a saint in heaven accepting worship, forgiving sin, acting as a mediator, or supplying the needs of people on earth. Saint worship is totally unscriptural and contrary to the will of God as expressed in His Word. The only Being we are to worship is the Deity Himself. Because Jesus Christ, the Father, and the Holy Spirit are the Deity, we are commanded to worship Him, seeking His forgiveness for our sins and asking for His guidance, wisdom, and strength in the affairs of our everyday lives.

How Then Do We Explain the Appearances of Mary and the New Age Masters?

There can be no doubt that people in various places around the world have seen genuine spirit apparitions. But these apparitions are not Mary or other dead human beings. They are evil spirits impersonating Mary and dead humans.

What is the origin of these spirit beings? First, we should point out that heavenly angels are sinless beings whom God created to inhabit His perfect universe. They willingly and lovingly cooperate with the Lord in His efforts to save humans from sin.

The myriads of heaven's angels were created by God (Col. 1:16; Heb. 1:2; 12:22; Ps. 68:17; Dan. 7:10). By comparison with humans, they are spirit beings with power and glory far in excess of anything we experience. They are totally loyal to God and Christ, worshiping them continually, willingly carrying out their divine commands, and never aspiring to a position of equality with the Deity (Ps. 103:20; 148:2; Heb. 1:4-6; Rev. 7:11, 12). Humans were created with less power, glory, and ability than the angels (Heb. 2:6, 7; 2 Peter 2:11). Never are humans said to be equal to the angels; quite the contrary, they are very much dependent upon them for protection, guidance, and instruction (Heb. 1:14; Ps. 91:11; Matt. 18:10; Acts 12:7). Yet, as we have already seen, we are specifically instructed in the Bible that we are never to worship angels. Like us they are created beings. Our worship belongs only to the Lord. The angels worship Christ as Lord of the universe, and we are instructed to do the same. We are not to pray to angels but only to the Lord.

Angels are not immortal spirits of dead human beings. No passage of Scripture teaches such a view. Nor does the Bible depict any dead human as existing in spirit form and appearing to the living with any kind of message.[37]

The Bible explains that Satan and his demons were once heavenly angels who were perfect beings living in a state of joyful service for God. Then they chose to rebel against God. As one of the cherubim in heaven with the special privilege of dwelling in the presence of God, Lucifer was a being of magnificent beauty and intelligence (Ezek. 28:12-17; Isa. 14:12-15; Ps. 80:1). Tragically he chose to covet the position and power of the Deity. Not satisfied with his own privileged status, he fostered pride and selfishness in his own heart until he made himself a demon completely divorced from righteousness, purity, and love. Unfortunately he was successful in captivating the affections of one third of heaven's angels; a huge number considering that there are countless myriads of angels. The only choice left to God was to cast out these dissenters who were destroying the peace and happiness of heaven (Rev. 12:4, 7-9).

There was war in heaven, and Satan and his hosts of supporting angels were cast out. Peter explains that they were cast out to "hell" (2 Peter 2:4). The Greek word he uses in the verse is *tartaroo*. It means "to hold captive in tartarus." To the ancient Greeks, Tartarus was the place of punishment of the wicked dead. It corresponded to Gehenna in Jewish thought. Since Peter was writing to Christians, many of whom were Gentiles, he uses a Greek term to symbolize the total rejection of Satan and his demons. His use of the word *tartaroo* does not, however, indicate that the Greek or Hebrew idea of death at that time was correct, or that he believed it. Peter's concern was to demonstrate that Satan and his demons, who since the creation of our world have been able to tempt and delude mankind, are reserved by God in a place of total isolation from heaven until the judgment at the end of time will result in their eternal destruction. Compare Jude 6: "The angels who did not keep their own position, but left their proper dwelling, he has kept in eternal chains in deepest darkness for the judgment of the great Day."

Satan and one third of the angels who were cast out with him are now roving around our world with the one intention of dragging as many humans as possible into the eternal ruin facing them. "Discipline yourselves, keep alert. Like a roaring lion your adversary the devil prowls around, looking for someone to devour. Resist him, steadfast in your faith, for you know that your brothers and sisters in all the world are undergoing the same kind of suffering" (1 Peter 5:8, 9). "Woe to the earth and the sea, for the devil has come down to you with great wrath, because he knows that his time is short!" (Rev. 12:12). Satan and his demons are not yet in a place of burning; they are occupied in an all-out attempt to destroy humanity.

These fallen angels who are now demons are able to impersonate Mary and the saints and other dead humans. Spiritualism in whatever form it takes is a wicked and masterful deception practiced by demons who are totally alienated from God and are determined to destroy for eternity as many humans as they can. Misery loves company! Satan and his demons deceive for the purpose of involving others in their ruin.

Through Moses, the Lord warned Israel that there would be dire results of preserving and giving heed to those who professed to communicate with the dead (Lev. 19:31; 20:27; Deut. 18:9-14). Israel was left in no doubt that the supposed living dead were in fact evil spirits who were bent on deception and destruction. Isaiah, Zechariah, and other prophets warned the people of the dangers of spiritualism and of the lies of false prophets who had received their communications from demons (Isa. 8:19, 20; 28:15-18; Zech. 10:2; 13:2, 3).

A vital part of Jesus' ministry involved combating evil demons who had taken possession of the minds and bodies of sick and sinful people (Matt. 8:28-34; 9:32, 33; 10:1; 12:22, 23; Mark 7:25, 26, 29). Jesus healed the insane and the physically ill by casting out the demons who were destroying their lives. He also gave His disciples the power to cast out evil spirits and commanded His followers to allow the Holy Spirit to work through them for the deliverance of those who were victims of Satan and his demons (Matt. 10:8). The book of Acts indicates that the apostles followed Jesus' instruction. Through the mighty power of Christ they were enabled to deliver suffering people from the harassment and possession of evil spirits (Acts 8:7-13; 16:16-18).

The Holy Spirit warns us that "in the latter times some shall depart from the faith, giving heed to seducing spirits, and doctrines of devils" (1 Tim. 4:1, KJV; cf. Eph. 6:12; 1 John 4:1-5). This prophecy is being fulfilled by the great increase in the popularity of the occult in our era. As never before in history spiritualism, in many different forms and represented in many different religious organizations, is exerting a powerful influence. The unbiblical doctrine that man's spirit lives on after death is the basis of a massive deception. Supposedly orthodox Christian churches are being swept into the rushing tide of spiritist delusions because they insist that the dead loved ones of their members are still living and able to communicate with them.

Little do such churches, their leaders, and their members realize the danger of infatuation with spiritualism. The supposed spirits of dead loved ones, who are actually evil spirits, say they are enjoying heaven. Even those who died unready to meet the Lord appear and give the message that they, and many others like them, are safe from harm and suffering in the blessed realm of the eternal spirits. The result is that people are deceived into believing that there is no difference between righteousness and wickedness; everyone goes to the same place whatever the record of the life. Such universalism is totally unscriptural (Heb. 12:14; 2 Peter 2:9; Jude 11-13).

The evil spirits impersonating the dead teach many other doctrines contrary to the Bible. First they gain confidence by teaching some things that are consistent with Scripture; then they teach error. Christ is placed on a level with the spirits, His unique Deity is denied, and His special saving work for man is depreciated. The Christianity of the Bible is destroyed by so-called Christian spiritualism.

The Apostle Paul's prediction of the last great deceptions of Satan should lead everyone to search the Scriptures very carefully. The final great deception will be with "all power, signs, lying wonders, and every kind of wicked deception for those who are perishing, because they refused to love the truth and so be saved" (2 Thess. 2:9, 10). People who refuse to receive Christ's truth will be permitted to accept "a powerful delusion, leading them to believe what is false, so that all who have not believed the truth but took pleasure in unrighteousness will be condemned" (verses 11, 12). There is terrible danger in clinging to sin at this time of crisis in our world. The deceptions of spiritualism will be attractive to those who refuse to receive the Holy Spirit into their hearts and to put away all sin from their lives.

John the Revelator agrees entirely with Paul, and adds the warning with great insistence. The false religious union of the last days will be a miracle working power (Rev. 13:13, 14). Satan will operate through professed Christians who have accepted a religion that is a counterfeit to that of the Bible.

21

They will perform outstanding miracles as a means of convincing earth's inhabitants that their beliefs are genuine. The only safety will be to cherish the Word of God and its teachings. "If they speak not according to this word, it is because there is no light in them" (Isa. 8:20, KJV).

In vision, John saw symbolized "the spirits of devils, working miracles, which go forth unto the kings of the earth and of the whole world, to gather them to the battle of that great day of God Almighty" (Rev. 16:14, KJV). That battle is Armageddon (verse 16), the final battle between the armies of heaven and the armies of earth at the second coming of Christ (Rev. 17:14; 19:11-16). Before this takes place, evil spirits are intensely deceiving the leaders and peoples of earth's nations, preparing them for destruction when Jesus appears. Because they will not accept God's final message of love and warning (Rev. 14:6, 7), multitudes will be captivated by spiritualism, convinced by demons that their unbiblical teachings are true. Their tragic plight is described graphically in the book of Revelation. We can imagine the tears in the eyes of the Lord Jesus Christ as He warns that those deceived by spiritualism will cry out to the mountains and rocks, "Fall on us and hide us from the face of the one seated on the throne and from the wrath of the Lamb" (Rev. 6:16).

Because He is "not willing that any should perish, but that all should come to repentance" (2 Peter 3:9, KJV), Jesus sends the last great warning message to the world: "Fallen, fallen is Babylon the great! It has become a dwelling place of demons, a haunt of every foul and hateful bird, a haunt of every foul and hateful beast" (Rev. 18:2). The great end-time "Babylon" is that false religious union of the last days that has turned away from the Bible and has accepted the deceptions of evil spirits. Christ cries out longingly and mercifully to every inhabitant of earth, "Come out of her, my people, so that you do not take part in her sins, and so that you do not share in her plagues" (Rev. 18:4).

What Will Be Satan's Crowning Act of Deception?

Just before the second coming of Jesus, Satan will attempt to anticipate that event by appearing as though he is the Christ. The warning of this final deception is clearly given in Scripture. The word will go out that Christ has come and that He can be seen in such and such a place.

The final great tribulation just before Jesus' coming will be more serious than anything the world has ever known (Matt. 24:21). For the sake of the elect it will be cut short (verse 22). As the tribulation is drawing to a close, there will be many rumors that Christ has already come (verse 23). Many false prophets will arise, inspired by Satan, who will try to demonstrate by miracles that they are Christ (verse 24). There will be reports that Christ is in this or that location, and people will be urged to go out and see him (verse 26). Only Satan, transformed into an angel of light (2 Cor. 11:14), could successfully deceive most people into believing that Christ has come. By a masterful impersonation of Christ, Satan will finally turn the impenitent world away from the Lord and Bible truth.

Christian believers do not have to be misled. Satan will not be permitted to counterfeit the manner of Christ's advent. Jesus' coming will not be localized; He will not appear in any one part of the earth at any one time. "For as the lightning comes from the east and flashes as far as the west, so will be the coming of the Son of man" (Matt. 24:27). Jesus comes with the matchless glory of the Father, accompanied by all the holy angels (Matt. 16:27). His coming will be viewed by every individual of every nation on earth (Matt. 24:30; Rev. 1:7). He does not touch the earth at this time. His faithful followers are caught up to meet Him in the sky and are then taken to be with Him in heaven (Matt. 24:31; 1 Thess. 4:16-18; John 14:1-3). Satan will not be able to counterfeit this glorious public appearing of Jesus Christ in the heavens.

Finally, at the end of the 1,000 years after Jesus' coming, Satan and his demons, along with all those humans who have followed his plans for their lives, will be destroyed eternally by fire (Rev. 20:7-10). The "sorcerers" (Greek: *pharmakos*) who are destroyed with Satan (Rev. 21:8; 22:15) are those who practice magic or witchcraft. These are the spiritualists who communicated with evil demons and convinced millions that they were the immortal spirits of the dead. Thus spiritualism with all its lies and false doctrines will be destroyed for eternity.

Jesus warns us to "watch" (KJV), to "keep awake (NRSV) (Mark 13:35). That means to study His Word regularly and pray constantly. To live with Jesus in your heart by the Holy Spirit is the only way to avoid the great spiritualistic deceptions of the last days. None of us is clever or wise enough to outsmart the devil. For many centuries he has been perfecting his deceptive arts. Only the grace and power of the Lord Jesus Christ can save us from these terrible delusions.

Are you living daily in a state of total surrender to Christ? Are you allowing the Holy Spirit to teach you the meaning of the Bible and allowing Him to so control your mind and body that there is no room for Satan and his demons to overcome you? Let us pray now and every day from now on that Jesus will dwell with us and protect us from the terrible evils that Satan wants to bring upon us.

Notes
1. Oscar Cullmann, *Immortality of the Soul Or Resurrection of the Dead? The Witness of the New Testament* (London: Epworth Press, 1958).
2. *Ibid.*, p. 9.
3. *Ibid.*, pp. 19-27.
4. *Ibid.*, pp. 25, 26.
5. *Ibid.*, p. 26.
6. Ted and Maureen Flynn, *Thunder of Justice: The Warning, the Miracle, The Chastisement, The Era of Peace* (Sterling, Virginia: MaxKol Communications, 1993).
7. *Ibid.*, pp. 4, 5.
8. *Ibid.*, p. 7.
9. *Ibid.*, pp. 21-38.
10. *Ibid.*, p. 27.
11. *Ibid.*, p. 203.
12. *Ibid.*
13. *Newsweek*, August 25, 1997, p. 49.
14. *Ibid.*
15. *Ibid.*, p. 51.
16. Will Baron, *Deceived by the New Age* (Boise, Idaho: Pacific Press, 1990), pp. 62-66.
17. *Ibid.*, p. 67.
18. *Ibid.*
19. *Ibid.*, p. 68.
20. *Ibid.*
21. Walter Martin, *The New Age Cult* (Minneapolis, Minnesota: Bethany House Publishers, 1989), p. 19.
22. Alice A. Bailey, *The Reappearance of the Christ* (New York: Lucis Publishing Company, 1948), p. 147, quoted by Walter Martin, *The New Age Cult*, p. 33.
23. Will Baron, *Deceived by the New Age*, pp. 105-109.
24. *Ibid.*, pp. 99-104, 110-124.
25. *Ibid.*, pp. 137-158.
26. *Ibid.*, pp. 159-169.
27. *Ibid.*, pp. 170-175.
28. *Ibid.*, pp. 176-192.
29. *Ibid.*, pp. 193, 197.
30. See Francis Brown, S. R. Drive, and Charles A. Briggs, *A Hebrew and English Lexicon of the Old Testament* (Oxford: Clarendon Press, 1906, 1951), s.v. *shakab.*
31. See William F. Arndt and F. Wilbur Gingrich, *A Greek-English Lexicon of the New Testament* (Cambridge: University Press, 1957), s.v. *koimao.*
32. Gerhard Kittel (ed.), *Theological Dictionary of the New Testament,* trans. by Geoffrey W. Bromiley (Grand Raids, Michigan: Wm. B. Eerdmans, 1968), vol. 6, pp. 360-362.
33. Gerhard Kittel (ed.), *Theological Dictionary of the New Testament,* vol. 9, p. 620.
34. My translation. The relevant phrase reads in the Greek text: *psuchen sosai:* "to save a soul" or "to save a life."
35. My translation.
36. "An Extract Out of Josephus's Discourse to the Greeks Concerning Hades," in Josephus, *Complete Works,* trans. by William Whiston (Grand Rapids, Michigan: Kregel, 1960), pp. 637, 638.
37. The spirit that appeared to King Saul (1 Sam. 28:7-19) was not the immortal spirit of the dead Samuel. It was an evil spirit impersonating Samuel. For a full explanation of the this Bible story see my next chapter.

Chapter 2
Does the Bible Teach
the Immortality of the Soul?

A s we have seen in the previous chapter, the dead do not have consciousness of any kind; they know nothing and they feel nothing. People who die do not go to heaven or hell where they live on in a state of consciousness. They go to the grave where their bodies disintegrate because the life force has been removed. They are sleeping, without any awareness of what is happening on earth or in heaven. The Bible clearly establishes that the righteous dead are not in heaven, and the wicked dead are not in a place of burning. They are in the dust of the earth, waiting for the resurrection day. That day for the righteous will be the second coming of Christ. For the wicked it will be at the end of the millennium, at which time they will be raised for judgment and put to sleep for eternity.

The purpose of the present chapter is to examine Bible passages that are used as evidence by those who believe in the immortality of the soul. It will be shown that the true meaning of each passage in its Scriptural context rules out any suggestion that the soul is immortal.

According to Jesus, Where Can Both Soul and Body Be Destroyed?

Jesus said: "Do not fear those who kill the body but cannot kill the soul; rather fear him who can destroy both soul and body in hell" (Matt. 10:28).

Immortal-soul advocates use this verse to point out the distinction between soul and body. They argue that the soul is the real self that dwells within the body during life, but lives on separate from the body after death. The problem for their view is that this verse proves that the soul, like the body, can be destroyed in hell. If the soul can be destroyed, it is not immortal, and it will not suffer eternally in hellfire. The message of the text is that, although we should not fear man who can destroy the body, we should fear God who is able to destroy both soul and body in hell, and who will destroy the wicked at the end of time (Rev. 20:9, 14, 15; 2 Thess. 1:7-10).

The Greek word for "soul" (*psuche*) used in Matthew 10:28 means "life." It is the same word that is used four times in Matthew 16:25, 26. In the King James Version it is translated "life" in verse 25 and "soul" in verse 26: "For whosoever will save his life [*psuche*] shall lose it: and whosoever will lose his life [*psuche*] for my sake shall find it. For what is a man profited, if he shall gain the whole world, and lose his own soul [*psuche*]? or what shall a man give in exchange for his soul [*psuche*]?" Note how the translators have varied the translation of the same Greek word. Verse 25 indicates that one could lose his soul for Christ's sake. That would not be possible if the soul were an immortal entity within man. The loss of the soul for the immortal-soul advocate means going to hell. Obviously no one goes to hell for Christ's sake. It is possible, however, to lay down ones life for Christ's sake. The translators, who believed in the immortality of the soul, saw the problem for their view and translated the word *psuche* by "life," even though they translated it "soul" in verse 26.

The real message of Matthew 16:25, 26 is that eternal life will be lost for those who substitute selfish desires for the service of Christ. But eternal life will be given to those who love and serve Christ. The next verse puts the statement into its context: "For the Son of man shall come in the glory of his Father with his angels; and then he shall reward every man according to his works" (verse 27, KJV). Matthew 25:46 is parallel. Contrasting the wicked with the righteous, Jesus said: "And these shall go away into everlasting punishment: but the righteous into life eternal" (KJV). "Everlasting punishment" is eternal loss of life, not an eternal life of loss (Matt. 16:25, 26). It is not a continuation of life in hell.

Matthew 10:28 is thoroughly consistent with Jesus' overall teaching that the "soul" or "life" of the unbeliever will be destroyed eternally. That being the case the soul is not immortal.

What Did Paul Mean When He Said that "Our Inner Nature Is Being Renewed Day by Day"?

"So we do not lose heart. Even though our outer nature is wasting away, our inner nature is being renewed day by day" (2 Cor. 4:16).

Believers in the immortality of the soul argue that the "inward man" (KJV) or "inner nature" (NRSV) is the immortal soul within the body. This text, they say, clearly proves a distinction between soul and body.

Undoubtedly there is a distinction between soul (or spirit) and body in the Bible. Since "soul" means "life" or "life force," as it does in Matthew 10:28, obviously it is something different from the body. The word "soul" in Scripture does not always mean what it does in Genesis 2:7, where "a living soul" is comprised of both body and life force (breath).

In his first letter to the Corinthians, Paul wrote: ". . . glorify God in your body, and in your spirit, which are God's" (1 Cor. 6:20, KJV). Textual evidence favors the omission of the words, "and in your spirit which are God's."[1] That is why these words are omitted in the New Revised Standard Version, the New International Version, the New American Standard Bible, and the New English Bible.

In the New Testament, the "spirit" of a human (Greek *pneuma*) often refers to the mind or the emotions. For example, 1 Corinthians 2:11: "For what human being knows what is truly human except the human spirit that is within?" The "spirit" here is the knowing part of a person, the faculty of comprehension, the mind. The New Revised Standard Version translates 2 Corinthians 2:13: ". . . but my mind [*pneuma* = spirit] could not rest because I did not find my brother Titus there." Note also 2 Corinthians 7:13: "In addition to our own consolation, we rejoiced still more at the joy of Titus, because his mind [*pneuma* = spirit] has been set at rest by all of you."

But in Scripture, the "spirit" or "soul" is never a separate, immortal part of the person, existing within the body, and living on after the death of the body. Minds and emotions (spirits) do not go on functioning after the body expires (Eccl. 9:5, 6, 10), and the "soul" or "life" is lost when the body dies (Matt. 16:25, 26). God reserves the righteous for eternal life, and reserves the wicked for eternal death (Rom. 6:23). But, as our previous studies have demonstrated, there is no continuing, conscious life for any individual after the extinction of the body.

Paul also wrote to the Corinthians that, though he was "absent in body," he was "present in spirit" (1 Cor. 5:3). Of course, he was not a split personality, having his body in Ephesus while his real self was over in Corinth. He obviously meant what we mean today when we say that we are with someone in spirit. His thoughts, concerns, and prayers were much with the Corinthians, even though his entire person remained in Ephesus.

Second Corinthians 4:16 simply means that the inner spiritual life of a person is renewed day by day as he or she turns to Christ for strength to face life's challenges. Jesus said, "The words that I have spoken to you are spirit and life" (John 6:63). As we receive His word into our hearts by the Holy Spirit every day (John 16:13), we are renewed spiritually and given grace to live for Christ. The same spiritual renewal is spoken of in Ephesians 3:16, 17: "That he would grant you, according to the riches of his glory, to be strengthened with might by his Spirit in the inner man; That Christ may dwell in your hearts by faith" (KJV). Christ lives out His life through the person who receives His Spirit into the life every day (Gal. 2:20).

Second Corinthians 4:16 does not teach the immortality of the soul. It teaches that our inner spiritual life must be renewed as we come to Christ every day.

Because Jesus and Stephen Committed Their Spirits to the Care of God, Do We Have Evidence of Their Immortality?

"Then Jesus, crying with a loud voice, said, 'Father, into your hands I commend my spirit'" (Luke 23:46).

"While they were stoning Stephen, he prayed, 'Lord Jesus, receive my spirit'" (Acts 7:59).

The Scriptural background to these prayers goes way back to Genesis 2:7: "And the Lord God formed man of the dust of the ground, and breathed into his nostrils the breath of life; and man became a living soul" (KJV). The body plus the breath of life produced a living soul. The word for "breath" in Genesis 2:7 is *n^eshamah* in the Hebrew original and *pnoe* in the Greek translation (the Septuagint). These words mean "breath, wind."[2] The breath that God breathed into the inanimate body gave it life. This same breath of life is spoken of in Job 33:4: "The spirit [*ruach*] of God has made me, and the breath [*n^eshamah*] of the Almighty gives me life." The breath of life (*n^eshamah*) is, therefore, the spirit (*ruach*) that God breathed into Adam's nostrils. The word *ruach* means "breath, spirit, wind." Referring to himself during life, Job said, ". . . as long as my breath [*n^eshamah*] is in me and the spirit [*ruach*] of God is in my nostrils. . . ." (Job 27:3). Once again the "breath" and the "spirit" are identified. When this spirit or breath returns to God the individual dies: "If he [God] should take back his spirit to himself, and gather to himself his breath, all flesh would perish together, and all mortals return to dust" (Job 34:14, 15).

The Psalmist expressed the same thought when he described what happens to man in death: "When their breath [*ruach* = spirit] departs, they return to the earth; on that very day their plans perish" (Ps. 146:4).

This explains the description of death as given in Ecclesiastes 12:7: "Then shall the dust [body] return to the earth as it was: and the spirit [*ruach* = breath] shall return unto God who gave it" (KJV). This simply reverses the process as described in Genesis 2:7. Now God takes the life force back to himself and the dead body disintegrates. The "spirit" or "breath" that goes back to God cannot possibly be man's immortal soul. If that were so the spirit or soul of all humans, righteous and wicked, would go to heaven when they die — an unbiblical conclusion. Moreover, the Bible teaches that animals have exactly the same breath of life as man, and this also goes back to God when they die: "For that which befalleth the sons of men befalleth beasts; even one thing befalleth them: as the one dieth, so dieth the other; yea, they have all one breath [*ruach* = spirit]; so that a man hath no preeminence above a beast [in this respect]: for all is vanity. All go unto one place; all are of the dust, and all turn to dust again" (Eccl. 3:19, 20, KJV). The next verse is a rhetorical question that he has already answered. His meaning may be paraphrased like this: "Whoever imagines that the spirit of man goes up to heaven, and the spirit of an animal goes down to the earth?" He has just asserted that such is not the case.

Of course there are some very vital differences between mankind and animals. Even though they both have the same life force from God, the distinctions are dramatic. Man was made in the image of God, with a moral nature, and the capacity to have communion with His Creator. Humans will face God's judgment and either be taken to heaven or destroyed in hell. None of this applies to animals. Nevertheless, the life force in humans and beasts is the same. If that life force were an immortal soul, we would have to argue that animals have immortal souls; an absurd idea.

In the light of the foregoing, consider Luke 23:46 and Acts 7:59; specifically the prayers of Jesus and Stephen committing their "spirit" or life force to God. They knew that they were dying. The life that came from God was being taken from them. That spirit or life force was the "breath" given to man at creation. If it were an immortal soul, then the soul of man must have existed prior to creation. This doctrine is acceptable to Mormons, but certainly not to those whose doctrinal understandings are based solely on Scripture.

The day Jesus died His human "spirit," "breath," or life force went back to God, but He certainly did not go to heaven as a conscious being that Friday afternoon. After His resurrection on Sunday morning, when He appeared to Mary Magdalene, He instructed: "Do not hold on to me, because I have not yet ascended to the Father" (John 20:17). Likewise Stephen did not ascend to heaven when the life force was taken from him. The righteous dead are not made immortal until they are raised at the second advent of Jesus (1 Cor. 15:51-54). Then they are taken to heaven to be with their Lord (1 Thess. 4:16-18). Jesus and Stephen were both praying that God would reserve them to eternal life with Him because they trusted wholly in Him. The prayer was answered for Jesus a couple of days later when He rose from the dead. Stephen's prayer will be answered when the saints are raised at the second advent of Jesus.

Jesus (as man) and Stephen did not have immortal souls that went to heaven when they died. They trusted God to give them back the breath of life (or life force) by raising them from the dead. In this sense they committed their lives into God's care.

What Does the Epistle to the Hebrews Intend to Teach When It Says that Christian Believers Have Come "to the Spirits of Just Men Made Perfect" (Heb. 12:23, KJV)?

The statement in context reads as follows: "But you have come to Mount Zion and to the city of the living God, the heavenly Jerusalem, and to innumerable angels in festal gathering, and to the assembly of the firstborn who are enrolled in heaven, and to God the judge of all, and to the spirits of the righteous made perfect, and to Jesus, the mediator of a new covenant, and to the sprinkled blood that speaks a better word than the blood of Abel" (Heb. 12:22-24, NRSV).

The Greek dictionaries define the Greek word translated "spirit" (*pneuma*) to mean, according to context, (i) a blowing, breathing, wind, breath; (ii) spiritual state; (iii) state of mind, disposition; (iv) spirit beings such as the Holy Spirit, angels, and evil spirits.[3]

Hebrews 12:18-29 is not written for people who are already in heaven, but for Christian believers on this earth who are confronted with the challenges and temptations of everyday life. Paul, who is thought to be the writer, reminds the Hebrew Christians that they have not been confronted with the remarkable experience of seeing God's glory on Mount Sinai, of hearing His mighty voice, and seeing the earth shake as the law was proclaimed (verses 18-21). Now that Christ has died and risen again, the divine love and glory are manifested in other ways.

Verses 22-24 emphasize that Christian believers on earth have come to: (i) "Mount Zion and to the city of the living God"; (ii) "the heavenly Jerusalem" (cf. Galatians 4:26 ff.); (iii) "innumerable angels"; (iv) "the assembly of the firstborn who are enrolled in heaven"; (iv) "God the Judge of all"; (v) "the spirits of the righteous made perfect"; (vi) "Jesus, the mediator of a new covenant"; (vii) "the sprinkled blood that speaks a better word than the blood of Abel." Then the instruction is given: "See that you do not refuse the one who is speaking" (verse 25).

Though some of the things or beings to which believers have come are in heaven and some on earth, the believers themselves remain on earth. If they were in heaven they would not need the intercession of the Mediator, nor would they be instructed not to refuse Christ who is speaking to them from heaven. Moreover, the church of the firstborn is still on this earth. Paul refers elsewhere to his "fellowlaborers, whose names are in the book of life" (Phil. 4:3, KJV). Jesus instructed His disciples to "rejoice that your names are written in heaven" (Luke 10:20). Those who are eventually translated to heaven at the second coming of Jesus are those whose names are retained in the book of life (compare Dan. 12:1; Rev. 3:5; 20:12; 21:27).

"The spirits of the righteous made perfect" (Heb. 12:23) are not disembodied spirits in heaven. In fact, there is no evidence in Scripture that there are any disembodied spirits of humans in heaven. The Hebrew Christians belonged to the church of the firstborn on this earth and have fellowship with those who have been made complete (or perfect) in Christ (Col. 2:10). Speaking of Christ's death a little earlier in the same letter to the Hebrews, Paul wrote: "But when Christ had offered for all time a single sacrifice for sins, 'he sat down at the right hand of God,' and since then has been waiting 'until his enemies would be made a footstool for his feet.' For by a single offering he has perfected for all time those who are sanctified" (Heb. 10:12-14). The point is that there is cleansing from sin and present perfection in Christ for those who are indwelt by the Holy Spirit and who are being progressively sanctified. (See also Rom. 6:18-22; 8:3, 4, 9, 10). Such a church of believers who are enjoying the indwelling righteousness of Christ by the Holy Spirit are accurately spoken of as "the spirits of the righteous made perfect" (Heb. 12:23). Their spiritual life has been brought into harmony with the will of God. They have become "servants" or "slaves" of righteousness (Rom. 6:18). The "righteousness of the law" is fulfilled in them (Rom. 8:4), and Christ, dwelling in their hearts by the Holy Spirit, is their righteousness within. The Hebrew Christians had the privilege of fellowshiping with genuinely born-again believers in the Church of Christ on earth. And Paul wanted the Hebrew Christians themselves to be "righteous [people] made perfect." (Compare Heb. 9:14; 10:19-22).

Every Christian believer, because of his or her relationship with Christ, may have such a vibrant spiritual life that the phrase, "the spirits of the righteous made perfect," may apply to his or her experience. This is Christ's ideal for His children.

To What Did Paul Refer When He Wrote of "a Man, (Whether in the Body, or Out of the Body, I Cannot Tell: God Knoweth;)" (2 Cor. 12:3, KJV)?

In context, the statement reads as follows: "It is necessary to boast; nothing is to be gained by it, but I will go on to visions and revelations of the Lord. I know a person in Christ who fourteen years ago was caught up to the third heaven — whether in the body or out of the body I do not know; God knows. And I know that such a person ... was caught up into Paradise and heard things that are not to be told, that no mortal is permitted to repeat. On behalf of such a one I will boast, but on my own behalf I will not boast, except of my weaknesses" (2 Cor. 12:1-5, NRSV).

First, we should note that Paul was speaking about himself. He was explaining how God had given him "visions and revelations" (verse 1; cf. verses 6-11). His purpose was to convince the Corinthians that he was a genuinely inspired apostle (verses 11, 12). In vision Paul had been caught up into paradise (verse 4), the third heaven (verse 2). Paradise is where God's throne is, and where the tree of life is (Rev. 2:7; 22:1, 2). Paul was not certain whether he was actually in bodily form in heaven, or only there in vision while his body remained on earth. The point is that Paul was still a human being living on this earth at the time he received his visions and revelations from God. He was not a disembodied spirit whose body had died and whose spirit was now dwelling in heaven. There is no evidence for the immortality of the soul in the passage.

The Lord sometimes gives inspired prophets visions and dreams in which they seem to be far away from their earthly place of dwelling. But such revelations do not prove that man has an immortal soul.

Why Did Jesus Speak of the Dead by Saying, "God Is Not the God of the Dead, but of the Living" (Matt. 22:32, KJV)?

Jesus said to the Sadducees: "For in the resurrection they neither marry nor are given in marriage, but are like angels in heaven. And as for the resurrection of the dead, have you not read what was said to you by God, 'I am the God of Abraham, the God of Isaac, and the God of Jacob?' He is God not of the dead, but of the living" (Matt. 22:30-32).

The whole passage of which this verse is a part (Matt. 22:23-32) is a discussion between Jesus and the Sadducees about the resurrection. They denied that there would be a resurrection of the dead (verse 23). They posed a hypothetical case of a woman who married seven brothers in turn and asked Jesus which of the brothers would be her husband after the resurrection. Jesus' answer focused on the resurrection: "*For in the resurrection* they neither marry nor are given in marriage, but are like the angels in heaven" (verse 30, italics supplied). Then he added: "And as for *the resurrection* of the dead, have you not read what was said to you by God, 'I am the God of Abraham, the God of Isaac, and the God of Jacob?' He is God not of the dead, but of the living" (verses 31, 32, italics supplied). Jesus' point was that God is the God of the living because the dead will be raised in the resurrection, not because the dead are living in spirit form in heaven now. Mark introduces the statement with the phrase: "And as for the dead being raised . . . ." (Mark 12:26). Luke quotes Jesus as saying: "*And the fact that the dead are raised* Moses himself showed, in the story about the bush, where he speaks of the Lord as the God of Abraham, the God of Isaac, and the God of Jacob. Now he is God not of the dead, but of the living; for to him all of them are alive" (Luke 20:37, 38, italics supplied).

The last phrase of Luke 20:38 may be translated: ". . . for to him [God] all are living." God views the things that will be as though they already are. Paul spoke of "God, who quickeneth [makes alive] the dead, and calleth those things which be not as though they were" (Rom. 4:17, KJV). Paul also wrote: "For none of us liveth to himself, and no man dieth to himself. For

33

whether we live, we live unto the Lord; and whether we die, we die unto the Lord: whether we live therefore, or die, we are the Lord's. For to this end Christ both died, and rose, and revived, that he might be Lord both of the dead and living" (Rom. 14:7-9, KJV). The Lord knows which of the dead belong to Him, and these are the ones whom He will raise at the second advent of Christ (1 Thess. 4:13-18; John 5:28, 29).

The living believer in Christ need have no fear of death because even after his death Christ is still his Lord, who has a complete record of his faithfulness and plans to raise him on the resurrection day.

What Did Paul Mean When He Wrote: "We Are Confident, I Say, and Willing Rather to Be Absent from the Body, and to Be Present with the Lord" (2 Cor. 5:8, KJV)?

The immortal-soul advocates use this passage (2 Cor. 5:1-10) to prove that Paul was looking forward to being a disembodied spirit in heaven. The context indicates otherwise. The three possible states to which he refers are: (i) "our earthly house" (verse 1); (ii) the "naked" or "unclothed" state (verses 3, 4); (iii) "a building of God, an house not made with hands, eternal in the heavens" (verse 1, KJV). The "unclothed" state is, in fact, the intermediate condition between the earthly and heavenly state. In the earthly state the believer has an earthly body. In the heavenly state he will have an immortal, incorruptible body. But in the "naked," or "unclothed" state he will have no body at all because it has gone back to the dust, and the life force has been removed by God. As we have seen above, this life force is not a conscious, immortal entity.

Paul was looking forward to the resurrection of the body at the second advent (Rom. 8:11, 22, 23; Phil. 3:20, 21; 1 Cor. 15:4-44). His focus was not on being a disembodied spirit after death but on being with Christ on the resurrection morning (2 Tim. 4:8; 1 Cor. 15:51-54).

Paul wrote: "For to me, living is Christ and dying is gain. If I am to live in the flesh, that means fruitful labor for me; and I do not know which I prefer. I am hard pressed between the two: my desire is to depart and be with Christ, for that is far better; but to remain in the flesh is more necessary for you" (Phil. 1:21-24). He does not, however, tell us in this passage when he will be with Christ. As far as the dead person is concerned the interval between the moment of death and the resurrection at Christ's coming is no time at all. After death the next thing he knows is that he is in the presence of Christ. Hence, Paul's desire to lay down his burden was not in view of a wish to be a disembodied spirit being in heaven after death. It was in view of his wish to be raised to be with Christ on the resurrection day.

For the Christian believer death is a state of unconsciousness followed by eternity with Christ. Death is rest from labor, and the resurrection is an eternity of restfulness. What greater blessings could the Lord bestow upon us?

How Do We Answer the Argument that, Since Man Is Made in the Image of God, and God Is Immortal, Therefore, Man Is Immortal (Gen. 1:26, 27)?

When man was made in the image of God he was not, therefore, given all of the characteristics of God. God is omnipotent (all-powerful) and omniscient (all-knowing). Of course man does not have, and never did have, these characteristics, even though he was made in God's image. Humans were made in the image of God in outward resemblance and in character. (See Gen. 5:1; Exod. 33:22, 23; Ezek. 1:26-28; James 3:9.) Our first parents had continuing life with no deterioration or expectation of death until the point at which they chose to sin (Rom. 5:12-19; 1 Cor. 15:21).

Never in Scripture are the words "immortal" or "immortality" used in reference to mankind in his earthly, fallen existence. Christian believers "seek for glory and honour and immortality, eternal life" (Rom. 2:7, KJV). They do not have immortality now; they are looking forward to it. Immortality at the second advent (1 Cor. 15:51-54) is possible because Christ earned it for us on Calvary (2 Tim. 1:10). By comparison with earthly humans, God "only hath immortality" (1 Tim. 6:16, KJV).

Every believer has the assurance that Christ will bestow immortality upon him at the second advent.

The Old Testament Speaks of the Souls of Dying People Departing. What Does that Mean (Gen. 35:18; 1 Kings 17:17, 21, 22)?

Genesis 35:18 describes the death of Rachel: "And it came to pass, as her *soul* was in departing, (for she died) that she called his name Benoni . . . ." (KJV, italics supplied). The Hebrew word translated "soul" in this verse is *nephesh*.

1 Kings 17:17-22 describes the death of the widow's son at Zarephath and Elijah's prayer that resulted in God raising him from the dead. When he died, "there was no *breath* left in him" (verse 17, KJV, italics supplied). The Hebrew word for breath used in this verse is *n*e*shamah*. Elijah's prayer to God resulted in the child being raised from the dead: "I pray thee, let this child's *soul* [*nephesh*] come into him again. And the Lord heard the voice of Elijah; and the *soul* [*nephesh*] of the child came into him again, and he revived" (verses 21, 22, KJV, italics supplied).

The Hebrew word translated "breath" in 1 Kings 17:17, *n*e*shamah*, according to the Hebrew dictionaries, means "breath," "breathing thing," "spirit of man."[4] It is the word used in Genesis 2:7: "And the Lord God formed man of the dust of the ground, and breathed into his nostrils the breath [*n*e*shamah*] of life; and man became a living soul" (KJV). Hence, the life force that was given to man by God when He created him left the widow's son when he died. *N*e*shamah* does not refer to a conscious, immortal part of the child that went on living when he died. It simply refers to the life from God that was taken away from the child at death.

As we have seen, both Genesis 35:18 and 1 Kings 17:21-22 use the Hebrew word *nephesh*, translated "soul" in the King James Version. Rachel's "soul" left her at death, and the child's "soul" came back into him when Elijah prayed for him. It is important to know what the Hebrew word *nephesh* means. According to the Hebrew dictionaries it means: "breath," "respiration," "life," "soul," "spirit," "mind," "living being," "creature," "a person," "self."[5] Never does *nephesh* refer to a part of an individual that can have conscious existence independent of the body. Kittel's *Theological Dictionary of the New Testament* has an excellent article on *nephesh*, as the Hebrew equivalent of the Greek word *psuche*. We quote part of the article for the purpose of clarifying the true meaning of *nephesh*. (The Hebrew words will be transliterated in brackets):

"The deciding mark of the living creature is breathing, and its cessation means the end of life. Hence the root . . . in the form of the noun . . . which occurs 755 times in the Hbr. Bible, denotes 'life' or 'living creature'. . . . In 1 K. 17:17 lack of . . .[*n*e*shamah* or breath] causes the departure of . . .[*nephesh*] which returns when the prophet gives the child breath again, for . . . [*nephesh*] alone is what makes a living creature into a living organism. . . . Yet one should not conclude that the . . . [*nephesh*] is an immaterial principle which can be abstracted away from its material substructure and which can lead an independent existence. The departure of the . . . [*nephesh*] is a metaphor for death; a dead man is one who has ceased to breathe. . . . [*Nephesh*] is the usual term for man's total nature, for what he is and not just what he has. . . . The . . . [*nephesh*] is almost always connected with a form. It has no existence apart from the body. Hence the best translation in many instances is 'person' comprised in corporeal reality. The person can be marked off and counted, Gn. 12:5; 46:18; Jos. 10:28; 11:11. Each individual is a . . . [*nephesh*], and when the texts speak of a single . . . [*nephesh*] for a totality, the totality is viewed as a single person, a 'corporate personality.' Hence . . . [*nephesh*] can denote what is most individual in human nature, namely, the ego, and it can become a synonym of the personal pronoun, Gn. 27:25."[6]

In fact, a lifeless body is sometimes spoken of as a *nephesh* in the Old Testament. It is a dead individual. (See Num. 5:2; 9:6, 10; Haggai 2:13.)

Summarizing the above, we arrive at these conclusions: (1) the root meaning of the word *nephesh* is "breath"; (2) because breath is essential to life, *nephesh* came to mean "life"; (3) because life is enjoyed by each living person, *nephesh* came to apply to an individual; it came to be used for the personal pronoun; (4) never does *nephesh* refer to a quality or a part of an individual that exists separate from the body.

Now it is very easy indeed to understand Genesis 35:18 and 1 Kings 17:21, 22. Rachel's "soul" (*nephesh*) that departed when she died was simply her breath or life. She ceased to be a living individual because the life force had departed. Just so, the widow's son died when the breath of life left him. When Elijah prayed for the boy, God gave him back his life (*nephesh*), and once again he became a living, breathing individual.

A study of the Hebrew and Greek words for "soul" in Scripture reveals that the word never means a disembodied, conscious entity. A soul is either the total personality, including body and life force, or it may refer to the life force (breath) itself, or to some other aspect of human personality that is always connected to the body. In fact, at times a dead body is spoken of as a "soul," simply because the body represents the person who has expired. Therefore, Rachel and the widow's son died when life departed from them, and the boy was raised up when God gave him life again.

Why Does the Book of Revelation Depict the Souls of Dead Martyrs Crying Out for Vindication (Rev. 6:9-11)?

First, it should be pointed out that the book of Revelation is full of prophetic symbolism. No one would wish to conclude, for example, that the four living creatures or the 24 elders, or the Lamb, of chapters 4 and 5 appear exactly in heaven as John saw them in vision. God gave John a series of symbolic visions which we can accurately interpret by comparing Scripture with Scripture.

Second, if we are to regard the "souls under the altar" of Revelation 6:9 as literal, we have a strange picture indeed. Why are they congregated under the altar in heaven? Their lot really does not seem to be very pleasant after all; they seem to be very unhappy people in dire need of vindication.

Third, why should these dead martyrs be crying out for God to "avenge" the injustice done to them, if their wicked enemies went to hell at death, as the immortal-soul advocates believe? Surely the vengeance against those who killed the martyrs was already being poured out, if the immortal souls of the wicked go to hell when they die.

Fourth, it is very important to understand that the "altar" of Revelation 6:9 is not the altar of incense in heaven. It is an allusion to the altar of burnt offering that was in the court of the ancient Israelite sanctuary or temple (Exod. 27:1-8; 29:12-18; 38:1-7). How do we know this? John's vision was of people who had been sacrificed. The only place where Israelites were to offer sacrifices was by the altar of burnt offering in the court of the sanctuary (Lev. 17:1-9). In the offering of animal sacrifices, the excess blood was poured at the base of the altar of burnt offering (Lev. 4:7, 18, 25, 30). The life (Hebrew *nephesh* or Greek *psuche* = "life" or "soul") of the animal was in the blood (Gen. 9:4; Deut. 12:23; Lev. 17:10, 11). When the blood of the animal was poured beneath the altar, that represented life being poured out; the life of Christ poured out for us (Heb. 10:1-9; Ps. 22:14), and the lives of Christ's people being sacrificed for Him (Phil. 3:10; Heb. 11:37).

The souls under the altar of Revelation 6:9-11 do not refer to living, conscious, immortal souls of dead people in heaven. These "souls" or "lives" are a symbol of those whose blood was poured out for Christ's sake. Their blood is crying out to God from the ground in a metaphoric sense as the blood of Abel cried out for justice (Gen. 4:10). As we have seen above, the Hebrew and Greek words for "soul" (*nephesh* and *psuche*) never refer to a part of a person that can have existence separate from the body.

The message of Revelation 6:9-11 is a beautiful symbol of God's continuing concern for those who have laid down their lives for Him. He has a record of the injustice dealt to them, and this record cries out for their vindication. They are judged worthy in heaven and told to "rest yet for a little season" (verse 11, KJV). At the second coming of Jesus they will be awakened from the sleep of death and given their eternal inheritance (1 Thess. 4:13-18).

What Did Peter Mean When He Wrote that Christ Preached to the "Spirits in Prison" (1 Peter 3:18-20)?

Those who believe in the immortality of the soul interpret this passage to mean that when Christ died He went down to hell and preached to the wicked souls who had been destroyed in the flood. Why would Christ do that? To give them another chance? Then they must have been in a place like purgatory and not irrevocably lost at all! Unfortunately for this view, the Bible never teaches that those who die lost are given another chance.

Compare what else Peter has to say about the people who were lost in the flood (2 Peter 2:4-9).

Why would Christ preach only to those who were lost in Noah's day? Why didn't He preach to the rest of the lost? The truth is that the passage is not talking about Christ descending to a place of immortal lost spirits when He died. There is no such place described in Scripture. Death is a sleep, and when Jesus died He slept in the grave until the moment of His resurrection. When the wicked were destroyed in the flood, they were put to sleep, reserved "unto the day of judgment to be punished" (2 Peter 2:9, KJV).

The Holy Spirit used Noah as a preacher of righteousness for 120 years (2 Peter 2:5). The "spirits" to whom Noah and Jesus preached were living human beings, in prison spiritually because they had forsaken the only true God (see Isa. 42:7; 61:1; Luke 4:18-21). The Scriptures a number of times speak of living humans on this earth as "spirits" (Heb. 12:23; Num. 16:22; 27:16). Never in the Bible is a "spirit" (*pneuma*) the disembodied, immortal spirit of a human being in heaven or hell. The word *pneuma* means "wind," "breath," "spirit." It was used often in the sense of "person," or in reference to an aspect of personality inseparable from the person. (See 1 Cor. 16:18; Gal. 6:18; 2 Tim. 4:22; cf. Phil. 4:23).

Just as Christ, through the ministry of the Holy Spirit, pled with people before the flood, so He pleads with us today to be reconciled to Himself (1 Peter 3:18).

Did Jesus Tell the Dying Thief that He Would Be in Paradise that Day (Luke 23:43)?

The immortal-soul advocates argue that Jesus preached to the spirits in hell after His death (1 Peter 3:18-20; discussed above). But, on the basis of Luke 23:43, they assert that Jesus went to paradise when He died? Exactly where was Jesus after death?

Paradise is heaven (2 Cor. 12:2, 4; Rev. 2:7; 22:1, 2). Jesus did not go to paradise that Friday afternoon of the crucifixion. On the next Sunday morning, after He had risen from the dead, He said to Mary Magdalene: "Touch me not; *for I am not yet ascended to my Father*" (John 20:17, KJV, italics supplied).

The punctuation of Luke 23:43 in English and in modern Greek Bibles does not represent the punctuation of the original author. There was no such punctuation in the ancient Greek manuscripts. The correct punctuation of the text is as follows: "Verily I say to you today, you will be with me in paradise." Jesus promised this dying believer that he would be in heaven with Him on the resurrection morning at His second coming (1 Thess. 4:13-18; 1 Cor. 15:51-54).

Praise the Lord, every believer in Christ can claim the promise made to the dying thief. Even though we should die, we will be raised to be with Christ in paradise.

If the Soul Is Not Immortal, How Do We Explain that after His Death Samuel Appeared to King Saul (1 Sam. 28:7-19)?

A number of facts establish certainly that this passage does not teach the immortality of the soul:

1. Saul went to the witch of Endor because "the Lord answered him not, neither by dreams, nor by Urim, nor by prophets" (1 Sam. 28:6, KJV). Because of his persistence in rebellion against God, the Lord withdrew from Saul and left him to the control of evil demons. (Compare 1 Samuel 16:14-16). In conversation with the spirit that the witch called up for him, Saul admitted: "God is departed from me, and answereth me no more, neither

by prophets, nor by dreams: therefore I have called thee, that thou mayest make known unto me what I shall do" (1 Sam. 28:15, KJV).

Had Saul repented of his sin, God would have heard his prayers and delivered him from his enemies. A later Bible writer explained why God allowed Saul's life to be taken: "So Saul died for his transgression which he committed against the Lord, even against the word of the Lord, which he kept not, and also for asking counsel of one that had a familiar spirit, to enquire of it; and enquired not of the Lord: therefore he slew him, and turned the kingdom unto David the son of Jesse" (1 Chron. 10:13, 14, KJV).

Since God had departed from Saul and would not answer his prayers, and since God later condemned Saul for going to the witch of Endor, it is inconceivable that God would use the witch to give Saul an inspired message. Since Samuel was a prophet of God during his lifetime, we can assume that the being which appeared to the witch of Endor was not Samuel, but an evil spirit impersonating Samuel. God was not speaking to Saul, and He never speaks at the request of mediums controlled by evil spirits.

2. The witch of Endor is described in the King James Version as one having "a familiar spirit" (1 Sam. 28:7). The Hebrew words for "familiar spirit" are *ba'alath-'ob*. *'Ob* means "necromancer," or "medium." This is a person who claims to foretell the future through alleged communication with the dead; a conjurer, wizard, sorcerer. God had specifically commanded that such evil spirit mediums should be put to death in Israel. Any one consulting spirit mediums was to be cut off from Israel. (See Lev. 19:31; 20:6, 27; Deut. 18:10, 11.) Saul had previously obeyed the divine commands in this respect by expelling the spirit mediums: "And Saul had put away those that had familiar spirits, and the wizards, out of the land" (1 Sam. 28:3, KJV). Are we now to believe that God would speak to Saul through a witch, the very kind of person that He had commanded should not be permitted to live? Such an idea is unthinkable!

3. In response to the witch's incantations, "Samuel" came up, not down (1 Sam. 28:11, 13, 14, 15). If the appearance had been truly Samuel's immortal soul, it would have come down from heaven, not up from the depths of the earth. The evil spirit impersonating Samuel was called Samuel by the Bible writer only because the story is told as the events were perceived by those present.

4. Saul did not see the spirit being. He only had the word of the witch that it was Samuel (verses 13, 14). What Saul "perceived" (verse 14) was

what he understood, even though he did not see the manifestation. Are we to believe the word of a condemned practicing witch that Samuel was actually present?

5. "Samuel" appeared as an old man bowed with his face to the ground. Do immortal souls retain the bodily appearance they had in old age on earth?

6. "Samuel" told Saul: ". . . and to morrow shalt thou and thy sons be with me" (verse 19, KJV). The next day Saul committed suicide (1 Sam. 31:4). If he went to be with Samuel's immortal soul, surely he would have gone to heaven. Do wicked men who are rejected by God and who commit suicide go to heaven when they die?

Saul turned away from God and consulted a medium of evil demons. Because Saul's life was in the devils's hands, the devil could predict what would happen the next day. When the evil one is in charge of a life he can destroy it at will. An evil demon impersonating Samuel predicted Saul's eternal doom.

What Is Meant by Isaiah's Description of the Destruction of the Wicked: "Their Worm Shall Not Die, Neither Shall Their Fire Be Quenched" (Isa. 66:24, KJV)?

The fire that destroys the wicked is unquenchable because, like the fire that burned old Jerusalem, nothing can put it out until it has done its job of consuming the lost (Jer. 17:27).

Why does Isaiah speak of the saved in the new earth viewing the "carcases" of the wicked? (Isa. 66:24). Note first that he does not describe the saved as viewing disembodied immortal souls suffering in hellfire. The Hebrew word translated "carcases" means "dead bodies," or "corpses." In Isaiah's description, worms and fire are devouring dead bodies, not immortal souls.

What is meant by the phrase, "for their worm shall not die"? Some would have us believe that the undying worm is the immortal soul. That would be a strange way indeed for the inspired prophet to describe the soul. In the Hebrew poetry of the text, the "worm" is parallel with the "fire." They are the forces of destruction, not the objects being destroyed. Hence, the meaning of the passage is that, when they are being viewed by the righteous, the dead bodies of the wicked are still in process of being consumed. The simple imperfect tense of the Hebrew verbs suggests the following translation: ". . . their worm had not died yet, nor had their fire been quenched." At the time at which the dead bodies of the wicked are being viewed by the saved, they have not yet been consumed.

Why does Isaiah depict the saved as viewing the burning of the dead bodies of the wicked? It must be understood that Isaiah's description of the new earth (Isa. 65:17 - 66:24) would have been fulfilled in every detail if Israel had not failed in the mission given it by God. Since Israel rejected Christ, and the Christian Church inherited its spiritual blessings and evangelistic program, Isaiah's prophecy must be interpreted in the light of later revelation concerning the new earth state. Whereas Isaiah's new earth for Israel incorporated such things as old age and death (Isa. 65:20), the final new earth foreseen by John the Revelator contains no suffering, death, or destruction of any kind (Rev. 21:1-5). And whereas in Isaiah's new earth, the righteous would see the dead bodies of the wicked, in John's new earth the wicked have been finally consumed (Rev. 20:14, 15). The long life followed by old age and death, and the burning of the wicked in Isaiah's prophecy can now be viewed as metaphoric descriptions of the eternal life of the righteous in a world where there is no death, and where no wicked person dwells. Before the establishment of the final new earth the wicked will be reduced to ashes (Mal. 4:1), for their mortal souls will perish. "The soul that sinneth, it shall die" (Ezek. 18:4, KJV).

Praise the Lord that each one of us can have a part in the earth made new where sin, suffering, and death are no more! If we die before Jesus comes again, we will be raised and given immortality (1 Cor. 15:51-54). If we live until His coming, we will be made immortal beings with the privilege of spending eternity in a universe free from the curse of evil.

How Do We Explain the Bible Statements that Refer to the "Everlasting Destruction" of the Wicked?

A number of times in the New Testament the destruction of the wicked is said to be "everlasting" or "eternal." For that reason some interpreters of the Bible have assumed that the immortal souls of the wicked will burn in hellfire for eternity.

Speaking of the destruction of the wicked, Jesus said: "The chaff he will burn with unquenchable fire" (Matt. 3:12). "Then he will say to those at his left hand, 'You that are accursed, depart from me into the eternal fire prepared for the devil and his angels'" (Matt. 25:41). "And these [the lost] go away into eternal punishment" (Matt. 25:46).

Paul wrote of the kind of destruction that will be meted out upon unbelievers: "These will suffer the punishment of eternal destruction, separated from the presence of the Lord and from the glory of his might, when he comes to be glorified by his saints" (2 Thess. 1:9, 10).

Do these statements of Jesus and Paul imply that the wicked will burn eternally? The answer is no. The fire is unquenchable because, like the fire that burned old Jerusalem, nothing can put it out until it has done its job of consuming the lost. Jeremiah presented God's prediction to His rebellious people: "If you do not listen to me, to keep the sabbath day holy, and to carry in no burden through the gates of Jerusalem on the sabbath day, then I will kindle a fire in its gates; it shall devour the palaces of Jerusalem and shall not be quenched" (Jer. 17:27). Jerusalem was destroyed as Jeremiah had predicted, and the fire burned out. "They burned the house of God, broke down the wall of Jerusalem, burned all its palaces with fire, and destroyed all its precious vessels. . . . to fulfill the word of the Lord by the mouth of Jeremiah" (2 Chron. 36:19, 21).

Sodom and Gomorrah suffered "a punishment of eternal fire" (Jude 7). But the wicked people in those cities are not still burning. Those cities and their inhabitants were reduced to ashes. "By turning the cities of Sodom and Gomorrah to ashes he condemned them to extinction and made them an example of what is coming to the ungodly" (2 Peter 2:6).

At the end of time, the wicked will be reduced to ashes. "See the day is coming, burning like an oven, when all the arrogant and all evildoers will be stubble; the day that comes shall burn them up, says the Lord of hosts, so that it will leave them neither root nor branch. . . . And you shall tread down the wicked, for they will be ashes under the soles of your feet, on the day when I act, says the Lord of hosts" (Mal. 4:1-3). Where would the ashes come from if the wicked went on suffering in the flames for eternity?

In speaking of the punishment of the wicked, both Jesus and Paul used the adjective "eternal" or "everlasting." The Greek adjective used in the New Testament is *aionios*. This adjective and its corresponding noun *aion* (eternity), do not necessarily mean never ending. Often they refer to a period of limited duration. For example, this present "world" or "age" that is coming to an end is a number of times spoken of as this *aion* (Matt. 13:39; Eph. 1:21; 2 Tim. 4:10; 1 Cor. 2:7).

Kittel's *Theological Dictionary of the New Testament* points out that "the meaning of . . . [*aion*] merges into that of a long but limited stretch of time. In particular, . . . [*aion*] in this sense signifies the time or duration of the world, i.e., time as limited by creation and conclusion. At this point we are confronted by the remarkable fact that in the Bible the same word . . . [*aion*] is used to indicate two things which are really profoundly antithetical, namely, the eternity of God and the duration of the world. This twofold sense, which . . . [*aion*] shares with the Heb. . . . [*'olam*], points back to a concept of eternity in which eternity is identified with the duration of the world."[7]

Thus in the New Testament, the words "everlasting" and "eternal" may mean a period of limited duration. Paul wrote to Philemon concerning the slave Onesimus: "Perhaps this is the reason he was separated from you for a while, so that you might have him back forever" (Philemon 15). The word "forever" translates the Greek adjective *aionios*. It does not mean that Philemon would have the services of Onesimus for eternity. It means that Onesimus would serve Philemon until he died.

Liddell and Scott's *Greek English Lexicon* comments on *aion* (eternity) and *aionios* (eternal) that the noun may mean a "period of existence. . . . lifetime, life. . . . space of time clearly defined and marked out, epoch, age. . . . this present world." The adjective *aionios* (eternal) may refer to "holding an office or title for life, perpetual. . . ."[8]

Thus "eternity" may refer to a period of unending duration or a period of limited duration. And "eternal" may mean as long as the nature of the subject allows.

What is the nature of those who are taken to heaven at the second coming of Jesus? They are given immortality when Jesus appears (1 Cor. 15:51-54). Therefore they live eternally, because beings who are immortal can never die (John 3:16, 36; Matt. 25:46).

What is the nature of the wicked upon whom the fire is rained at the end of the millennium? They are still mortal beings! Paul taught that "the wages of sin is death, but the free gift of God is eternal life in Christ Jesus our Lord" (Rom. 6:23).

The eternal punishment of the lost is eternal death, the opposite of eternal life. Because the lost are mortal, they can die and will die in the fires of the last great day. If they lived on in the fire for eternity, they would have eternal life, not eternal death. In the phrase "eternal fire" the word "eternal" refers to the limited period of intense suffering which comes to an end when the wicked die. The fire is eternal because it brings the world (*aion*) to an end. The fire is eternal in its results. The death of the wicked is an eternal (never-ending) death. That is what Jesus meant when He said of the lost: "These go away into eternal punishment" (Matt. 25:46).

"Forever" does not always mean without end throughout eternity. It is an English translation of *aion* or *aionios* (Greek) or *'olam* (Hebrew), which we have seen sometimes mean a period of limited duration. Jonah spoke of his experience in the belly of the whale: "I went down to the land whose bars closed upon me *forever*" (Jonah 2:6, italics supplied). But he was in the belly of the whale "three days and three nights" (Jonah 1:17). Gehazi and his seed were to be lepers "forever" (2 Kings 5:27). They were lepers until death. Israel was instructed to observe the Passover "for ever" (Exod. 12:24, KJV). But the Passover ceased to have significance when Jesus died on the cross (1 Cor. 5:7).

These facts enable us to explain the statements in the book of Revelation that speak of the sufferings of the wicked at the end of the millennium: "And the smoke of their torment goes up forever and ever [*eis aionas aionon*] There is no rest day or night for those who worship the beast and its image and for anyone who receives the mark of its name" (Rev. 14:11). "And they will be tormented day and night forever and ever [*eis tous aionas ton aionon*] (Rev. 20:10).

In each case, the Greek phrase means as long as the nature of the subject allows. Because the wicked are mortal beings, they suffer forever in the sense that their suffering continues until their lives expire. They have no rest and no freedom from torment until they are reduced to ashes.

Jude 13 and 2 Peter 2:17 indicate that the lost will suffer blackest darkness "forever." What better way could there be to describe the darkness of eternal extinction? The Psalmist pointed out that no one will be able to discover where the wicked are after they have been destroyed, because they will have been entirely consumed. "Yet a little while, and the wicked will be no more; though you look diligently for their place, they will not be there" (Ps. 37:10). "The wicked perish, and the enemies of the Lord are like the glory of the pastures; they vanish — like smoke they vanish away" (verse 20).

God is merciful in bringing the sufferings of the wicked to an end. Certainly the period that Jonah was in the belly of the whale must have seemed to him like forever. And the sufferings of the lost will seem to them like forever. But the Lord is too loving and merciful to permit them to suffer unendingly, for eternity.

Are you willing to commit your life, as Stephen did, to the care of the eternal Life Giver? The Lord pleads with you to turn from fables to the truth of His Word, and to find in Christ your assurance of salvation. The doctrine of the immortality of the soul opens the door for the deceptions of spiritism and the errors of purgatory and eternal hellfire. We can rejoice that God's Word delivers us from these deceptions and errors. And we can rejoice that Christ suffered to deliver us from sin and destruction.

"For God so loved the world that he gave his only Son, so that everyone who believes in him may not perish but may have eternal life" (John 3:16).

Notes
1. Kurt Aland, et al, *The Greek New Testament* (New York: American Bible Society, 1966), 1 Cor. 6:20.
2. Francis Brown, S. R. Driver, Charles A. Briggs, *A Hebrew and English Lexicon of the Old Testament* (Oxford: Clarendon Press, 1906, 1951), s.v. *nᵉshamah*; William F. Arndt and F. Wilbur Gingrich, *A Greek-English Lexicon of the New Testament* (Chicago: University Press, 1957), s.v. *pnoe*.
3. See Arndt and Gringrich, *A Greek-English Lexicon of the New Testament*. See also Gerhard Kittel, ed., *Theological Dictionary of the New Testament*, trans. by Geoffrey W. Bromiley (Grand Rapids, Michigan: Wm. B. Eerdmans, 1968), vol. 6, pp. 332-451
4. See Brown, Driver, and Briggs, *A Hebrew and English Lexicon of the Old Testament*.
5. See Brown, Driver, and Briggs, *A Hebrew and English Lexicon of the Old Testament*.
6. Gerhard Kittel (ed.), *Theological Dictionary of the New Testament* (Grand Rapids, Michigan: Wm. B. Eerdmans, 1974), vol. 9, pp. 618-620.
7. *Ibid.*, vol. 1, p. 202.
8. Henry George Liddell and Robert Scott, *A Greek-English Lexicon* (Oxford: Clarendon Press, 1968), s.v. *aion, aionios*.

Chapter 3
Does the Bible Teach Trinitarianism?

The Bible doctrine of the Trinity teaches that there is one God in three Persons: Father, Son, and Holy Spirit. The Bible teaching, as we will see when we turn to the Scriptures, is distinctly monotheistic. That is to say, the Bible teaches that there is one God, not three. The three Persons who comprise our one God share the same essence and characteristics. The unity between them is so mysteriously close that it is true to say that they are one God. When we pray to the Father, we are praying to the Son and the Holy Spirit. When we pray to the Son or the Holy Spirit, we are praying to the other two Persons of the Deity.

We could draw a circle on a blackboard and call the entire circle "the Godhead," or "the Deity." Then we could divide the circle into three parts and call the parts "the Father," "the Son," and "the Holy Spirit." By so doing we would be seriously misrepresenting the Bible doctrine of the Trinity. The Father is the full Deity, not a third of it. Likewise, the Son and the Holy Spirit are both the fullness of the Deity. Thus there are three fullnesses, but only one God. Each member of the Deity is the total Deity. The Persons are not separate and distinct in exactly the same way that human persons are. They are united in a mysterious bond so that all three together comprise the fullness of Deity, and any one of the three is also the fullness of Deity. Father, Son, and Holy Spirit are coequal and co-eternal. There is no indication in Scripture that, as God, the Son and the Holy Spirit are inferior to the Father, or that there ever was a time when they did not exist in infinitely close union with the Father. Our one God (Father, Son, and Holy Spirit) is our Creator and the Creator of our world and universe. To Him we owe complete allegiance because He gave us life and sustains our life.

Because this Bible teaching is so mysterious and, thereby, beyond the capacity of human beings to grasp completely, some Bible students react by saying that it is confusing, illogical, and unbiblical. As Robert M. Bowman has pointed out, among those religions whose members react in this way are "Unitarianism, Mormonism, New Thought, Christian Science, Unity School of Christianity, Theosophy (which is one of the principal sources of the contemporary New Age movement), modern spiritism (another major precursor to the New Age movement)—and Jehovah's Witnesses."[1]

Bowman adds: "The JWs will no doubt be offended to be included in such a list, and there are, of course, differences among these various religions. But all of them have in common, besides their time and place of origin, a firm belief inherited from the Enlightenment that the orthodox Christianity of the previous fifteen centuries was no longer acceptable. In particular, all of them reject the Trinity."[2]

Bowman's book was written specifically to answer the antitrinitarianism of the Jehovah's Witnesses as presented in the pamphlet that they have widely distributed, *Should You Believe in the Trinity?*[3] Bowman has effectively demonstrated that this Jehovah's Witness publication has seriously misrepresented the modern and early church sources it cites.[4] The authors incorrectly represent the ante-Nicene Fathers as largely in support of their antitrinitarian concepts. Moreover, they cite modern theologians as rejecting the doctrine of the Trinity. As Bowman has pointed out, the quotations provided by the Jehovah's Witnesses should be carefully examined in relation to their immediate contexts and to the overall contexts in the works from which they were taken.

What Do the Jehovah's Witnesses Believe about the Trinity?

What exactly do Jehovah's Witnesses teach on the subject of the Trinity? They write:

"If people were to read the Bible from cover to cover without any preconceived idea of a Trinity, would they arrive at such a concept on their own? Not at all.

"What comes through very clearly to an impartial reader is that God alone is the Almighty, the Creator, separate and distinct from anyone else, and that Jesus, even in his prehuman existence, is also separate and distinct, a created being subordinate to God."[5]

"Thus, Jesus had an existence in heaven before coming to the earth. But was it as one of the persons in an almighty, eternal triune Godhead? No, for the Bible plainly states that in his prehuman existence, Jesus was a created spirit being, just as angels were spirit beings created by God. Neither the angels nor Jesus had existed before their creation."[6]

As a man upon this earth, "Jesus, no more and no less than a perfect human, became a ransom that compensated exactly for what Adam lost—the right to perfect human life on earth. So Jesus could rightly be called 'the last Adam' by the apostle Paul, who said in the same context: 'Just as in Adam all are dying, so also in the Christ all will be made alive.' (1 Corinthians 15:22, 45). The perfect human life of Jesus was the 'corresponding ransom' required by divine justice—no more, no less. A basic principle even of human justice is that the price paid should fit the wrong committed. . . .

"It was only a perfect human, Adam, who sinned in Eden, not God. So the ransom, to be truly in line with God's justice, had to be strictly an equivalent—a perfect human, 'the last Adam.'"[7]

"Jesus never claimed to be God. Everything he said about himself indicates that he did not consider himself equal to God in any way—not in power, not in knowledge, not in age.

"In every period of his existence, whether in heaven or on earth, his speech and conduct reflect subordination to God. God is always the superior, Jesus the lesser one who was created by God."[8]

"The Bible's use of 'holy spirit' indicates that it is a controlled force that Jehovah God uses to accomplish a variety of his purposes. To a certain extent, it can be likened to electricity, a force that can be adapted to perform a great variety of operations."[9]

"There can be no compromise with God's truths. Hence, to worship God on his terms means to reject the Trinity doctrine. It contradicts what the prophets, Jesus, the apostles, and the early Christians believed and taught. It contradicts what God says about himself in his own inspired Word. Thus, he counsels: 'Acknowledge that I alone am God and that there is no one else like me.'—Isaiah 46:9, *TEV*."[10]

Bruce M. Metzger has provided the following summary of Jehovah's Witnesses' teaching regarding Christ: "According to the Jehovah's Witnesses, Christ before his earthly life was a spirit-creature named Michael, the first of God's creation, through whom God made the other created things. As a consequence of his birth on earth, which was not an incarnation, Jesus became a perfect human being, the equal of Adam prior to the Fall. In his death Jesus' human nature, being sacrificed, was annihilated. As a reward for his sacrificial obedience God gave him a divine, spirit nature. Throughout his existence, therefore, Jesus Christ never was coequal with God. He is not eternal, for there was a time when he was not. While he was on earth he was nothing more than a man, and therefore the atoning effect of his death can have no more significance than that of a perfect human being. Throughout there is an ill-concealed discontinuity between the preexistent spirit creature, the earthly man Jesus, and the present spirit existence of Christ Jesus."[11]

The Teachings of Arius Regarding Christ

The teachings of the Jehovah's Witnesses concerning Christ are quite consistent with the teachings of Arius (c. 250 – c. 336 A.D.), a presbyter in the church of Alexandria, who began to teach his distinctive views about the year A.D. 318. His fundamental idea was that only God the Father is absolutely unique and transcendent. He alone is eternal and the Source of all reality and existence. "Since it is unique, transcendent and indivisible, the being or essence (*ousia*) of the Godhead cannot be shared or communicated. For God to impart His substance to some other being, however exalted, would imply that He is divisible ... and subject to change ... which is inconceivable. Moreover, if any other being were to participate in the divine nature in any valid sense, there would result a duality of divine beings, whereas the Godhead is by definition unique. Therefore whatever else exists must have come into existence, not by any communication of God's being, but by an act of creation on His part, i.e. must have been called into existence out of nothing."[12]

Arius drew four conclusions regarding Christ[13]: (1) The Word, Christ, is a creature who, like other creatures, was formed by the Father out of nothing. (2) Christ, the Word must have had a beginning. "'We are persecuted', Arius protests, 'because we say the Son has a beginning whereas God is without beginning.'"[14] Arius and his followers liked to repeat their slogan, "'There was when He was not.'"[15] For Arius it was a contradiction of monotheism to say that Christ, like the Father, had eternity of existence. Hence, he taught that the Son was brought into existence by the Father back in the eternal ages before creation. (3) Because he is a creature, the

Son has no direct knowledge of the Father or communion with him in any sense other than that possible to other creatures. (4) Unlike God, the Son's nature is subject to change and the possibility of sin. Arius argued that the titles God and Son of God were merely courtesy titles given to Christ.

As we study the Scriptures regarding the nature of God and the Deity of Jesus Christ and the Holy Spirit, we quickly discover that we are treading on very sacred ground. There are many mysteries not explained to us mere mortals. But to attempt a solution to those mysteries based on philosophical arguments, instead of accepting the clear teachings of the Word of God, is to arrive at error that will ultimately undermine our faith in Christ. It is inconceivable that finite mortals could define or explain the infinite God. A god who is explainable by human beings is certainly not the God of the Bible. To deny Bible teaching on the subject of the Godhead because it is beyond our understanding, confusing, and illogical is to attempt to bring God and His Word down to our limited intellectual and spiritual grasp.

What does the Bible teach regarding the eternity of Christ and the Holy Spirit and their relationship with the Father. Are there three Gods, one supreme and the other two inferior? Is there one supreme God, a second god who is a created being, and a force that emanates from both, called the Holy Spirit? Or is there only one God—the Father, the Son, and the Holy Spirit?

There Is Only One God

The Bible doctrine of the Trinity does not in any way compromise the Bible teaching that there is only one God. There can be no question that the Bible writers were all monotheists, that is, believers in the existence of only one God. But they did not arrive at their monotheism as Arius did and the Jehovah's Witnesses do, by insisting that the Son and the Holy Spirit are not supreme Deity. The Bible writers never attempted to explain the nature of God in philosophical terms, nor did they spell out a systematic doctrine of the Trinity. They simply recorded the truths the Lord revealed to them and faithfully accepted the fact that "the secret things belong to the Lord our God" (Deut. 29:29). The result was the clear teaching that the Deity is One in three Persons. We will begin by emphasizing the Bible's monotheistic teaching.

The Hebrew of Deuteronomy 6:4 reads literally: "Jehovah [Yahweh] our God, Jehovah [is] One." Unlike the nations around them, who were polytheists, the Jews were monotheists, believing in only one true God. Moses reminded ancient Israel, "To you it was shown so that you would acknowledge that the Lord is God; there is no other besides him" (Deut. 4:35).

Consistently God revealed Himself to the prophets as One. The Psalmist wrote: "Let them know that you alone, whose name is the Lord [Yahweh], are the Most High over all the earth" (Ps. 83:18). "For you are great and do wondrous things; you alone are God [*Elohim*]" (Ps. 86:10).[16]

Isaiah declared that no God ever preceded the one true God, and no other has ever come into existence to share His glory. "You are my witnesses, says the Lord, and my servant whom I have chosen, so that you may know and believe me and understand that I am he. Before me no god was formed, nor shall there be any after me. I, I am the Lord, and besides me there is no savior" (Isa. 43:10, 11). "Thus says the Lord, the King of Israel, and his Redeemer, the Lord of hosts: I am the first and I am the last; besides me there is no god" (Isa. 44:6).

Whatever we believe about Jesus Christ and the Holy Spirit, we must not contradict the Scripture teaching that there is only one God. Jesus, Paul, and James taught the same truth, and it was believed consistently by the early Christian Church. When one of the scribes asked Jesus, "'Which commandment is the first of all?'" He answered, "'The first is, Hear, O Israel: the Lord our God, the Lord is one [Deut. 6:4]; you shall love the Lord your God with all your heart, and with all your soul, and with all your mind, and with all your strength.'" (Mark 12:28-30).

The apostle Paul reiterated the monotheistic teaching of the Hebrew-Christian tradition by asserting: "We know that 'no idol in the world really exists,' and that 'there is no God but one'" (1 Cor. 8:4). "One Lord, one faith, one baptism, one God and Father of all, who is above all and through all and in all" (Eph. 4:5, 6).

James underlined the point: "You believe that God is one; you do well. Even the demons believe – and shudder" (James 2:19).

The doctrine of the Trinity taught in Scripture does not contradict the truth that there is only one God. This doctrine does not teach that there are three separate Gods who are only morally and spiritually in perfect agreement. But what evidence is there that our one God is comprised of the Father, the Son, and the Holy Spirit?

There Is Only One Creator: the Father, the Son, and the Holy Spirit

The creatorship of God is a prominent Scriptural truth. Our one God made man in His own image. The passages that speak of the Creator emphasize His oneness. Yet our one Creator comprises the Father, the Son, and the Holy Spirit.

The Bible teaches that we have only one Creator. "Have we not all one father? Has not one God created us?" (Mal. 2:10). 1 Peter 4:19 speaks of "a faithful Creator."

This faithful Creator speaks of Himself in the plural: "Then God said, 'Let *us* make humankind in *our* image, according to *our* likeness'" (Gen. 1:26, italics supplied). After Adam and Eve fell into sin, they were driven from the garden of Eden lest they should eat of the tree of life and become immortal sinners (Gen. 3:22-24). "Then the Lord God said, 'See, the man has become like one of *us*, knowing good and evil.'" (Gen. 3:22, italics supplied). When the tower of Babel was being built, God said, "'Come, let *us* go down, and confuse their language there, so that they will not understand one another's speech.' So the Lord scattered them abroad" (Gen. 11:7, 8). Why did God speak of Himself in the plural in these passages? To suggest that it was because He was speaking in counsel with the angels does not answer the question. God did not make mankind in the image of the angels, nor is there evidence that angels know good and evil as God does. God's depiction of Himself as One who is plural is only adequately explained by comparing the New Testament with the Old. Our one Creator in whose image mankind was made was the Father, the Son, and the Holy Spirit.

The Father's role in creation is described in many Bible passages. For example: "In the beginning God created the heaven and the earth" (Gen. 1:1, KJV). "Know that the Lord [*Yahweh* or *Jehovah*] is God. It is he that made us, and we are his" (Ps. 100:3).

The Son is also described as the Creator. "Yet for us there is one God, the Father, from whom are all things and for whom we exist, and one Lord, Jesus Christ, through whom are all things and through whom we exist" (1 Cor. 8:6). "All things came into being through him [the Word, Christ], and without him not one thing came into being" (John 1:3). "For in him all things in heaven and on earth were created, things visible and invisible, whether thrones or dominions or rulers or powers — all things have been created through him and for him. He himself is before all things, and in him all things hold together" (Col. 1:16, 17). "In these last days he has spoken to us by a Son, whom he appointed heir of all things, through whom he also created the worlds. He is the reflection of God's glory and the exact imprint of God's very being, and he sustains all things by his powerful word" (Heb. 1:2, 3).

Likewise the Holy Spirit is presented as the Creator. "And the Spirit of God moved upon the face of the waters" (Gen. 1:2, KJV). "The Spirit of God has made me, And the breath of the Almighty gives me life" (Job. 33:4, NASB). "Thou doest send forth Thy Spirit, they are created" (Ps. 104:30, NASB).

The point is that the Creator who is one Deity, not three, comprises three divine Persons: the Father, the Son, and the Holy Spirit.

Like the Father, Christ Is Jehovah (*Yahweh*) Eternal God

There is no clearer teaching in Scripture than that Jesus Christ is the Deity, equal with the Father in authority and power, having exactly the same nature as well as eternity of existence.

Paul's statements in Colossians 1:19 and 2:9 establish conclusively that the full and complete nature of the Deity dwells in Christ. "For in him all the fullness of God was pleased to dwell" (Col. 1:19). "For in him the whole fullness of deity dwells bodily" (Col. 2:9). The word "fullness" translates the Greek word *pleroma* that means "*sum total, fullness*, even (*super*)*abundance . . . of someth*".[17] Arndt and Gringrich translate Colossians 2:9: "*the full measure of deity*." [18] Kittel's *Theological Dictionary of the New Testament* comments: "Col. 1:19: It has pleased God that the whole fullness of essence should take up dwelling (aor.) in Christ. According to the context, in a combination of thoughts from 2 C. 5:19 and 8:9 etc., the reference is to the historical Jesus . . . and hence to the fullness of the essence of the God of love. In Col. 2:9 the whole fullness of Godhead, understood from the standpoint of power, is ascribed (pres.) to the exalted Lord; this belongs wholly and undividedly to Christ."[19] The word "Godhead" (Col. 2:9) translates the Greek word that means Deity (*theotes*).[20] Thus the total Deity dwells in Christ.

Jesus claimed equality with God. Because He had healed a man on the Sabbath day (John 5:1-16), the Jewish religious leaders objected and "started persecuting" (verse 16, NRSV) Him. "But Jesus answered them, 'My Father is still working, and I also am working.' For this reason the Jews were seeking all the more to kill him, because he was not only breaking the sabbath, but was also calling God his own Father, thereby making himself equal to God. Jesus said to them, 'Very truly, I tell you, the Son can do nothing on his own, but only what he sees the Father doing; for whatever the Father does, the Son does likewise.'" (verses 17-19).

The objection is sometimes raised that, because the Jews *interpreted* Jesus as "making himself equal to God," does not prove that He was intending them to interpret Him in that way. But neither Jesus nor John, the Gospel writer, in any way denied the interpretation that He was making Himself equal with God. It would have been very simple for Jesus to correct such a misapprehension. In fact, His following discourse simply underlined His claim to equality with God. "Whatever the Father does, the Son does likewise" (verse 19). "Indeed, just as the Father raises the dead and gives them life, so also the Son gives life to whomever he wishes. The Father judges no one but has given all judgment to the Son, so that all may honor the Son just as they honor the Father" (verses 21-23). If Jesus had been only a perfect human while He was on earth, as the Jehovah's witnesses claim, He never could have made statements like that. It was precisely because they thought He was a mere human making divine claims for Himself that the Jews were seeking to kill Him.

C. K. Barrett comments: "God is essentially and unchangeably creative . . . ; what God does Jesus also does (v. 19). . . . The Jews are not slow to see the implications of Jesus' argument, and are when they see them the more anxious to kill him. . . . Sabbath-breaking, though important, was a comparatively trivial offence. . . . Jesus had called God his *own* father . . . a form of speech which did not arise out of liturgical custom or the notion of Israel as God's child; and the assumption of a uniform activity common to Jesus and to God could only mean that Jesus was equal to God. This inference John of course himself admits, but rightly presents it as extremely provocative to the Jews."[21]

In writing his Gospel, John could easily have corrected the Jews' mistaken interpretation, if, indeed, it had been mistaken. He later corrected a misinterpretation of Jesus' words (John 21:22, 23). But on this occasion,

He simply recorded Jesus' claim to the same honor and power possessed by the Father. We can only conclude that Jesus claimed equality with the Father.

This claim became more insistent in following discussions with the Jewish leaders. "Jesus said to them, 'Very truly, I tell you, before Abraham was, I am.' So they picked up stones to throw at him, but Jesus hid himself and went out of the temple" (John 8:58, 59). Jehovah's Witnesses would have us believe that Jesus was claiming preexistence, but not *eternal* preexistence. It is questionable whether the Jewish leaders would have immediately taken up stones to take His life if He had not been identifying Himself with the Father. Obviously they recognized the name I AM as a title of Deity. And rightfully so. This was the name by which *Yahweh* identified Himself to Moses. "God said to Moses, 'I AM WHO I AM.' He said further, 'Thus you shall say to the Israelites, I AM has sent me to you.' God also said to Moses, 'Thus you shall say to the Israelites, The Lord, the God of your ancestors, the God of Abraham, the God of Isaac, and the God of Jacob, has sent me to you: This is my name forever, and this my title for all generations.'" (Exod. 3:14, 15).

Similar "I Am" statements occur in Isaiah referring to *Yahweh*. Bowman comments: "Most biblical scholars who have written extensively on the subject agree that these 'I am' sayings in Isaiah are even more relevant to John 8:58 than the words of God in Exodus 3:14. The NWT [New World Translation of the JWs] renders these sayings as 'I am the same' or 'I am the same one,' which further hides the parallel. In Hebrew they read literally 'I [am] he,' and in the Septuagint were translated *ego eimi*, 'I am' (Isa. 41:4; 43:10; 46:4; 52:6; see also 45:18)."[22]

R. C. H. Lenski contrasts the tenses of the Greek verbs in Jesus' statement of John 8:58, "Before Abraham was [aorist or past tense, *genesthai*], I am [present tense, *eimi*]." Lenski points out: "As the aorist [past tense] sets a point of beginning for the existence of Abraham, so the present tense 'I am' predicates absolute existence for the person of Jesus, with no point of beginning at all. That is why Jesus does not use the imperfect . . . 'I was'; for this would say only that the existence of the person of Jesus antedates the time of Abraham and would leave open the question whether the person of Jesus also has a beginning like that of Abraham (only earlier) or not. What Jesus declares is that, although his earthly life covers less than fifty years, his existence as a person . . . is constant and independent of any beginning in time as was that of Abraham. For what Jesus here says about himself in comparison with Abraham is in the nature of the case true of him in comparison with any other man, no matter how far back the beginning of that man's existence lies. 'I am' = I exist. Thus with the simplest words Jesus testifies to the divine, eternal preexistence of his person."[23]

No wonder the Jews took up stones to stone Him. Because Jesus was claiming to be Yahweh, they regarded Him as a blasphemer worthy of death. The Jehovah's Witnesses and others react differently; they deny His claim by misinterpreting His words.

The eternal preexistence of Christ is taught in other passages of Scripture. For example, in predicting the Messiah's birth in Bethlehem, Micah wrote: "But as for you, Bethlehem Ephrathah, Too little to be among the clans of Judah, From you One will go forth for Me to be ruler in Israel. His goings forth are from long ago, From the days of eternity" (Micah 5:2, NASB). The prophet was not predicting that the Messiah who would be born in Bethlehem had a beginning somewhere back *within* the days of eternity. He was emphasizing that *throughout* the days of eternity, the Messiah had continuing existence.[24]

The same thought is expressed in Hebrews 7:2, 3. King Melchizedek of Salem, priest of the Most High God to whom Abraham paid tithes when he returned from battle is likened to Christ, the Son of God. We are not told who Melchizedek was, but we are told that he was "without father, without mother, without genealogy, having neither beginning of days nor end of life, but resembling the Son of God, he remains a priest forever" (Heb. 7:3). Whatever the passage is intended to tell us about Melchizedek, it is clear that the writer's purpose is to say that the Son of God had "neither beginning of days nor end of life." Christ's eternity of existence is underlined.

In Revelation, chapter 1, the Father is spoken of as "him who is and who was and who is to come" (verse 4). In verse 8, the Father is identified as "the Alpha and the Omega," "who is and who was and who is to come, the Almighty." The Father's eternity of existence is clearly pinpointed. The Jehovah's Witnesses are correct in reminding us that the title "Alpha and Omega" is not claimed by Christ in verse 11. These words do not occur in the Greek text. But in Revelation 22:12-16, the title Alpha and Omega is claimed by Christ. "And, behold, I come quickly; and my reward is with me, to give every man according as his work shall be. I am Alpha and Omega, the beginning and the end, the first and the last. . . . I Jesus have sent mine angel to testify unto you these things in the churches" (KJV). The same designation of His eternity of existence claimed by Jehovah in Revelation 1 is claimed by Jesus in Revelation 22 (compare Isa. 44:6).

When Jesus was born in Bethlehem in fulfillment of the Old Testament prophecies, in His Person God came to be with mankind. Matthew interpreted Isaiah 7:14 as a messianic prophecy referring to Jesus. "Now all this was done, that it might be fulfilled which was spoken of the Lord by the prophet, saying, Behold a virgin shall be with child, and shall bring forth a son, and they shall call his name Emmanuel, which being interpreted is, God with us" (Matt. 1:22, 23, KJV). Baby Jesus (the child and man He became) was not a mere perfect human. He was fully God and fully man. "Immanuel" in Isaiah 7:14, the passage that Matthew quotes in reference to Jesus, is speaking of Jehovah (*Yahweh*). Thus, according to Matthew, Jesus was "Jehovah with us."

Forecasting the coming of the Messiah, Isaiah spoke of Him as "Wonderful Counselor, Mighty God, Everlasting Father, Prince of Peace" (Isa. 9:6). This does not mean that the Father and the Son are the same Personality. It means that, though having a distinct personality, Jesus was, and still remains the "exact imprint of God's very being" (Heb. 1:3). As the Father is worshipped, so Christ was to be worshipped when He came to earth in human form: "And again, when he brings the firstborn into the world, he says, 'Let all God's angels worship him'" (Heb. 1:6). The Father addresses the Son as the Deity: "'Your throne, O God, is forever and ever, and the righteous scepter is the scepter of your kingdom'" (Heb. 1:8). The Father speaks of His Son as "Lord": "'In the beginning, Lord you founded the earth, and the heavens are the work of your hands'" (Heb. 1:10).

The writer of the epistle to the Hebrews identifies Jesus as God. "Yet Jesus is worthy of more glory than Moses, just as the builder of a house has more honor than the house itself. (For every house is built by someone, but the builder of all things is God.)" (Heb. 3:3, 4) Jesus who is God is "the builder of the house" in which Moses was "a servant" (verse 5). We are Christ's house "if we hold firm the confidence and the pride that belong to hope." (verse 6).

Two Jehovah's Witness ladies who were visiting my home refused to pray with me because I would pray directly to Jesus as Lord. They insisted that we should pray only to the Father. But if the angels are to worship Him

(Heb. 1:6), why should not we? After His humiliation on this earth and terrible death on the cross, "God also highly exalted him and gave him the name that is above every name, so that at the name of Jesus every knee should bend, in heaven and on earth and under the earth, and every tongue should confess that Jesus Christ is Lord, to the glory of God the Father" (Phil. 2:9, 10). When Stephen was being stoned "he prayed, 'Lord Jesus, receive my spirit'" (Acts 7:59). Bruce Metzger comments: "It is obviously both foolish and sinful to pray to anyone except God. If therefore the opinion of the Jehovah's Witnesses be correct, namely, that Jesus is only a spirit creature, then Stephen was an idolater in praying to one who was not truly God."[25]

Jesus identified Himself with the Father in a manner that established their equality as Deity and their unity of essence. "'If you know me, you will know my Father also. From now on you do know him and have seen him.' Philip said to him, 'Lord show us the Father, and we will be satisfied.' Jesus said to him, 'Have I been with you all this time, Philip, and you still do not know me? Whoever has seen me has seen the Father. How can you say, "Show us the Father"? Do you not believe that I am in the Father and the Father is in me? The words that I say to you I do not speak on my own; but the Father who dwells in me does his works. Believe me that I am in the Father and the Father is in me; but if you do not, then believe me because of the works themselves'" (John 14:7-11; compare John 10:30-38).

The passage teaches: (1) Knowing Jesus is knowing the Father. No mere man could have made such a claim. (2) The Father and the Son dwell within one another. Here is a statement of unity within the Deity that is beyond human explanation. But the statement has enormous implications. To speak to One is to speak to the Other. To worship the One as only Deity is to worship the Other as only Deity. (3) The Father's works are Jesus' works, and Jesus' works are the Father's works. Therefore, the love manifest by Jesus is the love of the Father. Christ's healing ministry is the Father's healing ministry. Christ's words of compassion and forgiveness come from the compassionate, forgiving heart of the Father. No wonder the prophet predicted that the Messiah would be "the Mighty God, Everlasting Father, Prince of Peace (Isa. 9:6).

The Father did not become the Son; they are distinct Persons. But their essential unity is so infinitely close that they are one God. With Jesus as infinitely loving Lord and Savior, we have the Father as infinitely loving Lord and Savior.

Thomas had no doubt of this when, convinced of Jesus identity after His resurrection, he exclaimed, "'My Lord and my God!'" (John 20:28).[26] To a Jew, a statement such as that was an unequivocal acknowledgment that Jesus was Jehovah God.

Titus 2:13 refers to "the blessed hope and the manifestation of the glory of our great God and Savior, Jesus Christ." Second Peter 1:1 speaks of "the righteousness of our God and Savior Jesus Christ." "These passages follow exactly the same construction as is found in the expressions 'our Lord and Savior Jesus Christ,' 'the Lord and Savior Jesus Christ,' and 'the Lord and Savior' (2 Peter 1:11; 2:20; 3:2, 18). This construction in Greek connects two nouns by using the Greek word for *and* (*kai*) and places a definite article "the" in front of the first noun but not in front of the second (e.g., 'the Lord and Savior'). In fact every occurrence of this construction, when the nouns are singular and are common nouns describing persons (Father, Son, Lord, Savior, brother, etc.), uses the two nouns to refer to the same person. Thus the construction used, and especially the way Peter uses it elsewhere, strongly supports the conclusion that in 2 Peter 1:1 [as also in Titus 2:13] Jesus is called 'God.'"[27]

First John 5:20 identifies Jesus as God: "And we know that the Son of God has come and has given us understanding so that we may know him who is true; and we are in him who is true, in his Son Jesus Christ. He is the true God and eternal life." The Son is the source of our eternal life (1 John 1:2; compare 5:11-13). We are in the Son Jesus Christ who "is the true God and eternal life."

Old Testament passages that refer to Jehovah (*Yahweh*) are sometimes applied to Jesus Christ in New Testament quotations. For example, Isaiah 40:3, "Prepare the way of the Lord [*Yahweh* or *Jehovah*]", is quoted in Matthew 3:3, "Prepare the way of the Lord" [*kurios,* which here refers to Christ]. Isaiah 8:13, 14 (KJV) depicts the Lord (*Yahweh* or *Jehovah*) as "a stone of stumbling" and "a rock of offence." Peter quotes the passage and applies it to Christ. "Unto you therefore which believe he [Christ] is precious: but unto them which be disobedient, the stone which the builders disallowed, the same is made the head of the corner, and a stone of stumbling, and a rock of offence" (1 Peter 2:7, 8, KJV). In Zechariah 12:10, Jehovah is spoken of as pierced (cf. verse 1): "They shall look upon me whom they have pierced" (KJV). In speaking of Jesus' side being pierced with a spear as He hung upon the cross, John writes: "And again another scripture saith, They shall look on him whom they pierced" (John 19:37, KJV; cf. verse 34). Once again, Jehovah is Christ. When Isaiah received a vision of Jehovah, he exclaimed: "My eyes have seen the King, the Lord of hosts!" (Isa. 6:5). John refers to the passage (Isa. 6:1-10) and adds, "Isaiah said this because he saw his glory and spoke about him" (John 12:41). It was the glory of Christ that Isaiah saw. But, as recorded in Isaiah 6, Isaiah saw the glory of Jehovah. The apostle Paul wrote of Christ: "For to this end Christ died and lived again, so that he might be Lord of both the dead and the living. . . . For it is written, 'As I live, says the Lord, every knee shall bow to me, and every tongue shall give praise to God'" (Rom. 14:9, 11). The Old Testament passage Paul quotes applies to Jehovah: "'To me every knee shall bow, and every tongue shall swear'" (Isa. 45:23; cf. Phil. 2:9-11).

The Septuagint, the Greek translation of the Old Testament, translates *Yahweh* by *Kurios*, Lord. *Kurios* occurs 749 times in the New Testament.[28] In the vast majority of cases it is applied to the Father or to Christ. Christ is spoken of in the New Testament as supreme Lord. "You know the message he sent to the people of Israel, preaching peace by Jesus Christ — he is Lord of all" (Acts 10:36). But according to both Old and New Testaments there is only one Lord (Deut. 6:4; Zech. 14:9; 1 Cor. 8:6; Eph. 4:5). Christ is Lord or Jehovah. Predicting the work of his son John the Baptist, Zechariah exclaimed: "And you child, will be called the prophet of the Most High; for you will go before the Lord to prepare his ways" (Luke 1:76). The Most High, the Lord for whom John the Baptist functioned as forerunner, was Jesus Christ (cf. Matt. 11:10; Mal. 3:1).

Jesus Christ is the Deity, one with the Father in essence, nature, authority, and power, possessing all of the characteristics and prerogatives of God. There never was a time when He did not exist. He was not brought into existence by the Father, but has eternity of preexistence. The Christ who bore our sins on the cross is the King of the universe.

Is Christ Subordinate to the Father?

Some New Testament passages refer to Christ's subordinate role when He was here on earth. As a God-man who had accepted the limitations of humanity, Jesus assumed a dependent role. For example, note His statement: "The Father is greater than I" (John 14:28). In the same chapter,

Jesus stated the divine mystery, "He that hath seen me hath seen the Father . . . Believest thou not that I am in the Father, and the Father in me?" (verses 9, 10, KJV). Since there was a divine oneness between the Son and the Father, Christ remained God in the fullest sense. Yet He had adopted the position of a human being so that He might be our example in the battle with sin (cf. 1 Peter 2:21). In His dependent position during the incarnation, it was true to say that His Father was greater; not greater than Christ who was the Deity but greater than the man Jesus who had placed Himself in a position of total dependence upon the Father.

A similar explanation may be given to such statements as the following: "But about that day or hour no one knows, neither the angels in heaven, nor the Son, but only the Father" (Mark 13:32). In His role of Messiah, the God-man who had taken on the limitations of humanity had laid aside divine knowledge which, as God, He naturally possessed. He deliberatively chose not to exercise some of the prerogatives and powers of Deity which were His by nature. Thus He placed Himself in a position to be our example in the battle with human existence and with sin.

Jesus Christ's subordinate role during His earthly existence is explained by the apostle Paul: "Let the same mind be in you that was in Christ Jesus, who, though he was in the form of God, did not regard equality with God as something to be exploited, but emptied himself, taking the form of a slave, being born in human likeness. And being found in human form, he humbled himself and became obedient to the point of death — even death on a cross" (Phil. 2:5-8).

The Jehovah's Witnesses mistranslate this passage (NWT) as follows: "Christ Jesus, who, although he was existing in God's form, gave no consideration to a seizure, namely, that he should be equal to God." In fact, the verse is more accurately translated: "Who being in the form of God, did not consider it a prize [to be retained] to be equal with God." Since Christ was already in the form of God, "equal with God" (John 5:18), the "I AM' (John 8:58), there was no question of His wishing to seize or rob equality with the Deity. He was already God in the fullest sense. The word translated "robbery" in the King James Version (*harpagmos*) may also mean "prize," "booty."[29] Christ did not consider His equality with the Deity a prize to which He should cling, but "emptied himself taking the form of a slave" (verse 7). If Christ had not already been equal with the Father, why was it necessary for Him to empty Himself? This does not mean that Christ ceased to be Deity; for the purpose of the incarnation, He laid aside some of His divine powers and prerogatives. Even so, He exercised His divine right to forgive people's sins (Mat. 9:6). Although during His earthly existence Jesus remained God in the fullest sense, He chose not to use those aspects of His divine power that would give Him an advantage over us in the battle with sin.

A few other passages in the epistles of Paul have been interpreted to mean that, since His return to heaven, Christ is subordinate to the Father. "And you belong to Christ, and Christ belongs to God" (1 Cor. 3:23). The Greek translates literally: "And you [are] of Christ, and Christ [is] of God." The passage is speaking about the unity of the church with its leaders. "So then let no one boast in men. For all things belong to you, whether Paul or Apollos or Cephas or the world or life or death or things present or things to come; all things belong to you, and you belong to Christ; and Christ belongs to God" (verses 21-23, NASB). Paul's point is that no leader should be exalted over another. The divisive commitments of the Corinthian believers to particular leaders (Paul, Apollos, Peter) were fragmenting the church. All the leaders belonged to the church members, and they were all to be one in Christ as Christ is one with God. Paul is not saying that "you are subordinate to Christ, as Christ is subordinate to God." Rather he is saying, "You are one with Christ, as Christ is one with God."

Another controversial passage is 1 Corinthians 11:3: "But I want you to understand that Christ is the head of every man, and the husband is the head of his wife, and God is the head of Christ." Giving this an extreme interpretation, it could be concluded that as Christ is the Lord and Master of every man, so a husband is to be lord and master over his wife, as God is Lord and Master over Christ. From this interpretation emanates the concept of the subordination of Christ to the Father. Certainly Christ's role as Savior, High Priest, and Mediator is a separate role from that of the Father. And Christ's role is under the direction of the Deity to which He belongs. The Deity (Father, Son, and Holy Spirit) decided the distinctive roles of the three members of the Godhead in the salvation process. And the roles of the Son and the Holy Spirit are under the direction and protection of the Deity. Just so, every man is under the direction and protection of Christ, and every Christian wife, although equal with her husband under God (see verse 11), accepts his role as leader and protector. Among equals there is often a head. A committee of equals may have a chairman who has a distinctive role, even though he is not superior to the committee members.

A third difficult passage in the writings of Paul is 1 Corinthians 15:28: "When all things are subjected to him, then the Son himself will also be subjected to the one who put all things in subjection under him, so that God may be all in all." We have established that Christ is God, equal with the Father in authority and power. At the end of time, Christ's distinctive role as Savior, High Priest, and Mediator will be complete. It will then be apparent that the Deity (Father, Son, and Holy Spirit) is responsible for man's salvation. Our One God (Father, Son, and Holy Spirit) will subject the separate redemptive functions of the Son and the Holy Spirit to the one unified function of King of Kings and Lord of Lords.

The Holy Spirit Is Also Jehovah (*Yahweh*) Eternal God

The Holy Spirit is not presented in the Bible merely as God's force or influence. Even though it is not possible for a human being to understand fully the nature of the Holy Spirit, enough is revealed so that we can be clear on two major points: (1) The Holy Spirit is a Person. (2) The Holy Spirit is Deity, equal with God the Father and God the Son in authority and power.

The Bible evidence is that, although the Holy Spirit does not possess a bodily form, He has the characteristics of personality. He is a Person who thinks, knows, feels, and communicates. The Holy Spirit has infinite intellect. He is a divine Teacher. In Old Testament times "you gave your good Spirit to instruct them" (Neh. 9:20). Jesus promised, "The Holy Spirit will teach you at that very hour what you ought to say" (Luke 12:12). "But the Advocate, the Holy Spirit, whom the Father will send in my name, will teach you everything, and remind you of all that I have said to you" (John 14:26).

The name "Advocate" (NRSV) or "Comforter" (KJV) translates the Greek word *parakletos* (Paraclete). The title is composed of the preposition *para* meaning "beside" and the adjective *kletos* meaning "called" or "one called." Hence, the literal meaning of *parakletos* is "one called to the side of." The Latin translators often rendered it by *advocatus* (advocate). But the words Advocate and Comforter do not adequately describe the Holy Spirit's work. He is the "Helper," the One who is called to our aid, the One summoned to assist and sustain us.

Like the Gospel writers, Paul presents the Holy spirit as the divine Teacher. "No one comprehends the thoughts of God except the Spirit of God. Now we have received not the spirit of the World, but the Spirit which is from God, that we might understand the gifts bestowed on us by God. And we impart this in words not taught by human wisdom but *taught by the Spirit*, interpreting spiritual truths to those who possess the Spirit" (1 Cor. 2:11-13, RSV, italics supplied).

When Jesus predicted the Spirit's coming as the divine Teacher, He referred to Him as "He." "When the Spirit of truth comes, he will guide you into all the truth; for he will not speak on his own, but will speak whatever he hears, and he will declare to you the things that are to come" (John 16:13). Even though *pneuma*, the word translated Spirit, is neuter gender in Greek, it is immediately preceded by the masculine personal pronoun *ekeinos*, because the Spirit is a Person. The same is true in John 15:26, "When the Advocate comes, whom I will send to you from the Father, the Spirit of truth who comes from the Father, he *[ekeinos]* will testify on my behalf."

The Holy Spirit experiences emotion. Ancient Israel "rebelled and grieved his Holy Spirit" (Isa. 63:10). We are counselled, "Do not grieve the Holy Spirit of God" (Eph. 4:30). Only persons can be grieved. Such language indicates the personality of the Holy Spirit.

The Holy Spirit is described in Scripture as exercising will. Writing of spiritual gifts, Paul identified their source: "All these worketh that one and the selfsame Spirit, dividing to every man severally as he will" (1 Cor. 12:11, KJV). Thus the Spirit wills to give spiritual gifts to each believer. When travelling through Asia Minor, Paul and his companions "went through the region of Phrygia and Galatia, having been forbidden by the Holy Spirit to speak the word in Asia. And when they had come opposite Mysia, they attempted to go into Bithynia, but the Spirit of Jesus did not allow them" (Acts 16:6, 7, RSV). At the Jerusalem Council (Acts 15), the letter drafted by the apostles and other church leaders to be sent to the Gentile believers included the words, "It seemed good to the Holy Spirit and to us to lay upon you no greater burden than these essentials" (Acts 15:28, NASB). The Holy Spirit has intellect, emotion, and will, the three marks of personality. No mere force could be said to think, teach, feel, and decide.

The activities of the Holy Spirit indicate personality. He hears (John 16:13). He speaks (Matt. 10:20; Acts 13:2; 1 Tim. 4:1; Rev. 14:13). He convicts (John 16:8; Gen. 6:3; 1 Chron. 12:18; Zech. 12:10; Rev. 22:17). He imparts love (Rom. 5:5). He imparts special skills (Exod. 31:3; 35:31; Judges 13:25; 14:6, 19). He encourages (Acts 9:31). He transforms (2 Cor. 3:18). He consecrates for special ministry (Acts 20:28; Num. 11:17, 25, 29; 1 Sam. 10:6, 10). He leads (Ezek 1:12, 20, 21; 3:12, 14; Matt. 4:1; Luke 2:27; Acts 8:29, 39; 10:19, 20; 13:2, 4; Rom. 8:14).

The characteristics of the Deity are the characteristics of the Holy Spirit. He is eternal (Heb. 9:14). He is omnipotent: (1) He is the Creator (Gen. 1:2; Job 33:4; Ps. 104:30). (2) Mary conceived the incarnate Christ by the Holy Spirit (Matt. 1:18, 20; Luke 1:35). (3) He empowered the ministry of Christ (Acts 10:38; Isa. 61:1, 2; Luke 4:18). (4) He raised Christ from the grave (Rom 8:11; 1 Peter 3:18). (5) He is a miracle worker (Rom. 15:19). (6) He gives eternal life (Gal. 6:8). (7) He gives spiritual power to God's servants (Micah 3:8; Acts 1:8; Rom. 15:13; 1 Cor. 2:4; 1 Thess. 1:5).

The Holy Spirit is omniscient; He knows all things. (1) He shares the thoughts of the Father (1 Cor. 2:10, 11). (2) He teaches "all things" (John 14:26). (3) He gave God's messages to the prophets (1 Peter 1:11; 2 Peter 1:21; Zech. 7:12; 1 Cor. 2:4; Eph. 3:5).

The Holy Spirit is omnipresent; He is everywhere at once (Ps. 139:7-12).

The Holy Spirit is identified with *Yahweh* of the Old Testament. In 2 Samuel 23:2, 3 the "Spirit of the Lord" is "the God of Israel." In Ezek 8:1, 3, the Lord God" is the "Spirit." "All Scripture is inspired by God" (2 Tim. 3:16), "because no prophecy ever came by human will, but men and women moved by the Holy Spirit spoke from God" (2 Peter 1:21).

The presence of the Spirit in the life of the Christian believer is the presence of the Father and the Son. David prayed, "Do not cast me away from Thy presence, And do not take Thy Holy Spirit from me" (Ps. 51:11, NASB). The presence of the Spirit is the presence of Jehovah. When promising the gift of the Spirit, Jesus said, "I will not leave you orphaned; I am coming to you" (John 14:18). In the same context, Jesus explained, "Those who love me will keep my word, and my Father will love them, and we will come to them and make our home with them" (John 14:23). So when the Holy Spirit is living in our hearts, the Father and the Son have made their home with us. The Deity (Father, Son, and Holy Spirit), the Creator of a billion galaxies condescends to take up His abode in the heart of every believer by the presence of His Holy Spirit.

In the New Testament, the Holy Spirit is identified as God. Second Corinthians 3:18 is correctly translated: "And all of us, with unveiled faces, seeing the glory of the Lord as though reflected in a mirror, are being transformed into the same image from one degree of glory to another; for this comes from the Lord, the Spirit." The Spirit is the Lord who progressively transforms our lives. Ananias and Sapphira lied to the Holy Spirit (Acts 5:3); they lied to God (verse 4).

A Few Texts Used Incorrectly by Jehovah's Witnesses

John 1:1. The text reads, "In the beginning was the Word, and the Word was with God, and the Word was God" (NRSV; see also KJV, RSV, NIV, NASB etc.). The Jehovah's Witnesses insist on translating the last clause of this verse, "and the Word was a god" (New World Translation). This translation is necessitated by their idea that Christ's divinity is inferior to that of the Father, since the Father created Him and made Him a subordinate god. The simple, undeniable truth is that the Greek of John 1:1 does not allow for the JWs' translation of the text.

Bruce M. Metzger makes the following pertinent observations concerning the Jehovah's Witnesses' interpretation of John 1:1: "It must be stated quite frankly that, if the Jehovah's Witnesses take this translation seriously, they are polytheists. In view of the additional light which is available during this age of Grace, such a representation is even more reprehensible than were the heathenish, polytheistic errors into which ancient Israel was so prone to fall.

"As a matter of solid fact, however, such a rendering is a frightful mistranslation. It overlooks entirely an established rule of Greek grammar which necessitates the rendering, '. . . and the Word was God.' Some years ago Dr. Ernest Cadman Colwell of the University of Chicago pointed out in a study of the Greek definite article that, 'A definite predicate nominative has the article when it follows the verb; it does not have the article when it precedes the verb. . . . The opening verse of John's Gospel contains one of the many passages where this rule suggests the translation of a predicate as a definite noun. The absence of the article [before *Theos*] does *not* make the predicate indefinite or qualitative when it precedes the verb; it is indefinite in this position only when the context demands it. The context makes no such demand in the Gospel of John, for this statement cannot be regarded as strange in the prologue of the gospel which reaches its climax in the confession of Thomas [John 20:28, 'My Lord and my God'].' "30

Robert W. Bowman comments: "Even Jehovah can be called 'a God' in the Bible, in passages using the exact same construction in Greek. . . . For example, in Luke 20:38 in the NWT we read that Jesus said, concerning Jehovah, 'He is *a God*, not of the dead, but of the living. . . .' Here 'a God' translates *theos* without the article and before the verb, just as in John 1:1. Thus, even if one wanted to translate *theos* in John 1:1 as 'a god,' that would not disprove that he is the true God."31 Bowman cites other New Testament passages in which "*theos* appears in the same context both with and without the definite article, yet with no change in meaning (John 3:2; 13:3; Rom. 1:21; 1 Thess. 1:9; Heb. 9:14; 1 Peter 4:10-11)."32

Colossians 1:15-17. The Jehovah's Witnesses translate the passage: "He is the image of the invisible God, the firstborn of all creation, because by means of him all [other] things were created in the heavens and upon the earth. . . . All [other] things have been created through him and for him. Also he is before all [other] things and by means of him all [other] things were made to exist." The four uses of the word 'other' in this translation are insertions by the translators. The word does not occur in the Greek text. The Jehovah's Witnesses interpret "the firstborn of all creation" (verse 15) to mean that Christ was the first being to be created by God. The Greek word used by Paul translated "firstborn" is *prototokos*. The same word is used in Revelation 1:5 which describes Christ as "the *firstborn* [*prototokos*] of the dead." But Jesus was not the first in point of time to be raised from the dead. Moses, Lazarus, the widow's son at Nain and others were raised from the dead before Jesus. "First born," or "first begotten" (*prototokos*) does not necessarily mean the first in point of time. It sometimes is used in a figurative sense meaning the strongest of its kind. Job 18:12, 13 speaks of a disease that was the "firstborn of Death." It was the strongest of its kind. Isaiah 14:30 refers to the "firstborn of the poor," that is, the poorest of the poor. Sometimes in the Greek Old Testament (the Septuagint) the "first-born" (*prototokos*) denotes status of dignity or honor invested on a person who is not the first son to be born in a family. For example, David was the youngest son of Jesse, but the Lord said of him, "I will make him my first-born [*prototokos*], higher than the kings of the earth" (Ps. 89:27; see LXX Ps. 88 [89]). We are told of Shimri, "though he was not the firstborn [*prototokos*], yet his father made him the chief [*archonta*]" (1 Chron. 26:10,

LXX). Jacob was slightly younger than his twin brother Esau, but the Lord called him "my firstborn [*prototokos*]" (Exod. 4:22, LXX). Manasseh was the firstborn son of Joseph, yet God called his brother Ephraim "my first-born [*prototokos*]" (Jer. 31:9, LXX [38:9]).

The point is that Christ is the "firstborn of all creation" (Col. 1:15) in the sense that He is the preeminent One over creation. He was the Creator (verse 16). As such He is supreme over all creation. In Revelation 1:5, He is the preeminent One to be raised from the dead (cf. Col. 1:18), because His resurrection makes possible all other resurrections.

Revelation 3:14. "These things saith the Amen, the faithful and true witness, the beginning [*arche*] of the creation of God" (KJV) The Greek word *arche* means "beginning," "origin," "first cause," "ruler," "authority," "rule."[33] In Luke 12:11 the word refers to the "rulers." In 1 Corinthians 15:24, *arche* means "ruler." Metzger's comment is very much to the point: "The New World Translation . . . makes the exalted Christ refer to himself as 'the beginning of the creation by God.'" The Greek text of this verse . . . is far from saying that Christ was created by God, for the genitive case . . . [*tou Theou*], means 'of God' and not 'by God' (which would require the preposition . . . [*upo*]). Actually the word . . . [*arche*], translated 'beginning,' carries with it the Pauline idea expressed in Col. 1:15-18, and signifies that Christ is the origin, or primary source, of God's creation (compare also John 1:3, 'Apart from him not even one thing came into existence')."[34]

Proverbs 8:22. "The Lord possessed me in the beginning of his way, before his works of old" (KJV). Jehovah's Witnesses regard the Wisdom spoken of here as a figure of speech referring to Jesus who, they say, was a spirit creature before He came to earth. They translate the verse, "Jehovah himself produced me as the beginning of his way" (New World Translation). Thus, they assert that Jesus was a created being. As Robert Bowman points out, the Hebrew word translated "produced" or "created" is *qanah*. It does not mean "to create"; it means "to get," "to acquire," "to possess," "to buy."[35] "This word is used frequently in Proverbs, never with the meaning 'create,' but always 'get' or 'buy,' that is, get with money (Prov. 1:5; 4:5, 7; 8:22; 15:32; 16:16; 17:16; 18:15; 19:8; 20:14; 23:23). That is also its consistent meaning in the some seventy instances in which it is used elsewhere in the Old Testament."[36]

Bowman also points out that "'wisdom' is personified, not only in Proverbs 8:22-31, but throughout Proverbs 1-9. Nothing in Proverbs 8:22-31 suggests that this is a different 'wisdom' than is spoken of in the preceding and following chapters. Therefore, if we take 8:22 to speak literally about Christ, we must also assume that Christ is a woman who cries in the streets (1:20-21), and who lives with someone named 'Prudence' (8:12) in a house with seven pillars (9:1)!"[37]

The message of the text is that wisdom existed eternally with God. The next verse underlines the point. "From everlasting I was established. . . ." (Prov. 8:23, NASB). "The phrase *from everlasting* is the same phrase used of God in Psalm 90:2, where the JWs recognize that God is being described as having no beginning."[38]

The Bible teaching is very clear that there is only one God: the Father, the Son, and the Holy Spirit. This is the doctrine of the Trinity. Orthodox Christians are trinitarian monotheists. Christ and the Holy Spirit are not inferior Beings. They are the Deity in the fullest sense. The Bible leaves us with the divine mystery unexplained that our one God comprises three distinct Persons. Only in the heavenly Kingdom will we understand more fully the nature of God.

Have you accepted Jesus Christ as your Lord and God, as Thomas did? (John 20:28). Can you pray to Him as your supreme Lord, as Paul urged us to? (Phil. 2:10, 11).

Notes

1. Robert M. Bowman, Jr., *Why You Should Believe in the Trinity: An Answer to Jehovah's Witnesses* (Grand Rapids, Michigan: Baker Book House, 1989), p. 46.
2. *Ibid.*
3. *Should You Believe in the Trinity: Is Jesus Christ the Almighty God?* (New York: Watchtower Bible and Tract Society, 1989).
4. Robert M. Bowman, *Why You Should Believe in the Trinity*, pp. 23-34
5. *Should You Believe in the Trinity? p. 12.*
6. *Ibid.*, p. 14.
7. *Ibid.*, p. 15.
8. *Ibid.*, p. 16.
9. *Ibid.*, p. 20.
10. *Ibid.*, p. 31.
11. Bruce M. Metzger, *The Jehovah's Witnesses and Jesus Christ: a Biblical and Theological Appraisal* (Princeton, N.J.: Theological Book agency, 1953; originally published in *Theology Today*, April, 1953), p. 70. See also George D. McKinney, Jr., *The Theology of the Jehovah's Witnesses* (Grand Rapids, Michigan: Zondervan, 1962); Anthony A. Hoekema, *Jehovah's Witnesses* (Grand Rapids, Michigan: William B. Eerdmans, 1973); Walter R. Martin and Norman H. Klann, *Jehovah of the Watchtower* (New York: Biblical Truth Publishing Society, 1953); Gordon R. Lewis, *The Bible, the Christian, and Jehovah's Witnesses* (Grand Rapids, Michigan: Baker Book House, 971).
12. J. N. D. Kelly, *Early Christian Doctrines* (New York: Harper & Row, 1960), p. 227.
13. *Ibid.*, pp. 227–229.
14. *Ibid.*, p. 228.
15. *Ibid.*

16. Although *Elohim* is a plural word meaning "gods," it is often used throughout the Old Testament with a singular meaning applying to the one and only true God, *Yahweh*. See Francis Brown, S. R. Driver, and Charles A. Briggs, *A Hebrew and English Lexicon of the Old Testament* (Oxford: Clarendon Press, 1906, 1951), s.v. *Elohim.*

17. William F. Arndt and F. Wilbur Gingrich, *A Greek-English Lexicon of the New Testament and Other Early Christian Literature* (Cambridge: University Press, 1957), s.v. *pleroma.*

18. *Ibid.*

19. Gerhard Kittel (ed.), *Theological Dictionary of the New Testament* (Grand Rapids, Michigan: Wm. B. Eerdmans, 1968), vol. 6 (edited by Gerhard Friedrich), pp. 303, 304.

20. Arndt and Gingrich, s.v. *theotes.*

21. C. K. Barrett, *The Gospel According to St John: an Introduction with Commentary and Notes on the Greek Text* (London: S.P.C.K, 1962), pp. 213, 214.

22. Robert M. Bowman, *Why You Should Believe in the Trinity,* p. 100. See also Barrett, *The Gospel According to John,* pp. 282, 283.

23. R. C. H. Lenski, *The Interpretation of St. John's Gospel* (Columbus, Ohio: Lutheran Book Concern, 1942), pp. 670, 671

24. *'Olam* translated "eternity" may refer to a period of limited duration as in Exod. 21:6 and 1 Kings 1:31. But the word often designates a period without beginning or end. See Ps. 10:16; 90:2; 93:2; 103:17, all of which refer to God's timeless existence. Compare Prov. 8:23.

25. Bruce M. Metzger, *The Jehovah's Witnesses and Jesus Christ,* p. 71.

26. The Greek reads: *Ho kurios mou kai ho theos mou,* which translates literally, "The Lord of me and the God of me."

27. Robert M. Bowman, *Why You Should Believe in the Trinity,* pp. 104, 105.

28. J. B. Smith, *Greek-English Concordance to the New Testament* (Scottdale, Penn.: Herald Press, 1965), s.v. *Kurios.*

29. Arndt and Gingrich, s.v. *harpagmos.*

30. Bruce M. Metzger, *The Jehovah's Witnesses and Jesus Christ,* p. 75; quoting E. C. Colwell, "A Definite Rule for the Use of the Article in the Greek New Testament," *Journal of Biblical Literature,* LII (1933), 12-21. See also B. M. Metzger, "On the Translation of John i:1," *Expository Times,* LXIII (1951-52), 125 f., and C. F. D. Moule, *The Language of the New Testament,* Inaugural Lecture, delivered at Cambridge University on May 23, 1952, pp. 12-14.

31. Robert M. Bowman, *Why You Should Believe in the Trinity,* pp. 92, 93.

32. *Ibid.,* p. 94.

33. Arndt and Gingrich, *A Greek-English Lexicon of the New Testament,* s.v. *arche.*

34. Bruce M. Metzger, *The Jehovah's Witnesses and Jesus Christ,* pp. 79, 80.

35. Brown, Driver, and Briggs, *A Hebrew and English Lexicon of the Old Testament,* s.v. *qanah.*

36. Robert M. Bowman, *Why You Should Believe the Trinity,* p. 60.

37. *Ibid.*

38. *Ibid.,* p. 61.

Chapter 4
Is There a Correct View
of Salvation?

In 1829 George Wilson was sentenced by a United States Court in Pennsylvania to be hanged for mail robbery and murder. President Andrew Jackson pardoned him, but Wilson refused to accept the pardon. He argued that if he did not accept it, he was not pardoned. The President appealed to the Supreme Court for a decision in the case.

Chief Justice John Marshall gave the following decision of the court: "A pardon is a paper, the value of which depends upon its acceptance by the person implicated. It is hardly to be supposed that one under sentence of death would refuse to accept a pardon, but if it is refused, it is no pardon. George Wilson must be hanged." And he was hanged.

"Provisionally the gospel of Christ which is the power of God unto salvation is for every one irrespective of what he may be or what he may have done. Potentially, it is only to "every one that believeth."[1]

But not all churches and theologians accept that understanding of the gospel. Some believe that everyone, good or bad, was justified at the cross. Others believe that no one can have the certainty of justification and salvation. Some argue for legal-only justification. They say that salvation is God's heavenly declaration of pardon, not transformation of heart. Others object, asserting that salvation is the new birth experience. Yet others consider that salvation is both legal and experiential; God both declares and makes a believer righteous.

Because there are so many different views of salvation held by Christians today, it would be unusual if someone did not ask, "How can we know which view is correct? If the scholars cannot agree, how can we be expected to understand salvation?"

Protestants and Catholics have dramatically different interpretations of the Bible teaching on salvation. Within Protestantism the various denominations rather strenuously contradict one another. The non-Christian looks on skeptically as the various Christian churches hammer away at their theological opponents or ignore them as unworthy of charitable fellowship. Even worse, within any one communion there is so much confusion on the issue of salvation that the members have difficulty identifying the distinctive teachings of their church.

How did the Christian Church get into this mess? Why are there so many contradictions? Is the Bible so difficult to interpret on this most fundamental issue that confusion is inevitable? If that is so, how can any of us be saved? If it is so hard to understand how to be saved, many will give up in despair. They will blunder along hoping that, despite their confusion and the unsatisfactory nature of their spiritual lives, God will be merciful enough to take them to heaven.

In this chapter we will compare the teachings of Jesus and Paul on the subject of salvation. As we do so, we ask, did they agree? What did Jesus mean by the new birth, and what did Paul mean by justification? Why are these experiences such good news for Christians today?

In His interview with Nicodemus (John 3), Jesus presented five principles of salvation. The legalistic Pharisee expressed wonder and doubt when he heard Jesus' explanation of how he could be saved. But the seed sown then bore fruit later. Those five principles became the guiding precepts of Nicodemus' life. And the same five principles were accepted and taught by the apostle Paul. Jesus and Paul used different imagery to describe salvation, but they taught the same good news. Peter thought Paul wrote some things difficult to understand (2 Peter 3:15, 16). And so he did. But when we compare Scripture with Scripture and prayerfully seek to understand Paul's writings, we discover his meaning to be much more simple than some learned scholars' interpretations and delightfully relevant to our spiritual need.

What were Jesus' five principles of salvation which Paul accepted and promoted?

The Cross Is Central to Our Salvation

The focal point of the picture of salvation that Jesus painted for Nicodemus was the vision of Himself hanging on the cross, bearing the sins of the world. "And just as Moses lifted up the serpent in the wilderness, so must the Son of Man be lifted up, that whoever believes in him may have eternal life. For God so loved the world that he gave his only Son, so that everyone who believes in him may not perish but may have eternal life" (John 3:14-16).

On the cross, eternal God the Son was separated from eternal God the Father and eternal God the Holy Spirit. Because the unity of the Deity was severed, the suffering of the Deity was infinite. The Bible teaches that there is only one God (Deut. 6:4; Mal. 2:10; 1 Cor. 8:4; Eph. 4:5, 6). The Father, the Son, and the Holy Spirit are so mysteriously united that together they are one God. But when Jesus was dying on the cross, He was separated from His Father and from the Holy Spirit because He was bearing the guilt of human sin.

Isaiah predicted that the Messiah would suffer the penalty for all the sins of mankind: "He was wounded for our transgressions, crushed for our iniquities; upon him was the punishment that made us whole, and by his bruises we are healed. All we like sheep have gone astray; we have all turned to our own way, and the Lord has laid on him the iniquity of us all" (Isa. 53:5, 6). Looking back on the cross, Peter took up the refrain: "He himself bore our sins in his body on the cross" (1 Peter 2:24). John chimed in with exultant praise: "He is the atoning sacrifice [expiation] for our sins, and not for ours only but also for the sins of the whole world" (1 John 2:2). And Paul added his voice to the chorus: "For our sake he made him to be sin who knew no sin, so that in him we might become the righteousness of God" (2 Cor. 5:21). "While we were still weak, at the right time Christ died for the ungodly. . . . God proves his love for us in that while we still were sinners Christ died for us" (Rom. 5:6, 8).

None of us can begin to understand the infinite intensity of Christ's suffering when separated from the Father because He was bearing our guilt. He cried out in agony that is beyond our comprehension, "My God, my God, why have you forsaken me?" (Mark 15:34). Eternal God was separated from eternal God because of your sin and mine. And the suffering involved was sufficient to atone for all human sin no matter how long time should last.

This was the first principle of salvation Jesus presented to Nicodemus, and it was the most important truth that Paul proclaimed as he evangelized throughout the Mediterranean world. He wrote to the Corinthians:

"I handed on to you *as of first importance* what I in turn had received: that Christ died for our sins in accordance with the scriptures, and that he was buried, and that he was raised on the third day in accordance with the scriptures " (1 Cor. 15:3, 4; italics supplied). No aspect of Paul's teaching could compare with this in importance. If there had been no cross, God the penalty for sin would not have been paid, there would be no salvation, and you and I would be destitute. Because Jesus successfully endured the suffering of the cross and rose again, we have hope. Eternal life is ours for the asking. "If Christ has not been raised, your faith is futile and you are still in your sins. . . . But in fact Christ has been raised from the dead. . . . for as all die in Adam, so all will be made alive in Christ. . . . Christ the first fruits, then at his coming those who belong to Christ" (1 Cor. 15:17-23).

The Cross Makes Forgiveness Possible

The second principle of salvation Jesus gave Nicodemus was that, because Jesus suffered our penalty for sin, we can be forgiven. "Indeed, God did not send the Son into the world to condemn the world, but in order that the world might be saved through him. Those who believe in him are not condemned" (John 3:17, 18). If we are not condemned, we are forgiven. Praise God, because of the cross, we can be forgiven! Paul underlined the same liberating truth: "There is therefore now no condemnation for those who are in Christ Jesus. For the law of the Spirit of life in Christ Jesus has set you free from the law of sin and of death" (Rom. 8:1, 2).

Forgiveness is what Paul meant by justification. In Acts 13:38, 39 Paul speaks of forgiveness available through Christ, and he identifies forgiveness with justification. The passage translates literally from the Greek text: "Let it be known to you, men, brothers, that through this man forgiveness of sins is being proclaimed to you, and from all things from which you were not able to be justified by the law of Moses, in this man all who believe are justified."[2] Forgiveness is justification.

Paul emphasized the same point in his epistle to the Romans. The person who does not try to earn his salvation by his own works, but "who believes in the One who justifies the ungodly, his faith is counted (reckoned, imputed) for righteousness" (Rom. 4:5).[3] The one "to whom God reckons [imputes, counts] righteousness apart from works" (verse 6) is the person "whose iniquities are forgiven" (verse 7). Paul quotes Psalm 32:1, 2. The individual to whom "the Lord imputes no iniquity, and in whose spirit

76

there is no deceit" (Psalm 32:2) is the "happy" person whose "transgression is forgiven" (verse 1). Paul's point is very simple. When the Lord forgives, He does not impute sin to a person. That is because He imputes or counts His righteousness. And this forgiveness which is the imputation of righteousness is justification. Thus in the passage we have three terms, all of which mean the same thing: (1) justification; (2) imputation of righteousness; and (3) forgiveness. When you are forgiven, you are justified, and Christ's righteousness is counted (imputed) to you.

What does God do for us when He forgives (justifies) us? The Greek word for forgiveness is *aphesis*. It means "*release* from captivity. . . . *pardon, cancellation* of an obligation, a punishment, or guilt."[4] During His earthly ministry Jesus provided forgiveness, deliverance from sin for His responsive hearers. Quoting Isaiah 61:1, 2, Jesus emphasized that His work was "to proclaim release [*aphesis*, forgiveness] to the captives" (Luke 4:18). The last phrase of the same text translates literally, "to send forth the crushed in forgiveness" (*aphesis*). When Jesus forgives, he releases Satan's captives from the dominion of sin that binds them. This is not just something that happens in heaven. It is *our spiritual experience* of being released from the power of sin.

Paul taught the same truth when he identified deliverance from "the power of darkness" with redemption and forgiveness. "He has rescued us from the power of darkness and transferred us into the kingdom of his beloved Son, in whom we have redemption, the forgiveness of sins" (Col. 1:13, 14). When we accept Jesus' sacrifice for us, He redeems us, buys us back from the slave-master who has bound us to lives of sin. And this deliverance from the mastery of sin occurs when God forgives us.

After his terrible sins of adultery and murder, David pled for forgiveness (Ps. 51:1). His understanding of forgiveness is revealed by the manner in which he asked for it. "Wash me thoroughly from my iniquity, and cleanse me from my sin. . . . Purge me with hyssop, and I shall be clean; wash me, and I shall be whiter than snow" (Ps. 51:2, 7).

God's forgiveness abolishes the guilt of our sin. But it does more than that. It cleanses our hearts, purifies our minds, delivers us from bondage. When God forgives, He transforms us. But, as we have seen, forgiveness is justification. Then justification involves both a legal and an experiential element. When God justifies us, He takes away our guilt and purifies our hearts.[5] When Jesus accepted the thief on the cross, he wiped out the guilt of his past sin and transformed his heart.

Some Christians speak of forgiveness as unconditional. But the Bible states a condition. "*If* we confess our sins, he who is faithful and just will forgive us our sins and cleanse us from all unrighteousness (1 John 1:9). Other passages of Scripture confront us with the same condition. "But if they confess their iniquity . . . then will I remember my covenant with Jacob" (Lev. 26:40-42). "When a man or a woman wrongs another, breaking faith with the Lord, that person incurs guilt and shall confess the sin that has been committed" (Num. 5:6, 7). "Now make confession to the Lord the God of your ancestors" (Ezra 10:11). "No one who conceals transgressions will prosper, but one who confesses and forsakes them will obtain mercy" (Prov. 28:13). "Only acknowledge your guilt, that you have rebelled against the Lord your God" (Jer. 3:13).

God's *love* is unconditional. "But God proves his love for us in that while we still were sinners Christ died for us" (Rom. 5:8). "And he is the atoning sacrifice for our sins, and not for ours only but also for the sins of the whole world" (1 John 2:2). Jesus draws all people to Himself (John 12:32), even those who, He knows, will choose never to respond to his love. That is unconditional love. *But forgiveness is conditional.* God wants us to confess our sins to Him and seek the cleansing that He is longing to bestow.

The Cross Makes It Possible for Christ's Righteousness to Be Counted for the Believer

This third principle of salvation that Jesus presented to Nicodemus is contained in John 3:14, 15: "And just as Moses lifted up the serpent in the wilderness, so must the Son of Man be lifted up, that whoever believes in him may have eternal life."

Jesus was referring to the story recorded in Numbers 21:4-9. The people complained to God and Moses because they did not have the food they wanted. They were not satisfied with what God had provided for them, and they hated the discomfort of the wilderness. The Lord withdrew His protection from these faithless people and allowed poisonous snakes to invade their camp and bite them. Many Israelites died. Suffering and terrified, the people appealed to Moses, "We have sinned by speaking against the Lord and against you; pray to the Lord to take away the serpents from us" (Num. 21:7). So Moses interceded with the Lord on behalf of his people. And God answered. He commanded Moses to make a serpent of brass and put it on a pole; everyone who would look to it would live. When those who were bitten by snakes looked to the brass serpent, they were immediately healed.

The brass serpent on the pole represented Christ. The serpent is a symbol of sin, and Christ became sin for us (2 Cor. 5:21). When we look to Him we have healing and life.

The major point is that when the people looked to the serpent, because they were exercising faith in God, their sin was forgiven. The life of God was imputed to them, counted for them. His life replaced their sickness. They were spiritually and physically healed. They had no life of their own; they were dying. God's life became their life.

Just so, when we look to Jesus, His life, His righteousness is counted for us. His life becomes our life; His righteousness becomes our righteousness.

By means of an example, Jesus taught Nicodemus the same doctrine of imputation of righteousness that the apostle Paul later taught in his epistle to the Romans: "Therefore his faith [Abraham's faith] 'was reckoned to him as righteousness.' Now the words, 'it was reckoned to him,' were written not for his sake alone, but for ours also. It will be reckoned to us who believe in him who raised Jesus our Lord from the dead, who was handed over to death for our trespasses and was raised for our justification" (Rom. 4:22-25).

The verb "to reckon" used in these verses may also be translated "to impute," or "to count." It is the Greek verb *logizomai*. This verb and its Hebrew equivalent *chashav* sometimes refer to a legal accounting of something. These verbs may also refer to a gift of something to someone. Both ideas are contained in a number of uses of *chashav* in the Hebrew Bible and of *logizomai* in the Greek translation of the Old Testament (the Septuagint).[6]

For example, 2 Samuel 4:2 reports that "Beeroth also was reckoned to Benjamin" (KJV). In the apportioning of the land to the various tribes, the town Beeroth was legally imputed, reckoned to the tribe of Benjamin. This *legal accounting* amounted to the *gift* of the town Beeroth to Benjamin.

Another Old Testament example of the use of the verb "to impute" is found in Numbers 18:27, 30. The tithe imputed to the priests was an actual gift of produce to them, one-tenth of which they paid as tithe and nine-tenths of which they and their families consumed.

In Romans, chapter 4, Paul takes the Old Testament concept of imputation and applies it to Christ's gift of His righteousness to the believer. Paul quotes Genesis 15:6: "For what does the scripture say? 'Abraham believed God, and it was reckoned to him as righteousness'" (Rom. 4:3). Abraham's faith union with God was reckoned, imputed, or counted as righteousness because God's righteousness was given to him by the Holy Spirit. (See Gal. 3:1-14.) The legal reckoning of the righteousness of God to the believer is accompanied by the gift of His righteousness to the heart by the presence of the Holy Spirit.

In Romans 4:4, Paul makes the point that wages are reckoned (imputed or counted; *logizomai*) to the one who works, because the wages have been earned. Verse 5 says that the gift of righteousness is reckoned (imputed or counted) to the one who has faith. In verse 4, the reckoning is a gift earned. In verse 5, the reckoning is a gift granted without any work on the part of the believer. In both verses the same verb is used (*logizomai*). There is a legal reckoning in both cases. In the case of righteousness by faith there is a legal reckoning of a gift that has not been earned, simply because believers have responded by faith to the grace of God extended to them.

Jesus and Paul are making the same point. Just as the life of God was reckoned to the dying Israelites who had been bitten by serpents, so the righteousness of Christ is reckoned to us who believe. The life of Christ, His righteousness becomes ours in a legal and an experiential sense. The perfect righteousness of Christ is legally counted for us, and it is bestowed upon us by the gift of the Holy Spirit. His life becomes our life, not in the sense that we are made righteous independently of Him, but in the sense that His presence in our hearts gives us new spiritual life. The legal accounting is accompanied by an actual gift to our hearts, a gift that makes us new creatures in Christ Jesus. (See 2 Cor. 5:17, 21.) "Christ redeemed us from the curse of the law by becoming a curse for us . . . in order that in Christ Jesus the blessing of Abraham might come to the Gentiles, so that we might receive the promise of the Spirit through faith" (Gal. 3:13, 14). The blessing of Abraham was the imputation of God's righteousness to him (Gal. 3:5-9). This blessing involved the gift "of the Spirit through faith" (verse 14). And the same gift is ours when Christ's righteousness is imputed to us. The Holy Spirit brings the righteous presence of Christ to our hearts, and He becomes to us "righteousness and sanctification and redemption" (1 Cor. 1:30).

The Cross Makes It Possible for Christ's Righteousness to Be Bestowed upon Us by the Holy Spirit

We have noted this already. But significantly this is the point with which Jesus began His instruction to Nicodemus. "Jesus answered him, 'Very truly, I tell you, no one can see the kingdom of God without being born from above'" (John 3:3). Nicodemus tried to evade the issue by pointing out the impossibility of physical rebirth. But Jesus would not be diverted. "'Very truly, I tell you, no one can enter the kingdom of God without being born of water and Spirit. What is born of the flesh is flesh, and what is born of the Spirit is spirit. Do not be astonished that I said to you, "You must be born from above." The wind blows where it chooses, and you hear the sound of it, but you do not know where it comes from or where it goes. So it is with everyone who is born of the Spirit'" (John 3:5-8).

The phrase "born from above" may also be translated as in the King James Version, "born again."[7] Jesus told Nicodemus that salvation depends on the new birth. He identified salvation with the new birth as Paul identified salvation with justification. Jesus did not say that the new birth is the *result* of salvation, as some would have us believe. The new birth *is* salvation. It is not our work but God's work *for* and *in* us. "You have been born anew, not of perishable but of imperishable seed, through the living and enduring word of God" (1 Peter 1:23). The "imperishable seed" through whom we are born is the Holy Spirit. That is why Jesus emphasized the importance of being born again by the Holy Spirit.

Jesus explained the meaning of the new birth by his allusion to the experience of the Israelites who were saved by looking to the brass serpent (John 3:14, 15). As we have seen, they received new life from God both legally and experientially. Legally, their sins were forgiven and the life of God was counted for them. At the same time, in personal experience the life of God became their life; they were healed spiritually and physically. They were born again, born of the Spirit, forgiven, changed in heart, renewed, transformed. The new birth (John 3:3-8) includes God's legal declaration that we are forgiven and that His life is counted for us. It also includes God's bestowal of the Holy Spirit upon us as a truly life-changing presence in our hearts.

The apostle Paul taught the same truth. When he spoke of the free gift of the righteousness of God (Rom. 3:21-26), Paul was defining justification. In His act of justifying believers in Christ, God, the heavenly Judge does two things for them: (1) He acquits them of their past sins and counts the righteousness of Christ for them; (2) He bestows His righteousness upon them by the gift of the Holy Spirit (Rom. 5:1-5; 8:9, 10). All that Jesus meant by the new birth, Paul meant by justification.

Ever since the latter half of the sixteenth century, some scholars have been asserting that justification is only a legal declaration of forgiveness and of the righteousness of Christ counted for believers who are never righteous. This was not the view of Luther and Calvin. They saw justification as involving two inseparable aspects: (1) The legal or forensic aspect is God's forgiveness of believers' sins and His crediting Christ's righteousness to their account. (2) The experiential aspect is Christ's gift of His righteousness to believers by the gift of the Holy Spirit. Christ within is the Spirit within is righteousness within.[8] In his later works, Melanchthon, Luther's close associate, is credited with promoting legal-only justification, the view that was accepted by the Lutheran Formula of Concord (1577). After 1577, orthodox Lutheranism consistently followed the Formula of Concord by adhering to the concept of legal-only justification. But this was not the understanding of the magisterial Reformers.[9]

Jesus taught Nicodemus that the gift of the Spirit to the heart is essential to salvation. And Paul identified justification with the gift of grace (Rom. 3:24), a gift that always involves the bestowal of spiritual power to the life of the believer by the outpouring of the Holy Spirit. (See 1 Cor. 1:4, 5; 15:10; 2 Cor. 8:1, 2; 9:8, 14; Gal. 2:9; 2 Tim. 2:1; Heb. 13:9; 2 Peter 3:18).

Justification, the gift of the righteousness of God, spoken of in Romans 3 is illustrated in Romans 4 by the imputation of righteousness to Abraham and to those who believe as he did. Similarly, Jesus' explanation to Nicodemus began with the gift of the Spirit (John 3:3-8) and continued with the imputation of God's life to the believer (verses 14, 15).

In Romans 5, justification by faith, by which we have peace with God (verse 1), involves "love . . . poured into our hearts through the Holy Spirit that has been given to us" (verse 5). In Romans 6, the death of the "old man," the old life of habitual sinning, is identified as justification. Verse 7 translates literally: "For he who has died has been justified from sin."[10] The result is that believers have been "set free from sin" and "have become slaves of righteousness" (verse 18). In Romans 7, justification is the death of the first husband (the "old man" of sin) and marriage to Christ (verses 1-6) which makes possible "the new life of the Spirit" (verse 6). In Romans 8, justification is described as "the law of the Spirit of life in Christ Jesus" that "has set you free from the law of sin and death" (verse 2). Now the Spirit within is Christ within, and He is your "life because of righteousness" (verses 9, 10).

The artificial outline imposed on the book of Romans by some scholars, by which they argue that chapters 3–5 discuss justification and chapters 6–8 discuss sanctification, does a gross injustice to Paul's meaning. Chapters 6–8 are just as much about justification as the earlier chapters.

In his epistle to Titus, Paul clearly defined justification as the new birth. "Not by works in righteousness which we have done, but according to His mercy He saved us, through the washing of rebirth (*paliggenesia*) and renewing of the Holy Spirit, whom He poured out upon us richly through Jesus Christ our Savior, so that having been justified by his grace, we might be heirs according to the hope of eternal life" (Titus 3:5-7).[11]

"He saved us . . . so that having been justified. . . ." Christ's saving act is His justifying act. He saved us by giving us the new birth experience, by pouring out the Holy Spirit upon us. Since the saving is the justifying, He justifies us by the new birth experience, by pouring out the Holy Spirit upon us. Justification is not only a legal declaration that Christ's righteousness is counted for us; it is also the transforming new birth experience that we enjoy when the Holy Spirit brings the presence of Christ to our hearts. Thus Paul repeated Jesus' message to Nicodemus, using different imagery, but identifying his imagery with that used by Jesus.

Paul spelled out the same message for the Galatian Christians. We are justified only by faith (grace), not by works (Gal. 2:16). When we were justified we "died to the law" so that we "might live to God." We were "crucified with Christ" (verse 19). Now Christ lives in us (verse 20). This experience of justification comes through God's gift of grace, not through our attempts to obey the law (verse 21).

We began our new walk with Christ when we were justified, because then the Holy Spirit came into our hearts (Gal. 3:3-5). This is the same experience that God gave Abraham (verses 6-9). And God has given

Abraham's experience to us "so that we might receive the promise of the Spirit through faith" (verse 14). For Paul, justification is what Jesus meant by the new birth.

Martin Luther, the great sixteenth-century Reformer, identified justification as both Christ's righteousness counted for us in a legal sense and His righteousness bestowed upon us by the transforming gift of the Holy Spirit. He wrote: "Then what does justify? Hearing the voice of the bridegroom, hearing the proclamation of faith — when this is heard, it justifies. Why? Because it brings the Holy Spirit who justifies."[12] (For further historical references, see endnote 8.)

The Cross Makes It Possible for Christ to Give Us the Power to Obey His Law

Jesus did not teach that when you are given present salvation by the new birth experience, you can live like the devil and sin to your heart's content. He did not say that once you have legal *standing* with God your spiritual *state* becomes irrelevant to your salvation. Quite the contrary, Jesus taught Nicodemus, "But those who do what is true come to the light, so that it may be clearly seen that their deeds have been done in God" (John 3:21). Once we are born again, our deeds, our works, our behaviors are "done in God." In other words, the Spirit in our hearts provides the power for works that are acceptable in the sight of God.

Paul taught the same truth. We are saved by grace through faith (Eph. 2:8), not by anything we do (verse 9). But when we are saved by grace, we are "created in Christ Jesus *for good works*, which God prepared beforehand to be our way of life" (verse 10; italics supplied).

Justification by faith (grace) does not release us from the requirement that we obey God's law; justification is the power to obey His law. The Spirit within is Christ within is righteousness within. There is no greater power available than the power of the Holy Spirit freely given to the person who believes in Jesus Christ. "Do we then overthrow the law by this faith? By no means! On the contrary, we uphold the law" (Rom. 3:31). Christ died "so that the just requirement of the law might be fulfilled in us, who walk not according to the flesh but according to the Spirit" (Rom. 8:3, 4). Christ's death does not make it possible for us to save ourselves by law keeping. His death makes salvation by grace available to every human being willing to receive the gift (Rom. 5:17). And this gift results in lives delivered from the bondage of evil, lives in harmony with the principles of God's holy law.

Jesus taught Nicodemus five timeless principles of salvation that were reiterated by Paul. These principles are just as essential for us as they were for first-century Christians: (1) the cross made our salvation possible; (2) because of the cross, our sins can be forgiven; (3) because of the cross, Christ's righteousness is imputed to us, put to our account and made part of our lives; (4) because of the cross, Christ's righteousness is bestowed upon us by the Holy Spirit; (5) because of the cross, we can have the power of Christ to enable us to overcome sin and keep God's law.

The submarine *Squalas* and its crew lay helpless at the bottom of the Atlantic Ocean. They were two hundred and forty feet below the surface. The crew sent up smoke flares trying to make known their location. Eventually they were located, and thirty-three survivors were brought to safety.

None of the thirty-three men objected when their rescuers arrived. None said, "I will think it over," or "I will wait for a more convenient time," or "I am in a good enough condition as I am," or "I will know better tomorrow what I should do." All instantly and gratefully accepted rescue from death.[13]

Why do we hesitate when Jesus offers us deliverance from eternal death? Is it because we doubt that we are under sentence of death? Is it because we don't think we need saving? Or is it because we think He will be merciful enough to save us despite our failure to commit to His love and the lifestyle He commands? Whatever the reason, it is irrational to close our minds to the conviction of the Holy Spirit and refuse the pardon and salvation that Jesus has earned for us.

Have you surrendered your heart to Christ? Have you allowed Him to transform your life through the power of the Holy Spirit? Have you claimed His righteousness as yours? Through the grace He willingly gives, are you enjoying a life of spiritual victory? By entering into the experience that Jesus outlined for Nicodemus, you can give a positive answer to each one of these questions.

Notes
1. Sunday School Times, quoted by Paul Lee Tan, *Encyclopedia of 7,700 Illustrations: Signs of the Times* (Rockville, Maryland: Assurance Publishers, 1979), pp. 1211, 1212.
2. The translation is mine. The Greek verb "to justify" (*dikaioo*) is used twice in the passage as an explanation of forgiveness (*aphesis*).
3. Translation mine. The Greek participle *dikaiounta* is identified with *logizetai . . . eis dikaiosunen*. The One who justifies is the One who counts, reckons, or imputes faith for righteousness. Hence, justification is the imputation of righteousness.

4. William F. Arndt and F. Wilbur Gingrich, *A Greek-English Lexicon of the New Testament and other Early Christian Literature*, 1957 ed., s.v. *aphesis*.

5. Arndt and Gingrich define *dikaioo*, the verb "to justify" as follows: "*show justice, do justice . . . to someone. . . . justify, vindicate, treat as just. . . . be acquitted, be pronounced and treated as righteous* and thereby become *dikaios, . . . make free or pure . . . be set free, made pure.*"

6. One prominent connotation of *chashav* and *logizomai* in the Hebrew and Greek Old Testament is "to impute," "count," "reckon to," "consider as belonging to," "regard as," "treat as," "credit to." The instances in which these verbs have these closely related meanings may be divided into six categories. (In the texts listed below, the Hebrew *chashav* is not always translated by *logizomai* in the Septuagint. But it is so translated often enough for the parallel between the two verbs to be clear.)

   (i) Things are sometimes reckoned as belonging to a specific class: Lev. 25:31; Num. 18:27, 30; Job 41:27, 29, 32 (verses 19, 21, 24 in the Hebrew Bible).

   (ii) The verb "to impute" is sometimes used in the sense of regarding (considering, counting) a person to be something which he is not. In every instance in which the verb is so used in the Old Testament human error is involved: Gen. 31:15; 38:15; 1 Sam. 1:13; Job 13:24; 19:11.

   (iii) The verb "to impute" in some instances refers to people being regarded as exactly what they are: Neh. 13:13; Num 23:9; Deut. 2:11, 20; Job 18:3; Ps. 106:30, 31; 88:4; Isa. 29:17; 32:15; 40:15, 17.

   (iv) In two cases the verb "to impute" is used to refer to non-imputation of an animal sacrifice to one who offered in a manner contrary to the will of God: Lev. 7:18; 17:4.

   (v) The non-imputation of iniquity was forgiveness of sin: 2 Sam. 19:19-23; Ps. 32:1, 2.

   (vi) The verb "to impute" on occasions is used in the Old Testament to designate a gift or the specification of actual ownership: Num. 18:27, 30; Joshua 13:3; 2 Sam. 4:2 (2 Kings 4:2, LXX).

   What is the specific relevance of these six points for a discussion of Genesis 15:6? (1) Abraham was categorized (counted) as righteous; (2) Abraham was not counted to be something that he was not; (3) the reckoning of righteousness to Abraham was a factual statement that God's righteousness had taken possession of Abraham's life; (4) iniquity was not imputed to Abraham; (5) the imputation of righteousness to Abraham was non-imputation of sin; (6) the imputation of righteousness to Abraham was the genuine bestowal of the righteousness of God upon him.

7. The Greek word *anothen* means both "from above" and "again" or "anew."

8. See *Luther's Works*, ed. Jaroslav Pelikan, 55 vols. (Philadelphia: Muhlenberg Press, 1960), vol. 22, p. 275; vol. 25. pp. 19, 30, 104; vol. 26, pp. 130, 132, 137, 167, 168, 208; vol. 34, pp. 152, 153, 177, 178. See also Paul Althaus, *The Theology of Martin Luther*, trans. Robert C. Schultz (Philadelphia: Fortress Press, 1966), pp. 226, 234, 235; Alister E. McGrath, *Iustitia Dei: a History of the Christian Doctrine of Justification* (Cambridge University Press, 1986), vol. 2, pp. 14, 126. See also John Calvin, *Institutes of the Christian Religion*, trans. Henry Beveridge (Grand Rapids, Michigan: Eerdmans, 1559, 1962), III. XI. 2, 3, 10.

9. See McGrath, vol. 2, pp. 23-26, 29, 32, 44, 45.

10. My translation. The Greek reads: *ho gar apothanon dedikaiotai apo tes hamartias. Dedikaiotai* is the 3rd person, singular, perfect, indicative, passive of the verb *dikaioo*, the verb "to justify." The perfect form used in the text means "has been justified." The sentence translates, "He who died (has died), has been justified from sin."

11. My translation. This is one sentence in the Greek text. In verse 5 *esosen* corresponds to *dikaiothentes* in verse 7. Hence, salvation is identified with justification. The result of the saving (the justifying) is that we are "heirs according to the hope of eternal life."

12. *Luther's Works*, 55 vols. (St. Louis, Missouri: Concordia, 1963), vol. 26, p. 208.

13. Adapted from Robert G. Lee, "Rescue of the Squalas," quoted by Paul Lee Tan, *Encyclopedia of 7,700 Illustrations: Signs of the Times* (Rockville, Maryland: Assurance Publishers, 1979), p. 1212.

Chapter 5
What Does Sanctification Have to Do with Salvation?

Queen Victoria once visited a large paper mill. She was shown the "rag room" where tons of filthy rages were stored. She asked, "How can these dirty rags be made white and pure?" The superintendent answered, "I have a chemical process by which I can remove all the grime and uncleanness from those rags and make them immaculately white."

Sometime later the Queen received a gift of some of the most beautiful writing paper she had ever seen. Accompanying the paper was a note that read: "Will Her Majesty be pleased to accept a specimen of my paper with the assurance that every sheet was manufactured out of the dirty rags which she saw?"[1]

The Bible says that "all our righteousnesses are as filthy rags" (Isa. 1:18, KJV). That is just another way of saying that we are naturally unrighteous people who are incapable of changing ourselves. But the thrilling news is, "though your sins be as scarlet, they shall be as white as snow; though they be red like crimson, they shall be as wool" (Isa. 1:18, KJV). And that is just another way of saying that our sins will be forgiven and our guilt washed away as we accept the free gift of Jesus' holiness.

We discovered in our previous chapter that justification includes two major aspects: (1) God forgives our sins and counts the righteousness of Christ for us; (2) God bestows Christ's righteousness upon us by the gift of the Holy Spirit.

What is sanctification, and what does it have to do with salvation? Since justification is salvation, why is sanctification necessary?

The Greek word for "sanctification" used in the New Testament also means "holiness."[2] The verb "to sanctify" means "to make holy."[3] When

God sanctifies believers, He does not only set them apart for a holy use, He makes them holy. Obviously believers cannot be set apart for holy uses unless they are first made holy people. Jesus was "sanctified and sent into the world" (John 10:36) in the sense that, because He was perfectly holy, He could be set apart for a special holy work, the work of saving the world from sin. When Jesus prayed, "Sanctify them in the truth; your word is truth" (John 17:17), He was asking that His followers should be made holy and, therefore, be useful for the holy work for which He had chosen them. First He made them holy, and then He "sent them into the world" (verse 18).

But how are believers sanctified? The apostle Paul addressed that question in his epistle to the Romans. "For just as you once presented your members as slaves to impurity and to greater and greater iniquity, so now present your members as slaves to *righteousness for sanctification*" (Rom. 6:19, italics supplied). "But now that you have been *freed from sin* and enslaved to God, the advantage you get is *sanctification*" (verse 22, italics supplied). The gift of righteousness sanctifies a person. In the book of Romans, Paul speaks of justification as the gift of the righteousness of God (Rom. 1:16, 17; 3:21-24; 4:22-25). This gift is what sanctifies or makes holy. When we are justified, we are "freed from sin" (Rom. 6:22), delivered from the impurity and iniquity that had been reigning in our lives (verse 19). The result of justification is that we are sanctified or made holy.

After something has been bestowed upon us, we then possess it. Justification is Christ bestowed. Sanctification is Christ possessed. Justification is Christ coming into our hearts every day as we surrender to Him. Sanctification is Christ dwelling in our hearts every day. Justification causes sanctification. Holiness (sanctification) in the heart is the result of Christ's gift of Himself to us by the Holy Spirit.

Never does the Bible say that we sanctify ourselves or that our works make us holy. The consistent teaching of Scripture is that the Holy Spirit makes us holy. Believers in Christ have been "sanctified by the Spirit to be obedient to Jesus Christ" (1 Peter 1:2). Our salvation is "through sanctification by the Spirit and through belief in the truth" (2 Thess. 2:13). Believing Gentiles are "sanctified by the Holy Spirit" (Rom. 15:16).

The gift of righteousness in justification sanctifies us or makes us holy, because in justification the Holy Spirit is poured into our hearts (Titus 3:5-7; Rom. 5:1, 2, 5; 8:9, 10; Gal. 3:3-14). This is why justification and sanctification are inseparable. If a rich man gives you a check for a million dollars, you deposit the check in your bank account, and you are now rich. It was the gift that made you rich. Just so, Christ's gift of Himself to us by the Holy Spirit makes us spiritually rich. His gift is justification; the result is holiness or sanctification. You cannot have one without the other. That is why it is incorrect to say that justification is righteousness by faith alone and sanctification is by faith plus works. Never in Scripture is holiness something earned by human works. It is the possession of those into whose hearts Christ has come. Sanctification is an inevitable, inseparable aspect of the experience of righteousness and salvation by faith (grace) alone.

Sanctification is both present holiness in Christ and growth in holiness in Christ. Sanctification is the immediate and long term work of the Holy Spirit in our hearts.

Sanctification—Present Holiness in Christ

Sanctification is often spoken of in Scripture as present holiness. Paul was sent to the Gentiles "so that they may receive forgiveness of sins and a place among those who are sanctified by faith in me" (Acts 26:17, 18). The last phrase of that text translates literally, "who *have been sanctified* by faith in Me" (italics supplied)[4] The reference is to those who have received the gift of sanctification and who are continuing to enjoy the results of the gift.

Paul addressed his letter to the Roman Christians "to all those who are in Rome, beloved of God, called saints (holy ones)" (Rom. 1:7)[5] They were called saints or holy ones because they had received justification involving the gift of the Holy Spirit to their hearts. Because they possessed the Holy Spirit, they were enjoying the blessings of present holiness (or sanctification) in Christ.

Toward the end of the same letter, Paul speaks of himself as "a minister of Christ Jesus to the Gentiles . . . so that the offering of the Gentiles might be acceptable, *having been sanctified* by the Holy Spirit" (Rom. 15:16, italics supplied).[6] As a Gospel minister, Paul wanted to present to God a people who had experienced and were still experiencing the blessings of sanctification.

Paul addressed his Corinthian letter "to the church of God that is in Corinth, having been sanctified by Jesus Christ, called saints" (1 Cor. 1:2).[7] Even though the Corinthian Christians were tragically divided, they had previously received the blessing of salvation (justification) in Christ and the accompanying gift of holiness (sanctification) in Christ. Paul's concern was that they were spoiling the gift that already had been given to them. Later in the same letter Paul reminded the Corinthian Christians of the purifying experience the Lord had provided them. "You were washed, you were sanctified, you were justified in the name of the Lord Jesus Christ and in the Spirit of our God" (1 Cor. 6:11).[8] They had received the cleansing involved in the inseparable experiences of justification and sanctification, and Paul wanted them to retain the blessings the Lord had so graciously bestowed.

To the Colossians, Paul wrote, "You have been made complete (full, perfect) in Him" (Col. 2:10).[9] The Greek verb *pleroo* used in this verse is translated "perfect" in the KJV, the RSV, and NRSV versions of Revelation 3:2. The person who accepts Christ as Savior and Lord is complete or perfect in Him in the sense that Christ is now dwelling in the heart and directing the thoughts, feelings, and aspirations. This person has received spiritual circumcision, "by putting off the body of the flesh in the circumcision of Christ" (Col. 2:11). This is the essence of sanctification. It is "Christ in you, the hope of glory" (Col. 1:27). We may have the blessings of sanctification, present holiness in Christ, at this moment. As we receive Christ into our hearts by the presence of the Holy Spirit, we have the gift of His holiness; we "become participants of the divine nature" (2 Peter 1:4). The thief on the cross had this gift the moment he accepted Christ. Hebrews 12:14 speaks of "holiness without which no one will see the Lord." But Jesus told the dying thief that he would be with Him in Paradise (Luke 23:43). Then the thief must have had the gift of holiness (sanctification), because without it he never could be with the Lord.

The same promise is for us. "We may share his holiness" (Heb. 12:10). The moment we accept Christ the divine miracle of justification (the new birth) takes place, and we are then complete in Him. This is salvation, the qualification for eternal life. Because Christ who is holy lives in our hearts, we have holiness now; and we have the gift of eternal life now (John 3:36; 1 John 5:11-13).

Sanctification—Growth in Holiness in Christ

Even though we enjoy the blessings of present holiness in Christ, we are still fallen human beings with propensities to sin. Paul was only too conscious of the weaknesses of his fallen nature. He was a born again, justified believer, but he knew that, unless he relied totally upon Christ for strength, he would give in to the demands of his fallen self and commit sin. That is why he wrote, "I punish my body and enslave it, so that after proclaiming to others I myself should not be disqualified" (1 Cor. 9:27). Paul did not attempt to earn his salvation by punishing and enslaving his body. What he meant was that he depended on Christ and the power of the Holy Spirit to control the natural urges of his fallen humanity.

Paul admonished the Galatian Christians, "Live by the Spirit, I say, and do not gratify the desires of the flesh. For what the flesh desires is opposed to the Spirit, and what the Spirit desires is opposed to the flesh; for these are opposed to each other, to prevent you from doing what you want. But if you are led by the Spirit, you are not subject to the law" (Gal. 5:16-18).

The whole point is that when we are justified, the Holy Spirit comes into our hearts. We are enjoying the blessings of present holiness because the Holy Spirit is dwelling in our hearts. But we are still fallen human beings who daily have desires that are contrary to the will of God. These desires *per se* are not sin. It is when we dwell on these desires and give in to them that we fall into sin. The Spirit in our hearts wars against our natural unholy desires, but we still have the power of choice. We can choose to submit to Christ (James 4:7, 8) and to live by the Spirit, or we can choose to resist the Spirit's conviction and power and give in to our unholy desires. If we choose the Spirit's way, we grow in holiness; if we choose sin we retrogress and bring ourselves under the condemnation of the law.

The simple truth is that a justified, born-again believer has two natures: a fallen nature which was inherited at birth (Ps. 51:5; 58:3; Eph. 2:3), and a spiritual nature because of the presence of the Holy Spirit in the heart. Sanctification as growth is the process by which we learn to depend on Christ every day, accepting and appropriating the power of His Holy Spirit. As we starve our fallen natures, keeping our minds focussed on Jesus and refusing to dwell on that which is evil, we "grow in the grace and knowledge of our Lord and Savior Jesus Christ" (2 Peter 3:18). We grow by beholding Him in His Word and by communing with Him in prayer. We have the experience so beautifully described in 2 Corinthians 3:18: "All of us, with unveiled faces, seeing the glory of the Lord as though reflected in a mirror, are being transformed into the same image from one degree of glory to another; for this comes from the Lord, the Spirit." The veil of unbelief has been removed; we love Jesus and love to contemplate the glory of His character. As we thus behold Him, He is able by His Spirit to transform us progressively from one stage of spiritual growth to a higher and higher stage. This is how we become more and more like Jesus. We become reflectors of His character beauty.

Paul emphasized this more and more experience in his first epistle to the Thessalonians. "May the Lord make you *increase and abound* in love for one another and for all, just as we abound in love for you. And may he so strengthen your hearts in holiness that you may be blameless before our God and Father at the coming of our Lord Jesus with all his saints. Finally, brothers and sisters, we ask and urge you in the Lord Jesus that, as you learned from us how you ought to live and to please God (as, in fact, you are doing), you should do so *more and more.* For you know what instructions we gave you through the Lord Jesus. For this is the will of God, your *sanctification. . . ."* (1 Thess. 3:12–4:3; italics supplied).

Thus, sanctification as growth involves an increase in holiness, a progressive development in the life of love and service for Christ and for others. We must learn to rely totally upon the perfect righteousness of Christ bestowed and not upon our own unaided efforts. We must be justified (born again) every day as the means of constant spiritual growth. Justification provides the power; growth in holiness (sanctification) is the result. The power of our fallen humanity is weakened as the power of Christ constantly subdues it, and the holiness that is Christ's gift and presence becomes our habitual experience.

Christian Perfection Before the Second Coming of Jesus

The Bible teaches that sanctification as growth in holiness is to result in victory over all sin before Jesus comes. This is not our achievement; it is Christ's gift. The power is justification; the result is sanctification and total victory.

The Bible standard is perfect holiness in Christ. The inspired apostle wrote: "Since we have these promises, beloved, let us cleanse ourselves from every defilement of body and spirit, *making holiness perfect* in the fear of God" (2 Cor. 7:1; italics supplied). Of course, Paul did not mean that we cleanse ourselves by our unaided human effort. We cleanse ourselves by depending on the transforming, empowering work of the Holy Spirit in our lives (Rom. 8; Gal. 5). This cleansing, the work of the Spirit, results in "making holiness perfect." It is not possible to express this in more comprehensive terms than the Bible does. We are to cleanse ourselves "*from every defilement of body and spirit.*" That means that our bodies and minds are to be free from acts of sin.

We are not told that we will cease to be fallen human beings with propensities to sin. We will be fallen, corruptible in nature until Jesus comes. "This perishable body must put on imperishability, and this mortal body must put on immortality.... then the saying that is written will be fulfilled: 'Death has been swallowed up in victory.'" (1 Cor. 15:53, 54). As long as we are in these mortal, perishable, fallen bodies, everything we do will be tinged with human imperfection. It is impossible for an imperfect mind and body to do anything absolutely perfectly. But the Bible message of salvation is permeated with the thought that fallen minds and bodies do not have to sin. The good news is that Christ died "so that the just requirement of the law might be fulfilled in us, who walk not according to the flesh but according to the Spirit" (Rom. 8:4).

Peter, who was so prone to indiscretions of one form or another, wrote of the importance of victory over sin. "As he who called you is holy, be holy yourselves in all your conduct; for it is written, 'You shall be holy, for I am holy'" (1 Peter 1:15). The Greek word translated "conduct" (*anastrophe*) means "behavior," "way of life." Through receiving the gift of Christ to our hearts, we are to be holy in *all* our behavior. This is not salvation by works; it is salvation received as a gift from Christ, the result of which is holiness of behavior. And behavior includes our thoughts, our feelings, our desires, and our motives. The Bible says that in all of this we are to be holy, because Christ whom we have received is holy.

Christ wants our works to be perfect. The message to the church of Sardis is for us: "I have not found your works perfect in the sight of my God." (Rev. 3:2). He would not make such a statement if He did not want our works to be perfect. The bride of Christ, His faithful people who are preparing to meet their returning Lord, is to "'be clothed with fine linen, bright and pure'—for the fine linen is the righteous deeds of the saints" (Rev. 19:7, 8). Only born-again (justified) believers are capable of doing deeds or works that are righteous in the sight of God. "You understand that every one who does righteousness has been born of Him" (1 John 2:29)[10] Such people are "righteous, just as he is righteous" (1 John 3:7), because, directed and controlled by the Holy Spirit, "their deeds have been done in God" (John 3:21). The presence of the Spirit in their hearts is the presence of Christ in their hearts. And He is the presence of righteousness in their hearts (Rom. 8:9, 10). Christ is their righteousness and the source of their spiritual victory.

When Jesus said, "Be perfect, therefore, as your heavenly Father is perfect" (Matt. 5:48), He provided the punch line of a sermon in which He had emphasized the right kind of behavior for the Christian. He had explained that anger and hate are tantamount to murder (verses 21, 22), and lustful looking comprises adultery (verses 27, 28). Swearing is ruled out for the Christian (verses 33-37), vengeance is to be replaced by submission to mistreatment and injustice (verses 38-42), and enemies are to be loved and prayed for (verses 43-47). Jesus' concept of perfection is doing righteous works because righteousness is in possession of the heart. He had stated, "Unless your righteousness exceeds that of the scribes and Pharisees, you will never enter the kingdom of heaven" (verse 20). The righteousness that God accepts is that which has been received by faith (Rom. 1:16, 17; 3:21-24; 5:1; 9:30–10:10; etc.) This alone is the basis of the kind of perfection that Jesus emphasized.

The adjective "perfect" used in Matthew 5:48 (*teleios*) is the same word that Paul uses in Ephesians 4:13: "Till we all come in the unity of the faith, and of the knowledge of the Son of God, unto a *perfect* [*teleios*] man, unto the measure of the stature of the fullness of Christ" (KJV). The word translated "perfect" in these verses means "*having attained the end or purpose, complete, perfect. . . . fully developed.*"[11] Some translations render it by "mature" (NIV) or "maturity" (NRSV). Giving the word that connotation, some scholars have argued that the term does not mean complete freedom from sinful behavior. On the other hand, of course, it would be hard to find a Christian who would argue that any one of his sins was mature.

The real meaning of the word is given in Ephesians 4:13: "unto a perfect man, unto the measure of the stature of the fullness of Christ" (KJV). What was Christ like? "For to this you have been called, because Christ also suffered for you, leaving you an example, so that you should follow in his steps. 'He committed no sin, and no deceit was found in his mouth.'" (1 Peter 2:21, 22). Perfection is Christlikeness! This does not mean that we can ever equal the infinitely perfect character of Christ. But like Christ, as we depend totally upon Him, we can be kind, merciful, compassionate, and free from sinful behavior.

According to Scripture, God's wish is that despite the tendencies of our fallen humanity and the imperfection with which all our works are tinged, we will stop sinning before Jesus comes. All sin is imperfection, but not all imperfection is sin. Everything we do is imperfect because we have imperfect bodies and minds. But not everything we do is sin. "Whatever does not proceed from faith is sin" (Rom. 14:23). When our works are the result of our faith in Christ, they are accepted by heaven, despite their human imperfection. Martin Luther put it biblically when he wrote: "Works that result from the Word and are done in faith are perfect in the eyes of God, no matter what the world thinks about them. . . ."[12]

This does not mean that God ever accepts or excuses sin. God forgives sin, but never does He excuse it. Imperfect works that are done in faith He accepts. Before the end of time, God's people are to be victors in the battle with sin. Since the Lord is willing to bestow Himself upon us in justification, and dwell within our hearts as the means of our sanctification (holiness), we have all the necessary power to be overcomers. To deny the possibility of victory over all sin is to contradict the Lord who says that He "is able to keep you from falling" (Jude 24) and who promises that with every temptation He will "make a way to escape, that ye may be able to bear it" (1 Cor. 10:13, KJV). When the Lord says that He is able to bring all our thoughts under the control of His Spirit, why should we doubt Him? (2 Cor. 10:4, 5). He offers us power for total victory. How can we do otherwise than accept His offer?

Years ago I was teaching at Avondale College in Australia. I had a young man in one of my classes who was not a professing Christian. He was brought up in a Christian home, and he respected his parents' faith, but he did not practice it. He was a constant problem to me and to some of the other students. Later he left the college and went to work in a nearby city. He met and fell in love with a lovely girl, but she didn't profess the faith that he knew was right. He asked a pastor if he would study the Bible with his girl friend, hoping that she would accept the faith. The pastor agreed on condition that he would accompany his girl friend to the studies. This he did, and his life was changed as he found in God's Word the answer to his own spiritual need. A few years later I met this young man in a church where I was taking meetings. He gripped my hand, looked me straight in the eye, and told me of the transformation he had experienced.

Only Jesus can change lives in this way. Only He can take a sinner and give that one victory over the crippling power of evil. Have you found Christ bestowed (justification) to be your power for victory over sin? Have you experienced present holiness and growth in holiness by receiving Christ into your heart daily? This experience can only result in that complete victory that is the qualification for meeting Jesus at His coming without seeing death. Like Enoch of old, God's people will be translated to heaven as a holy people (Rev. 7; 14) because they have allowed Christ to fill their minds and hearts. Justification is the constantly available power; sanctification is the immediate and long-term result; total victory over sin is the goal to be reached by a people who will go on growing spiritually until Jesus comes, and who will continue to grow throughout eternity.

Notes

1. Adapted from Paul Lee Tan, *Encyclopedia of 7,700 Illustrations: Signs of the Times* (Rockville, Maryland: Assurance Publishers, 1979), p. 1232.
2. The Greek word for "sanctification" is *hagiasmos*. Five times in the King James Version it is translated "sanctification" (1 Cor. 1:30; 1 Thess. 4:3, 4; 2 Thess. 2:13; 1 Peter 1:2). Five times the same word is translated "holiness" (Rom. 6:19, 22; 1 Thess. 4:7; 1 Tim. 2:15; Heb. 12:14). Arndt and Gingrich's *Greek-English Lexicon* defines the word as "*holiness, consecration, sanctification*; the use in a moral sense for a process, or, more often, its result (the state of being made holy) is peculiar to our lit."
3. The Greek verb "to sanctify" is *hagiazo*. This verb is used 29 times in the New Testament. Arndt and Gingrich define the word as meaning "*make holy, consecrate, sanctify. . . . treat as holy, reverence. . . . purify.*"
4. *Hegiasmenois* is the perfect, passive, participle of *hagiazo* (the verb "to sanctify"). *Tois hegiasmenois* means "those who have been sanctified." "The significance of the perfect tense in presenting action as having reached its termination and existing in its finished results lies at the basis of its uses. Emphasis, as indicated by the context or the meaning of the verb root, may be on either the completion of the action or on its finished results."—H. E. Dana and Julius R. Mantey, *A Manual Grammar of the Greek New Testament* (New York: Macmillan, 1927, 1955), p. 201.
5. My translation. The Greek reads *kletois hagiois*, "called saints," or "called holy ones." The verb "to be" is not in the Greek text.
6. My translation. The Greek reads *hegiasmene en pneumati hagio*, "having been sanctified by the Holy Spirit." *Hegiasmene* is the perfect, passive, participle of *hagiazo*. The participle is correctly translated, "having been sanctified" or "having been made holy."
7. My translation. Once again the Greek uses the perfect passive participle of the verb *hagiazo*. The phrase *hegiasmenois en Christo Iesou* may be translated "having been sanctified in Christ Jesus" or "to those who have been sanctified in Christ Jesus."
8. The Greek reads, *alla hegiasthete*. Here the verb is the aorist, indicative, passive of *hagiazo*. It refers to an event in the past. The Corinthians "were sanctified."
9. My translation. The Greek reads, *kai este en auto pepleromenoi*. Randolph O. Yeager comments: "The perfect periphrastic is decidedly durative. It matches the durative nature of *katoikei* in verse 9. Having been made complete in association with Christ we are now filled. Deity always resides in Him and since the believer is in constant association with Him (John 17:21) he, having been made complete, is always fulfilled with all the spiritual utility that has God as its source."—Randolph O. Yeager, *The Renaissance New Testament*, 18 vols. (Gretna, Louisiana: Pelican, 1985), 15:59. The verb *pleroo*, of which the perfect, passive, participle is used in Col. 2:10, means "*make full, fill. . . . of persons fill w. powers, qualities, etc. . . . fulfill. . . . complete, finish, bring to an end.*"—Arndt and Gingrich, s.v. *pleroo*.
10. My translation. The Greek reads: *ginoskete hoti kai pas ho poion ten dikaiosunen ex autou gegennetai*: ". . . you know (understand) that every one who does righteousness has been born of Him." *Gegennetai* is 3rd person, singular, perfect, passive, indicative of *gennao*, which means "beget," "bear," "bring forth." The person

who does righteousness "has been born" of Christ. The reference is to the new birth experience described in John 3.

11. Arndt and Gingrich, s.v. *teleios.*

12. *Luther's Works,* ed. Jaroslav Pelikan, 55 vols. (Saint Louis, Missouri: Concordia, 1961), vol. 3, p. 318.

Chapter 6
Did God Predetermine Our Salvation?

This question is especially relevant because millions of contemporary Christians hold the once-saved-always-saved belief, based on the doctrine of double predestination. This doctrine teaches that in the eternal ages before the creation of our world God decreed that certain ones will be saved and others lost. Those predestined to be saved are the elect to whom God gives His irresistible grace. Once they have responded to this grace, which they inevitably will, they cannot fall away from a right legal relationship with God and be lost. Those who were predestined to be lost cannot respond to God's grace and be saved.[1]

The doctrine of single predestination has the same effect but teaches slightly differently. God is supposed to have predestined only the elect to be saved. The rest are lost, not because God decreed that they should be but because He did not decree that they should be saved.

Writers who believe predestinarian teaching make statements like the following by Randolph O. Yeager: "The argument in Romans is devastating in its attack upon the notion that salvation can be earned by works produced by man. It also shows that while no amount of good works can bring the sinner into right relationships with God, once the sinner has that right relationship, by grace through faith, no amount of evil can separate Him from God, nor terminate his standing as God's child. However low, miserable and degrading our state may be, children of God never suffer any diminution of our standing."[2] This simply means that elect believers remain legally saved even if they should fall into the most degrading sins.

Of course every Christian believer wishes to have a settled assurance of salvation. The Bible teaches that if we believe in Christ we enjoy the beginnings of eternal life now (John 3:36; 1 John 5:11-13). But does it follow from this that disobedience to God's laws does not change a person's salvation status? Does it follow that no matter what professed believers do they still remain saved? Some Christians seem to have a sense of security that nothing can dispel. They regard obedience to laws as legalism. They declare that if the so-called elect want to turn away from Christ, they cannot. And temporary defection from a life of faith will inevitably be reversed. A once-saved person will most certainly be an inheritor of the eternal Kingdom of Christ.

We can see at a glance that such a doctrine could produce very lax Christians who do whatever they wish and still cling to the certainty of eternal security. Does the Bible teach that God requires obedience to His law? Certainly the Bible denies that we are saved by obedience (Rom. 3:20-22; Gal. 2:16). But does the Lord expect the saved soul to obey Him? Does He plan to save us *in* our sins or *from* our sins? And can a saved soul turn away from obeying God and be lost? Can a once-saved person choose to reject salvation?

These are the questions to which in this chapter we will seek the Bible answer. But first let us examine church history to discover the roots of predestinarian teaching.

Predestination in Church History

The question of predestination did not become a serious issue in the Christian church until the time of Augustine (A.D. 354-430), the famous Bishop of Hippo in North Africa. Augustine opposed Pelagius, a British monk who taught that man's will can accomplish much toward his own salvation without the assistance of divine grace. Augustine argued that any change in fallen man is solely the work of God's grace. Before the fall, Adam could do good because he had the help of grace. Since the fall, man's will can choose only sin. It is not possible for him to choose God's will until grace is active in his life. God gives His grace only to the elect, the ones whom He decides should have His unmerited favor. God's grace given to the elect is irresistible. A person who is predestined by God to salvation will receive His irresistible grace and will inevitably be saved. Those who are not so chosen by God are left in their perdition and will justly receive eternal damnation.[3]

Both Luther and Calvin, the great sixteenth-century Reformers, accepted a thoroughly biblical definition of justification. Their views of predestination, however, are highly suspect. First we will consider their views; then we will turn to the Scriptures.

Augustine strongly influenced the thinking of the sixteenth-century Reformers. They substantially accepted Augustine's doctrine of predestination, modifying it and adding to it according to their own understandings. In his 1525 book, *The Bondage of the Will*, Luther argued that all things that happen, whether good or evil, are the result of God's unchangeable will. There is no such thing as free will in humans. Luther contradicted two then current ideas on the free will of mankind: (1) that human beings have the power to choose what is right, and (2) that they have the power to put right choices into action. Luther said that man does not choose God; he is chosen by God. God chooses only the elect whom He has predestined to eternal salvation. The rest of humanity are predestined to eternal rejection.

In Luther's view, everything that God foresees must occur just as He foresees it. In fact, everything that He foresees to occur will happen *because He has willed it*. Luther wrote: "From this it follows irrefutably that everything we do, everything that happens, even if it seems to us to happen mutably and contingently, happens in fact nonetheless necessarily and immutably, if you have regard to the will of God."[4] Therefore, if God wills and foresees everything that happens, nothing is left to the free will of man. Even the evil in the world has been willed by God. Yet Luther argued that God is not responsible for evil. His omnipotence moves upon imperfect, fallen natures, and the result is that these natures do evil works. The evil is theirs not God's, and they are justly punished for their sins.

Even so, it is apparent that there is a contradiction in Luther's thought. If all that God foresees happens of necessity because He has willed it, in the final analysis He is responsible for evil. All Luther's attempts to resolve that problem were unavailing.

Luther went so far as to suggest that Adam's fall was willed by God. He wrote: "The same must be said to those who ask why he permitted Adam to fall, and why he creates us all infected with the same sin, when he could either have preserved him or created us from another stock or from a seed which he had first purged. He is God, and for his will there is no cause or reason that can be laid down as a rule or measure for it, since there is nothing equal or superior to it, but it is itself the rule of all things."[5]

Luther summed up his lengthy argument on the bondage of the will and divine predestination by writing as follows: "For if we believe it to be true that God foreknows and predestines all things, that he can neither be mistaken in his foreknowledge nor hindered in his predestination, and that nothing takes place but as he wills it (as reason itself is forced to admit), then on the testimony of reason itself there cannot be any free choice in man or angel or any creature."[6]

John Calvin (1509-64) placed the doctrine of double predestination at the center of his theological system. Because of Calvin's strenuous defense of the doctrine and its acceptance by leading European theologians in following centuries, it has become a standard Christian teaching for millions of Protestants.

Calvin summarized his teaching in the following terms: "We say, then, that Scripture clearly proves this much, that God by his eternal and immutable counsel determined once for all those whom it was his pleasure one day to admit to salvation, and those whom, on the other hand, it was his pleasure to doom to destruction. We maintain that this counsel, as regards the elect, is founded on his free mercy, without any respect to human worth, while those whom he dooms to destruction are excluded from access to life by a just and blameless, but at the same time incomprehensible judgment."[7]

Thus Calvin taught that, in the ages before the creation of our world, God decreed that certain humans would be saved (the elect) and others would be damned. Nothing can change these decrees; man's will chooses only that which God's decrees have previously decided. The elect receive the irresistible grace of God to choose and perform His will. They are saved solely by His grace, not by their own choice. The divine decree that others are lost is equally unchangeable. Even the fall of Adam was decreed by God. "The decree, I admit, is dreadful; and yet it is impossible to deny that God foreknew what the end of man was to be before he made him, and foreknew, because he had so ordained by his decree. . . . Nor ought it to seem absurd when I say, that God not only foresaw the fall of the first man, and in him the ruin of his posterity; but also at his own pleasure arranged it."[8]

When people responded to Luther and Calvin by pointing out the injustice of punishing the wicked who are as they are because of God's decree, they responded by arguing inconsistently that the lost are punished justly because of their own choice to sin. They said that we can never understand the hidden mystery of God's will. Our part is to believe in Him despite our inability to understand why He arbitrarily chooses some to salvation and others to damnation. Both Reformers argued strenuously against the teaching that God's decrees are based on His foreknowledge of human choice. To them, God predetermined man's choice; He did not foresee anything that He does not cause.

Jacobus Arminius (1560-1609), the celebrated Dutch Reformed theologian, strenuously opposed the earlier Reformers' doctrine of predestination.[9] He taught that God foresaw who would receive Christ and who would not. Each individual has been given the power to choose or to reject Christ. Those whom God foresaw would exercise their free choice by receiving Christ as Lord and Savior were predestined to salvation. Those whom He foresaw would reject Christ were predestined to eternal rejection. God does not will all things that happen. He had nothing to do with the origin of evil in the universe or in our world, and He does not will the sins of human beings. Nor does He will that anyone should be lost. His saving grace is given to those who choose to believe, and it is kept from those who choose not to believe.

In opposition to the Arminians, the Synod of Dort convened by the Dutch Reformed Church in 1618-19 decided in favor of the Calvinistic doctrine of predestination, and the Arminians were then persecuted.[10] The English Westminster Assembly (1643-49), which produced the "Confession" that gave official expression to the Presbyterian faith, also accepted Calvinistic predestination, but without the teaching that Adam's fall was decreed by God.[11] Since then Calvinistic predestination in one form or another has been very influential in many Protestant churches, even though Arminianism is more acceptable to many others.

God Does Not Will All that He Foresees

If God willed all that He foresaw would happen, as the Reformers taught, ultimately He would be responsible for all the evil in our world. It is true that He foresaw everything that would occur. He declared "the end from the beginning and from ancient times things not yet done" (Isaiah 46:10). But He did not will or cause humanity's sin, suffering, and misery.

Even though God has always foreseen the destruction of the wicked at the end of the world, it has never been His will that they should be lost. Peter wrote that God is "not wanting any to perish, but all to come to repentance" (2 Peter 3:9). Because our world is finally to be destroyed by fire, Peter urges all to lead "lives of holiness and godliness" (verse 11). So concerned was Peter that the believers to whom he was writing should be saved at the Second Advent, he urged that they beware of falling away into sin and of being lost at last (verse 17). Only God could foresee who would be true till the end and who would fall away, but He did not will that anyone should be lost. The point is that God's foreknowledge is not equivalent to His will for mankind.

Paul emphasized the same message. God's design is that all humanity should be saved. He "desires everyone to be saved and to come to the knowledge of the truth" (1 Tim. 2:4). The Lord knows that, because not all will choose Christ as Savior and Lord, not all will be saved. Only those who "*receive* the abundance of grace and the free gift of righteousness" will have "life through the one man, Jesus Christ." (Rom. 5:17, italics supplied). But God wishes that all would receive, and He does all that an infinitely loving God can do to make it so.

"For the grace of God that bringeth salvation hath appeared to all men" (Titus 2:11, KJV). God's grace has not been made available only to those whom He has predestined to salvation; it is readily available to all. As Jesus so beautifully explained it, "God so loved the world" that He planned for "the world" to be saved through Christ (John 3:16, 17). His grace and love were not reserved for a select class, while the rest were left untouched and unmoved. God has no favorites in respect to salvation. All people are His children, and He wishes to save them all.

This truth was forcefully proclaimed by the prophet Ezekiel. The ancient Israelites were urged to put away their sins and turn to the Lord precisely because God has "no pleasure in the death of him that dieth" (Ezek. 18:31, 32, KJV). There is no suggestion in Ezekiel's discussion that God's will in regard to humanity is fixed, with the righteous being arbitrarily chosen and the wicked irrevocably rejected. Quite the contrary, the Lord pled with His people on the basis of His willingness to forgive their sins and grant them eternal life if only they would repent. Ezekiel 33:11-16 teaches that if a righteous person turns away from the Lord and lives in sin again, he will be lost. But the repenting sinner will be saved. God most certainly did not will that some would be lost because He foresaw that it would be so. Despite God's foreknowledge of the ultimate damnation of the wicked (2 Thess. 1:7-10; Rev. 21:27), He moves upon their hearts with earnest entreaties. In fact, He foresaw and rejoiced that some wicked people would respond to His pleas and finally be saved.

Isn't it a terrible insult to the Deity to argue, as the predestinarians do, that all God foresees is His will for humanity? Did God *will* that Adam would fall into sin, that pre-Flood mankind would live in moral degradation and ultimately be destroyed, that the inhabitants of Sodom and Gomorrah would become so debased that He would have to rain fire and brimstone upon them, that the Jews would reject Christ's love and subject Him to merciless torture, and that the history of our world would be filled with the record of hatred, violence, disease, and death? To credit all that to the will of God is preposterous in the extreme! Such a doctrine drives people away from Christ because they cannot believe that a loving God would will such evil.

What God foresees will happen in the future is often not His will but the will of Satan and of those who reject Christ.

Christ Died for All Mankind, Not Only for the Elect

The predestinarians often teach that Christ died only for those whom He had decreed to save. He bore their guilt on the cross but did not bear the guilt of those whom He had decreed to damn. This is quite contrary to Bible teaching.

The beloved apostle John contended strongly that Christ died for all humanity. "He is the atoning sacrifice for our sins, and not for ours only but also for the sins of the whole world" (1 John 2:2). John had heard the Baptist announce that Christ is "the Lamb of God who takes away the sin of the *world*" (John 1:29; italics supplied). Even though God cannot finally remove the guilt of those who reject Christ, His loving purpose in having Christ die for all was that all should be saved.

Paul underscored the same thrilling message. He wrote that because "one has died for all; therefore all have died. And he died for all, so that those who live might live no longer for themselves, but for him who died and was raised for them" (2 Cor. 5:14, 15). In other words, Christ died for all, hoping that all would accept Him and be saved from sin. In this sense, "in Christ God was reconciling the world to himself" (verse 19). He foresaw that He would not be able to save all, because not all would accept Christ and repent of their sins (Rev. 2:21; 9:20, 21; 16:9, 11). Nevertheless, God provided all with the same wonderful opportunity by atoning for their sins and giving them the ability to choose Christ as their Substitute (see 2 Cor. 5:20, 21).

Paul announced that Christ's sacrifice made justification available for all humanity (Rom. 5:18), so that everyone willing to receive can have life (verse 17). Rejection of Christ is the greatest of sins because His infinite love led Him to suffer our eternal loss on Calvary. As those who are ultimately lost face the judgment throne of God at the end of time (Rev. 20:11-15), they can never argue that Christ did not love them, die for them, or make justification available to them. They can never claim that they were predestined to be damned and had no choice in the matter. Christ offers Himself as the Savior of the whole world (1 John 4:14; John 6:51; 12:47), not as a discriminating judge who, apart from human decisions, chooses some to life and the rest to eternal destruction.

Praise the Lord, all classes, races, and nationalities have a Savior from sin and destruction. Whoever you are, Christ offers you eternal life. Every provision has already been made that you might be saved. The only ingredient that the Lord awaits is your acceptance of His free offer of grace.

God's Predestination Is Based on His Foreknowledge of Human Choice

The Bible teaches that God first foresaw how people would decide; then He predestined to salvation those whom He knew would accept Christ. God did not impose arbitrary decrees upon humanity. He did not decide that some would be saved and others lost, irrespective of their personal choice. And He did not make it impossible for some to reject His grace and just as impossible for others to accept His grace.

Paul taught that those who were predestined to salvation were those whom God foreknew. "For those whom he *foreknew* he also predestined to be conformed to the image of his son" (Rom. 8:29; italics supplied).[12] The statement obviously means that divine foreknowledge of the individual came *before* divine predestination. Because in the ages before creation of our world God foresaw that certain ones would submit to Christ's loving authority, He predetermined that He would save them from sin, give them the new birth experience, and invest them with the glory of Christ's character (verse 30). These are the "elect" (verse 33) or the chosen ones.[13] Because they have been justified by faith, no one can bring a charge against them that carries any weight with God. "It is God who justifies" (verse 33).

The reason that they are God's choice ones, His chosen, select ones is precisely that they have responded by faith to His conviction and have received His justification. God predestined them to salvation because he foresaw their faith response to His love.

Peter reiterates Paul's teaching. He introduced his first epistle by writing: "Peter, an apostle of Jesus Christ to the *elect (chosen)* exiles of the dispersion of Pontus, Galatia, Cappadocia, Asia, and Bithynia, according to the *foreknowledge* of God the Father, by sanctification of the Spirit, for obedience and sprinkling of the blood of Jesus Christ" (1 Peter 1:1, 2, italics supplied).[14] The "elect (chosen) exiles" (verse 1) were chosen "according to the foreknowledge of God the Father" (verse 2). God foresaw their genuine faith (verse 7). He did not choose them because He foresaw their good works. Faith is not a work. God foresaw that they would respond in heart to the drawing, convicting ministry of the Holy Spirit. On the basis of this foreknowledge, God chose them for holiness, spiritual cleansing, and obedience to Jesus Christ.

In Romans, chapter 11, Paul discussed God's foreknowledge of the decisions of His people. When Paul wrote that "God has not rejected his people whom he foreknew" (Rom. 11:2), he did not mean that the whole Israelite nation was still God's chosen people. This is very clear from the context. The ones God "foreknew" were like the seven thousand in the time of Elijah who had not bowed the knee to Baal (verse 4). They were the "remnant according to the election of grace" (verse 5, KJV). Even though the nation Israel generally was blind, the elect remnant had received God's blessing (verse 7). The greater part of Israel was rejected by God because of unbelief (verse 20). They would be accepted again, as the Christian Gentiles were accepted, if they would believe in Christ (verse 23). Therefore, the remnant of Israel who were accepted by the Lord were those who had retained their faith. They were elect or predestined to salvation because God foresaw that, unlike the majority of their fellow Israelites, they would be faithful to Him. God's predetermination that the remnant should be saved was based on His foreknowledge of their belief in Christ.

Ephesians, chapter 1 must be interpreted in the light of what we have already discovered. Paul did not contradict his message to the Romans by what he wrote to the Ephesians. The earlier verses of this chapter are often taken in isolation from the later ones. God chose His people "before the foundation of the world" (verse 4). They were predestined to be His children (verse 5). But these verses do not say that God's choice of His people before the creation of the world was based upon His purely arbitrary decision, quite apart from His foreknowledge of their faith. Verse 11 repeats the point that Christians were "predestinated according to the purpose of him who worketh all things after the counsel of his own will" (KJV). But what was God's will? The next verse says it very simply: "That we should be to the praise of his glory, *who first trusted in Christ*" (verse 12, KJV; italics supplied). It was God's will to make holy those whom He foresaw would trust in Christ.

The Ephesian Christians trusted in Him after they had heard the preaching of the Gospel (verse 13). Then they were sealed by the Holy Spirit. They received the Holy Spirit only when they believed. It was then that God's predetermined will could be carried out in their lives. The passage does not say that God predestined their belief. He foresaw their belief, and, in view of it predestined them to an eternal inheritance.

Ephesians 1:19 speaks of "the immeasurable greatness of his power for us who believe." And the next chapter underlines the point. "For by grace you have been saved through faith, and this is not your own doing; it is the gift of God" (Eph. 2:8). Salvation is a gift of God's grace, but it must be received by faith (compare Rom. 5:17). Faith does not earn grace; it responds to it and receives it. There is no salvation for an individual unless he chooses to receive God's grace. God does not urge His grace upon us so forcibly that we cannot resist receiving it. This teaching of Augustine and the Reformers was unbiblical. We must choose to receive grace; and that choice is faith! Because God foresaw that choice He predestined us to salvation.

Peter wrote of Christ as "having been foreknown before the foundation of the world, but revealed in the last times for you" (1 Peter 1:20; compare 1 Cor. 2:2, 7, 8; Rev. 13:8).[15] Some interpreters have argued that Christ could not have failed in His divine mission by choosing to sin because He was predestined to succeed. This interpretation ignores the significance of the temptations confronting Jesus (Heb. 4:15). Unless there was a possibility of failure, there was no contest, and the fact of His victorious sinlessness would have no significance for us in our battle with sin. Peter also wrote that Christ is our "example, so that you should follow his steps" (1 Peter 2:21). Christ overcame in the same way that we may overcome (Rev. 3:21). We are instructed to "walk just as he walked" (1 John 2:6). Christ was "foreknown before the foundation of the world" (1 Peter 1:20) in the sense that God foresaw that He would not choose to sin. God did not foreordain that Christ could not fail; He foresaw His victory. Christ was foreordained to be our Savior because God foresaw that He would succeed in His mission, that because of the depth of His love He would prevail.

God Gives Everyone the Power to Choose Christ

The predestinarians argue that the only ones who can choose Christ are the elect to whom God has given irresistible grace. In the final analysis, they are saved because God chooses them, not because they choose Him. The rest of humanity have no ability to choose Christ and salvation.

But what does the Bible teach? The many Old Testament calls for God's people to choose Him and put away their sins imply that they have the power of choice. The blessings and curses that God put before Israel would have been meaningless unless the people possessed the ability to choose Him (Deut. 30:19; compare chapters 28, 29). Joshua's command to Israel, "Choose this day whom you will serve" (Joshua 24:15) would have been quite irrelevant if they had lacked the power to choose. The people chose God, He came into their lives, and they then had the power to obey. Of course, God's grace, in the form of divine conviction, engendered their choice in the first place. But His grace was available to all because all the people were invited to choose.

The book of Proverbs reminds us that failing to "choose the fear [reverence] of the Lord" results in rejection by God. If we turn away from God, rejecting His counsel and leading in our lives, we cannot expect Him to answer us in time of need (Prov. 1:28-30). But if we choose Him and walk in His way we will be blessed. The wise man added, "but those who listen to me will be secure and will live at ease, without dread of disaster" (verse 33). Such a promise would be meaningless if the predestinarians were correct in maintaining that human beings have no ability to choose God.

Isaiah completely shatters the idea that only the elect are called by God. "I will destine you to the sword, and all of you shall bow down to the slaughter; because, when I called, you did not answer, when I spoke, you did not listen, but you did what was evil in my sight, and chose what I did not delight in" (Isa. 65:12). God's grace led Him to call these people, but they chose evil rather than God's will. His grace was by no means irresistible! They resisted God's call, and He rejected them.

The Lord has taught us through the apostle Paul that "the righteousness of God through faith in Jesus Christ" is "for *all* who believe" (Rom. 3:22, italics supplied). We are not left in doubt about how many are offered this gift, for Paul adds, "for there is no distinction, since all have sinned and fall short of the glory of God" (verses 22, 23). The "all" who have sinned are offered without distinction the gift of Christ's righteousness if they will believe and submit to His love. The passage means nothing unless all sinners have the ability to choose to believe in Christ.

Before his conversion, Paul had the capacity to choose what was right but not the capacity to put into action the right choices he had made (Rom. 7:18). Only when he invited Christ to come into his heart was he able to be an overcomer (Rom. 7:24, 25). When he chose the righteous presence of Christ by the presence of the Holy Spirit in his heart, he had spiritual power and victory over sin (Rom. 8:9-14).

Jesus said that after His death He would "draw all people" to Himself (John 12:32). Jesus also said, "No one can come to me unless drawn by the Father who sent me" (John 6:44). But He draws all to Himself! That being so, all have the ability to come to Him by their own choice. That is why Jesus' very comforting invitation to burdened souls is given to *all* humanity (Matt. 11:28-30).

John the Baptist testified "that all might believe through him" (John 1:7). Jesus is "the true light, which enlightens everyone" (verse 9). Those who respond to the light are given "power to become children of God" (John 1:12). Isaiah had presented the same truth. He extended God's loving invitation to all. "Turn to me and be saved, all the ends of the earth!" (Isa. 45:22).

It is not Christ's will that only an elect group of arbitrarily chosen people should believe in Him. He wants the whole world to believe, for He says, "Let everyone who wishes take the water of life as a gift" (Rev. 22:17). Jesus prayed, ". . . so that the world may believe that you have sent me" (John 17:21; compare verse 23). His prayer implies that the whole world has the ability to believe.

Once Saved Believers Can Fall Away and Be Lost
The warning is all through the Bible that it is possible for believers to apostatize and be lost. This is why we are constantly admonished to watch, pray, study the Word, and daily surrender to Christ's loving will.

What did Paul mean by saying that he brought his fallen self into subjection lest, having preached to others, he himself should become a "castaway" (1 Cor. 9:27, KJV)? What is a castaway? The Greek word is *adokimos*. It means "*not standing the test . . . unqualified, worthless, base.*"[16] It is the word used in 2 Corinthians 13:5: "Know ye not your own selves, how that Jesus Christ is in you, except ye be *reprobates*?" (KJV; italics supplied). People who have lost the presence of Christ in their hearts are castaways or reprobates. The same word is used in Titus 1:16: "They profess that they know God; but in works they deny him, being abominable, and disobedient, and unto every good work *reprobate*" (KJV; italics supplied). This is the kind of person Paul did not want to become. He knew it was a very real possibility if he did not keep his fallen nature under the control of the Holy Spirit by daily yielding his will to Christ's loving authority.

Hebrews 6:4-6 does not mean that there is no hope for backsliders. It means that backsliders cannot be renewed again to repentance "while (as long as) they are crucifying to themselves the Son of God, and exposing Him to public disgrace."[17] The relevant point for our study is that people who "have once been enlightened, and have tasted the heavenly gift, and have shared in the Holy Spirit, and have tasted the goodness of the word of God and the powers of the age to come" can fall away and be lost. Unless they cease crucifying Christ by lives of sin, they cannot be renewed unto repentance and be saved. Once saved people can be lost in sin, and backsliders can be saved only if they repent by accepting Jesus as Lord of their lives.

Hebrews 10:23-38 makes a similar point. We are instructed to cling to our faith "without wavering" (verse 23) because if we waver and choose to live in sin again, there is nothing more the Lord can do for us. "For if we willfully persist in sin after having received the knowledge of the truth, there no longer remains a sacrifice for sins, but a fearful prospect of judgment, and a fury of fire that will consume the adversaries" (verses 26, 27). Toward the end of the chapter comes the very clear statement: "My righteous one will live by faith. My soul takes no pleasure in anyone who shrinks back" (verse 38). Such people who revert to a life of sin "are lost" (verse 39, NRSV); they "draw back unto perdition" (KJV). Then it is very possible for a once saved soul to fall away and be lost by rejecting Christ's repeated overtures of love.

Peter, who knew what falling is all about, warned born-again believers of the danger of lapsing into lives of sin. "For if, after they have escaped the defilements of the world through the knowledge of our Lord and Savior Jesus Christ, they are again entangled in them and overpowered, the last state has become worse for them than the first. For it would have been better for them never to have known the way of righteousness than, after knowing it, to turn back from the holy commandment that was passed on to them. It has happened to them according to the true proverb, 'The dog turns back to its own vomit,' and, 'The sow is washed only to wallow in the mud'" (2 Peter 2:20-22). Hence the instruction: "You therefore, beloved, since you are forewarned, beware that you are not carried away with the error of the lawless and lose your own stability" (2 Peter 3:17). By dependence upon Christ, we can constantly "grow in the grace and knowledge of our Lord and Saviour Jesus Christ" (verse 18).

In the parable of the sower, Jesus spoke of some seed falling on rocky ground. He illustrated the case of those who "in a time of testing fall away" (Luke 8:13) because they lack a wholehearted relationship with Christ.

The faithful servant of Christ who turns away from his faithfulness and reverts to a life of sin will be eternally rejected unless he repents. "The master of that slave will come on a day when he does not expect him and at an hour that he dos not know, and will cut him in pieces, and put him with the unfaithful" (Luke 12:46).

Jesus' parable of the unforgiving servant (Matt. 18:23-35) illustrates the fact that when God forgives our sins, he expects us to forgive others. If we refuse to forgive, He will revoke His forgiveness of our sins. The unforgiving debtor was severely punished. "So my heavenly Father will also do to every one of you, if you do not forgive your brother or sister from your heart" (verse 35).

Ezekiel 33:13, 18 specifically states that the Lord will reject and put to death people who once knew Him, if they turn away from a life of righteousness.

The Bible predicts that towards the end of world history "some will renounce the faith by paying attention to deceitful spirits and teachings of demons" (1 Tim. 4:1). Some former believers will be lost "because they have cast off their first faith" (1 Tim. 5:12, KJV). This is exactly the message of Revelation 2:4, 5. Believers who have lost their first love and have fallen into sin have rejected God. With tears of sorrow, God turns away, both rejected and disappointed.

King Saul was once filled with the Spirit of God (1 Sam. 10:6, 9). But he fell into sin, refused to repent, and died a suicide (1 Sam. 31:4). His experience proves conclusively that once-saved believers can apostatize and be lost. Apostate believers are not always restored to their former position of favor with God. Only as they respond anew to Christ's love, turning to Him for forgiveness and spiritual power can they have salvation again.

The Meaning of Romans, Chapter 9

Predestinarians use this chapter in an attempt to establish their view that, quite apart from any human choice, God decreed who should have mercy and who should be lost. Is this what the chapter really teaches?

What is meant by the statement of the Lord, "It is through Isaac that descendants shall be named for you" (Rom. 9:7, NRSV; Gen. 21:12)? In speaking thus to Abraham, the Lord did not mean that He had chosen Isaac for salvation and Ishmael for damnation. He meant that He had selected Isaac as the father of the chosen nation and the forefather of the Messiah. God promised to make a nation of Ishmael's descendants also, and He took care of Hagar and Ishmael in a miraculous way (Gen. 21:13-20). But Sarah was Abraham's true wife, and Isaac's birth when Abraham was a hundred years old and Sarah was ninety was a miracle. Therefore the Lord insisted that Isaac should be the one to have the birthright, making him the patriarch of the chosen people. Abraham had prayed that Ishmael might be the one chosen by God to inherit His special promises, but the Lord declared otherwise (Gen. 17:17-21). Even so, the Lord assured Abraham that He would make special provision for Ishmael (Gen. 17:20)—a promise that He kept.

The point is that Paul's use of this story in Romans 9 was not intended to establish that Isaac was predestined to be saved and Ishmael to be damned. Because Isaac was a child of promise, conceived miraculously in a manner quite contrary to normal physical possibilities, he is used in Scripture as a symbol of salvation by faith. God promised Isaac to Abraham and Sarah, they trusted Him implicitly, and God fulfilled the promise. Hence, Isaac is used by Paul as an analogy of those who rely upon faith in Christ for salvation. Many of the Jews tried to earn salvation by their works, as Abraham had tried to fulfill God's promise of a son by taking Hagar in place of Sarah. Therefore, Paul uses Ishmael, the child of human works, as an illustration of those who depend on works for salvation (compare Gal. 4:22-24, 29-31). A remnant of the Jews as well as the Gentile Christians accepted salvation by faith in Christ. It is these that Paul represents by his reference to Isaac (compare Gal. 4:27, 28; 3:28, 29).

In Romans 9, Paul uses a second illustration to explain salvation by faith/grace in contrast to salvation by works. Jacob, like Isaac, is used as the symbol of those who are saved by grace, not by their own works. And Esau is the symbol of those who are rejected by God. Paul's point is not that God arbitrarily gave salvation to Jacob and denied it to Esau. The statement to Rebekah at the birth of the boys, "the elder shall serve the younger" (Gen. 25:23), meant that God had chosen Jacob to have the spiritual birthright and to be the patriarch of the family. Both brothers would be guilty of serious sins (see Gen. 25:27-34; 27:1-41). Jacob repented and by faith accepted God's salvation, but Esau persisted in his rebellious way of life. Jacob was not chosen by God because of his future good works, but because the Lord foresaw (Rom. 8:29) that he would be a genuine believer who would receive the free gift of grace. Esau was rejected because God foresaw that he would not choose to receive divine saving grace. God offered salvation to both men (compare Isa. 45:22); one responded to the invitation, the other did not.

The passage does not teach that God's pre-election of Jacob was independent of Jacob's choice of grace; it teaches that God's predestination was independent of Jacob's good works (verse 11). Faith is not a work that saves us; it is a response to divine grace. We are not saved by our own wills (verse 16), but by God's grace. Even so, we must will to receive His saving grace (compare Rom. 5:17). Esau could have made the same response as did Jacob, but he chose not to. God did not "hate" him (verse 13) in the modern sense of the term. The Greek word (*miseo*) is sometimes used in the New Testament in the sense of "to love less," or "to put to one side" (see Luke 14:26; John 12:25; Matt. 6:24; compare Mal. 1:2-4).

The reference to Pharaoh (Rom. 9:17-21) is interpreted by some to mean that God deliberately hardened Pharaoh's heart because he was predestined to be lost. Our study has revealed that the ones upon whom the Lord chooses to have mercy (verse 18) are those who believe in Him. Pharaoh chose to defy God's warnings. He refused to believe God or to acknowledge His loving authority. Certainly God is often said to have hardened Pharaoh's heart (Exod. 4:21; 7:3 etc.), but Pharaoh is also said to have hardened his own heart (Exod 8:32; 9:34; 1 Sam. 6:6). The paradox is explained by two facts: (1) In Scripture God is often said to cause that which He allows, even though the real cause is the devil; (2) God's loving appeals will soften one heart and increasingly harden another because one will choose to accept them and another will not. Appeals rejected result in deepening alienation from the Lord.

Romans 9:17 quotes Exodus 9:16. God said that he had raised up Pharaoh, "to show you my power, and to make my name resound through all the earth." In context, God's statement is part of His rebuke for Pharaoh's tenacious unwillingness to respond to His appeals. The Lord added: "You are still exalting yourself against my people, and will not let them go" (Exod. 9:17). A little later Pharaoh admitted that God is righteous and that he and his people had sinned (verse 27). The divine purpose would have been fulfilled however Pharaoh had reacted to God's appeals. If Pharaoh had responded positively surely God's name would have been exalted in the earth. When Pharaoh chose to reject God, he separated himself from the source of life and was destroyed. The Lord's name was exalted because of His miraculous deliverance of His people from Pharaoh's power. There is, however, no suggestion that because Pharaoh was predestined to be lost, he had no choice but to react negatively to God's appeals. God wills to have mercy upon believers, and wills to reject unbelievers. The vessel made for "honor" (Rom. 9:21, KJV) is the one who chooses to believe; the vessel made for "dishonor" is the one who chooses not be believe.

The ones chosen for wrath (Rom. 9:22) are those who, like the ancient Israelites, sought righteousness by works instead of by faith (verses 31-33). The ones chosen for mercy are the ones who, like the Christian Gentiles, attained to righteousness by faith (Rom. 9:30). Verses 30-33 provide the punch line of the whole chapter. The elect are those who have faith in Christ; the damned are those who do not have faith.

Romans 9 must be interpreted in the light of the overall teaching of Scripture on the question of human choice and divine predestination. The message throughout the Bible is that God hoped all would accept His love but in sorrow predestined to salvation only those whom He foresaw would accept Him. He has given light and the power to choose to every human soul. People are not lost who accept Christ and allow His Spirit to reign in their hearts.

Have you chosen Christ as Lord of your life? There is forgiveness, power to become like Jesus, and eternal life with Christ available for you if you receive Him as Savior and Lord.

Notes

1. See Loraine Boettner, *The Reformed Doctrine of Predestination* (Nutley, New Jersey: Presbyterian and Reformed Publishing Company, 1932, 1968). Boettner clearly states the Calvinistic doctrine of predestination. He presents the five points of Calvinism: total inability, unconditional election, limited atonement, efficacious grace, the perseverance of the saints. His defense of the doctrine is unconvincing because it is exegetically unsound. ·

2. Randolph O. Yeager, *The Renaissance New Testament*, 18 vols. (Gretna, Louisiana: Pelican, 1983), 11:200. Even though Yeager's massive contribution of analyzing every word in the Greek New Testament is very valuable to the student, his Calvinistic theology should be critically examined on the basis of the overall teaching of Scripture.

3. See Justo L. Gonzalez, *A History of Christian Thought*, 3 vols. (Nashville, Tennessee: Abingdon Press, 1971), 2:44-47; Reinhold Seeburg, *The History of Doctrines*, 2 vols. (Grand Rapids, Michigan: Baker, 1895, 1977), 1:350- 353; G. W. H. Lampe, "Christian Theology in the Patristic Period," in *A History of Christian Doctrine*, ed. Hubert Cunliffe-Jones (Edinburgh: T. & T. Clark, 1978), p. 167; Bernhard Lohse, *A Short History of Christian Doctrine* (Philadelphia: Fortress Press, 1966), pp. 116, 117.

4. *Luther's Works*, ed. Helmut T. Lehmann, 55 vols. (Philadelphia: Fortress Press, 1972), 33: 37, 38.

5. *Ibid.*, 33:180, 181.

6. *Ibid.*, 33:293.

7. John Calvin, *Institutes of the Christian Religion*, trans. Henry Beveridge (Grand Rapids, Michigan: Eerdmans, 1559, 1962), III. XXI. 7.

8. *Ibid.*, III. XXIII. 7.

9. *The Writings of James Arminius*, trans. James Nichols and W. R. Bagnall, 3 vols. (Grand Rapids, Michigan: Baker, 1977), I:447-449; II:483-485.

10. *The Oxford Dictionary of the Christian Church*, 1958 ed., s.v. "Dort, Synod of."

11. *Ibid.*, s.v. "Westminster Assembly" and "Westminster Confession."

12. The verb "foreknew" translates the Greek *proegno*, which is the 3rd person, singular, aorist, active, indicative of *proginosko*, which means "*know beforehand, in advance, have foreknowledge (of) . . . some thing.*" —William F. Arndt and F. Wilbur Gingrich, *A Greek-English Lexicon of the New Testament and Other Early Christian Literature*, 1957 edition, s.v. *proginosko*. The verb "predestined" translates the Greek *proorisen*, which is the 3rd person, singular, aorist, indicative, active of *proorizo*, meaning "*decide upon beforehand, predestine . . . some one.*"—Arndt and Gingrich, s.v. *proorizo*.

13. The Greek adjective *eklektos* means "*chosen, select. . . . choice, excellent.*" —Arndt and Gingrich, s.v. *eklektos*. The corresponding noun is *ekloge*, meaning "*selection, election . . . choosing. . . . that which is chosen or selected.*"—*Ibid.*, s.v. The corresponding verb is *eklegomai*, meaning "*choose, select. . . . choose someone (someth.) for oneself.*"—*Ibid.*, s.v.

14. My translation. The "chosen ones," "the elect" (*eklektois*) were chosen "according to the foreknowledge (*prognosin*) of God the Father." They were not arbitrarily selected apart from any divine foreknowledge of their faith. Peter speaks of "the genuineness" of their faith (1 Peter 1:7). God did not choose them because He foresaw their good works. Faith is not a work. He foresaw their heart response to the convicting, drawing ministry of the Holy Spirit. On this basis they were chosen for "sanctification of the Spirit, for obedience" and the cleansing that results from the sacrifice of Jesus Christ.

15. My translation. The Greek reads: *proegnosmenou men pro kataboles kosmou. Proegnosmenou* is the perfect, passive, participle of *proginosko*, meaning "*know beforehand, in advance, have foreknowledge. . . .*"—Arndt and Gingrich.

16. Arndt and Gingrich, s.v. *adokimos*.

17. My translation. Two present participles are used in Hebrews 6:6: *anastaurountas . . . paradeigmatizontas.* "While (as long as, because) they are crucifying . . . and holding Him up to contempt (exposing Him to public disgrace)."

Chapter 7

Are the Ten Commandments
Still the Law for Christians?

Many Christians give a negative answer to this question. They believe that the Ten Commandments, like the ceremonial laws,
were abolished at the Cross. They apply the New Testament passages that speak of the ceremonial laws being done away at the Cross to the
moral law of Ten Commandments. They reason that, because Moses gave
all these laws to the Jews, they were intended only for the nation Israel
before the death of Jesus. Now we follow the teachings of Jesus and not the
requirements that were specifically intended for Jews only.

Some dispensationalists go a step further. They reason that before the
Cross salvation was by obedience to law. Since then it has been by grace
alone.[1] We are living in the dispensation of grace, while the Jews were living in the dispensation of law. Thus God used a different means of saving
humanity before the Cross than He uses for us today.[2] If we try to live by
the laws of the Old Testament, we become legalists and cannot be saved by
grace.

Some interpreters take the view that, although the Ten Commandments
were done away at the Cross, nine of them were reinstituted by Christ and
His apostles. They think it possible to discover all the commandments restated in the New Testament except the fourth, the Sabbath command.[3]
People who reason this way reveal their true motive for arguing that the
Ten Commandments were abolished at the Cross. They are not opposed to
nine of those commands, but they are opposed to the Sabbath. Because
they can find nine of the Ten Commandments restated in the New Testament, they have no burden to oppose them. But since they think the Sabbath command is not repeated in the New Testament, they oppose it strenu-

ously. Their dispensationalist theology provides a very handy method of doing away with the weekly seventh-day Sabbath.

Opposition to keeping God's law is called antinomianism (*anti* = against; *nomos* = law). The idea that salvation by grace alone rules out the importance of obeying the law of God fails to recognize the principle that Christ's gift of salvation is designed to bring us into accord with God's will. Of course, it is not true that salvation is by law keeping. We receive saving grace from God when, by faith, we accept Jesus Christ as Savior and Lord (Eph. 2:8, 9). But such faith always results in conformity to the will of God as expressed in His law (verse 10). Paul wrote that Christ died "so that the just requirement of the law might be fulfilled in us, who walk not according to the flesh but according to the Spirit" (Rom. 8:4). If we are not obeying the law of God, we cannot claim that its righteousness is fulfilled in us.

Legalism is not obedience to God's law; it is the attempt to obey His law without first having received the gift of His grace. Legalism is the attempt to save oneself by law keeping, instead of allowing Christ to save by crediting His righteousness to us and bestowing His righteousness upon us by the gift of the Holy Spirit. Once having received Christ's divine saving presence in the life, it is inevitable that the believer will want to follow all of Christ's commands. Grace is the means; obedience is the result. Obedience to the law of God is the sure consequence of the genuine new birth experience.

Let us turn now to the Scriptures and see what was done away at the Cross and what still applies for Christian believers today.

The Moral Law of Ten Commandments Was the Standard of Righteousness before the Cross

The means of righteousness and salvation has always been faith/grace. Faith is our belief and acceptance; grace is God's saving gift. Old Testament believers were saved in exactly the same way as New Testament believers. The *standard* of righteousness was the law of God, the Ten Commandments; the *means* by which they were to arrive at the standard was grace, the power of God readily bestowed upon them because they had accepted God's call and submitted faithfully to His loving will.

The New Testament teaching that in the salvation by faith experience the law of God is written on the believer's heart is a reiteration of Old Testament teaching. The New Testament writers underlined and reemphasized the Old Testament truth. Paul's teaching that "the one who is right-eous will live by faith" (Rom. 1:17) was a repetition of Habakkuk's mes-sage, "the righteous live by their faith" (Hab. 2:4). In explaining righteous-ness by faith, Paul quotes Moses. Romans 10:6-8 quotes Deuteronomy 30:11-14. "The righteousness that comes from faith says, 'Do not say in your heart, "Who will ascend into heaven?"' (that is to bring Christ down) 'or "Who will descend into the abyss?"' (that is, to bring Christ up from the dead). But what does it say? 'The word is near you, *on your lips and in your heart*' (that is, the word of faith that we proclaim)" (Rom. 10:6-8, italics supplied).

In other words, Paul taught exactly the same message of righteousness by faith that Moses taught. It is not true that under the Mosaic dispensa-tion salvation was by works of law while under the New Testament dispen-sation salvation is by grace. At every stage of history, God saves believers by grace. He mercifully writes His will on their hearts and lives out His right-eous life through them.

The New Testament teaching of heart circumcision repeated the Old Testament teaching. The Lord's instruction through Moses was "Circum-cise, then, the foreskin of your heart, and do not be stubborn any longer" (Deut. 10:16). "Moreover, the Lord your God will circumcise your heart and the heart of your descendants, so that you will love the Lord your God with all your heart and with all your soul, in order that you may live" (Deut. 30:6). Centuries later, Jeremiah repeated the same instruction. "Circum-cise yourselves to the Lord, remove the foreskin of your hearts, O people of Judah and inhabitants of Jerusalem" (Jer. 4:4).

Circumcision of the heart was then and still is the same spiritual expe-rience that Jesus illustrated by new birth (John 3). "Real circumcision is a matter of the heart — it is spiritual and not literal" (Rom. 2:29). "And ye are complete in him, which is the head of all principality and power: In whom also ye are circumcised with the circumcision made without hands, in putting off the body of the sins of the flesh by the circumcision of Christ" (Col. 2:10, 11, KJV). This is exactly the spiritual transformation that Jesus invited Nicodemus to receive when He said to him, "What is born of the flesh is flesh, and what is born of the Spirit is spirit. Do not be astonished that I said to you, 'You must be born from above'" (John 3:6, 7).

In the centuries before the Cross, salvation was always by faith/grace, and the standard of righteousness was always God's law of Ten Commandments. The experience of salvation by grace produced in the heart of Old Testament believers the desire and the power to obey God's law. Abraham is presented in the New Testament as the great example of the life of faith (Romans 4; Galatians 3). Yet, in his own day, the Lord praised Abraham because he "obeyed my voice and kept my charge, my commandments, my statutes, and my laws" (Gen. 26:5).

In the preface to the Ten Commandments, the Lord instructed Moses to tell the people, "Now therefore, if you obey my voice and keep my covenant, you shall be my treasured possession out of all the peoples" (Exod. 19:5). And through Solomon the Lord presented to Israel His unchanging standard of righteousness: "Therefore devote yourselves completely to the Lord our God, walking in his statutes and keeping his commandments, as at this day" (1 Kings 8:61). This was not legalism! To argue so is to accuse God of imposing a legalistic system upon His people and then punishing them for not doing the impossible, for not obeying His law in their own strength. Quite the contrary, God offered to save them by coming into their hearts. Once that relationship was established, the Lord expected them to obey His law. Then they had the right motivation and the power. Grace came first; obedience followed as an inseparable result.

The dispensationalist idea that between Sinai and the Cross humans were saved by works of law is unscriptural. The dispensationalist author, Charles F. Baker, admits that and proceeds to explain what dispensationalists really believe.

"We agree perfectly with Dr. Buswell and other reformed theologians that no man ever attained or could ever attain eternal life by legal obedience, but we do contend that the Bible states that perfect legal obedience would be rewarded by justification. The point that Buswell and others do not seem to understand about the dispensational view is that dispensationalists do not contend that God ordained the law dispensation to the end that Israelites might be saved by legal obedience, but rather to prove once and for all the impossibility of sinful flesh ever being able to do anything to please God. The law-flesh-works combination, having been proved a failure, God introduces His method, the grace-faith-spirit combination, which fulfills all of the righteous requirements of His holy law. Just as Israel had to go through Egypt and the wilderness to learn many valuable lessons, so they had to go through the dispensation of law before they inherited the promises."[4]

In Baker's view, the law-flesh-works dispensation existed until the time of the apostle Paul. "This law system was imposed upon Israel during the dispensation of Law, which was in force from Moses until the revelation given to Paul"[5] So from the giving of the law at Sinai until the salvation by grace dispensation began with Paul, Israel and the world were bound to a system of law under which no one could be saved. The logic of Baker's position is as follows: (1) No one can ever attain eternal life by legal obedience; (2) Israel and the world were bound to a system of legal obedience from Sinai to the time of Paul. Conclusion: Therefore no one could be saved from Sinai until the time of Paul. Quite the contrary, both Old and New Testaments teach that, in every age before the time of Jesus, salvation was by faith/grace alone. Obedience to God's law of Ten Commandments was and still is the result of that experience.

The Moral Law of Ten Commandments Remains the Standard of Righteousness for the Christian

There is no contradiction between the Old Testament and the New on the question of obedience to the law resulting from salvation by faith. In fact, as we have already seen, the New Testament writers referred to and quoted the Old Testament prophets in defense of their teaching regarding the law.

The moral law of Ten Commandments remains the standard of righteousness. The additional factor introduced in the New Testament is that the life of Jesus, which was a perfect exemplification of God's law, is a more effective demonstration of the divine standard than the written commandments. The method of arriving at the standard, of emulating Jesus' life of obedience, is the faith/grace relationship with the Lord.

The experience of salvation by faith does not obviate God's requirement that we obey His law. Quite the contrary, the New Testament explains that faith results in the law being established in the heart of the believer. Paul wrote to the Romans, "Do we then overthrow the law by this faith? By no means! On the contrary, we uphold the law" (Rom. 3:31). Because the law is the standard (although not the means) of righteousness, it points out our sin. Paul exclaimed, "If it had not been for the law, I would not have known sin. I would not have known what it is to covet if the law had not said, 'You shall not covet'" (Rom. 7:7). Paul saw the law as holy, just, good, and spiritual (verses 12, 14). There is no suggestion that he rejected the law because it was nailed to the Cross.

James agreed with Paul by teaching that disobedience to any one of the Ten Commandments is tantamount to rejection of the total law of God. James clarifies which law he is speaking of. "For whoever keeps the whole law but fails in one point has become accountable for all of it. For the one who said, 'You shall not commit adultery,' also said, 'You shall not murder.' Now if you do not commit adultery but if you murder, you have become a transgressor of the law. So speak and so act as those who are to be judged by the law of liberty" (James 2:10-12). Hence, the Ten Commandments are a law of liberty, not a burden.

This is exactly what John wrote: "For the love of God is this, that we obey his commandments. And his commandments are not burdensome, for whatever is born of God conquers the world. And this is the victory that conquers the world, our faith. Who is it that conquers the world but the one who believes that Jesus is the Son of God?" (1 John 5:3-5). Conquering the world is obeying God's commandments, and the one who has this conquering power is the born-again believer.

Jesus left us in no doubt about His standard of righteousness. We are not even to think that He came to abolish the law. "Do not think that I have come to abolish the law or the prophets; I have come not to abolish but to fulfill" (Matt. 5:17). Anyone who dares to teach that one of God's established commandments is not binding will be rejected by heaven (verse 19). We know what set of laws Jesus meant because he quoted the Ten Commandments (verses 21, 27).

Some have argued that Jesus' interpretation amounted to an abolition of the Ten, because He emphasized the importance of the spirit of the law rather than the letter. The fact is that Jesus gave a more strict interpretation of the law than was generally accepted. The spirit of the law does not exclude the letter; it goes beyond it to show what the commandments really mean. The command that says, "You shall not murder" means that Christians are not to lose their tempers with their neighbors or cherish hatred in their hearts (Matt. 5:21, 22). The command, "You shall not commit adultery" means that impure thoughts must not be cherished (verses 27, 28). Jesus exalted the standard far above what many of His contemporaries thought necessary. He did not abolish the Ten Commandments; He established them permanently as God's standard of righteousness.

The New Testament teaching regarding the new covenant experience is based firmly on the Old Testament. Hebrews 8:10-12 quotes Jeremiah 31:31-33. The good news is that under the new covenant the law of God is written on believers' hearts. There can be no doubt that the reference is to the Ten Commandment law, for this was the standard of righteousness accepted by Jeremiah (see Jer. 11:1-8).

The New Testament like the old promotes righteousness and salvation by faith in Christ. It is God's grace that saves and grace alone, but grace received is never alone. God's grace includes His gift of spiritual power (1 Cor. 1:4-9). It always results in obedience to the Ten Commandments. God's law is not merely ten suggestions that may be lightly set aside. It is an established, immutable standard of righteousness, obedience to which is made possible by the free gift of His grace.

The Ceremonial Law Ceased at the Cross

By the ceremonial law we mean the ministry associated with the ancient Israelite earthly sanctuary or temple. In the wilderness during the exodus, God gave through Moses instructions regarding the sanctuary and its services. These were carried out at that time, and later on an even greater scale in the temple built by Solomon. In the time of Jesus, the animal sacrifices and services of the temple were still being regularly performed. This ceremonial system was the gospel before the Cross. It comprised a series of ceremonies that pointed forward to the death and ministry of Jesus Christ. Once He had died on the cross and ascended to heaven, it was no longer necessary to have such a set of earthly ceremonies. Now type had met its antitype, the shadow was transcended by the substance, the example was replaced by the reality. The ministry of Jesus in the heavenly sanctuary replaced the ministry of priests in the earthly sanctuary.

When Jesus expired on the cross, the veil of the Jerusalem temple was torn from top to bottom by a divine hand (Matt. 27:50, 51). The significance of the earthly ministry had come to an end. Jesus' death fulfilled the type or analogy that daily for centuries had been enacted in the temple. Every animal sacrifice pointed forward to "the Lamb of God who takes away the sin of the world" (John 1:29). Every temple service typified some aspect of Jesus' ministry for sinful humanity. Every item of sanctuary furniture represented an aspect of Jesus' work for us. When Jesus died on the cross the penalty for sin was paid (Isa. 53:6; 2 Cor. 5:21; 1 Peter 2:24). When

He ascended to the heavenly sanctuary, the ministry began to which the service of the earthly priests had pointed (Heb. 9:11-14).

In his letter to the Ephesians, Paul wrote that the Gentile believers who once had no hope of salvation now have equal hope with Jews who believe in Christ (Eph. 2:11-13). "For he is our peace; in his flesh he has made both groups into one and has broken down the dividing wall, that is, the hostility between us" (verse 14). What was that dividing wall? The next verse explains: ". . . having abolished the law of commandments in ordinances, so that he might create the two in himself into one new man making peace" (Eph. 2:15).[6] What was "the law of commandments in ordinances" that Christ abolished? If Paul had been suggesting that the Ten Commandments were abolished by Christ, he would have been contradicting what he had written to the Roman Christians (Rom. 3:31; 7:7, 12, 14; 8:3, 4). The Ten Commandments still functioned for Paul and, in his inspired understanding, will be the standard on the basis of which all humanity ultimately will be judged (Rom. 2:13). In his epistle to the Ephesians, Paul was referring to the ceremonial laws that were a barrier separating Jew and Gentile. Once Christ had died on the cross, this barrier was abolished. Now Gentiles could join Jews in worshiping Christ without the hindrance of having to enter into a set of ceremonial observances.

Hebrews 7:11-28 teaches that Christ's heavenly high-priesthood has replaced the ministry of earthly priests in the ancient Israelite temple. Jesus Christ belonged to the tribe of Judah, not the tribe of Levi from which the earthly priests were drawn. But Jesus became the heavenly High Priest whose work was typified by the ministry of every earthly Levitical priest. When Jesus became our heavenly High Priest after his death, resurrection, and ascension, it was no longer necessary for the earthly priests to function. The ministry to which their ministry pointed forward had begun. Moreover, the animal sacrifices that the earthly priests regularly offered in the earthly temple no longer had any significance with the Lord. The one sacrifice of Christ to which the earthly sacrifices pointed had occurred. "Unlike the other high priests, he has no need to offer sacrifices day after day, first for his own sins, and then for those of the people; this he did once for all when he offered himself. For the law appoints as high priests those who are subject to weakness, but the word of the oath, which came later than the law, appoints a Son who has been made perfect forever" (Heb. 7:27, 28).

Hebrews, chapter 8, tells us that there is a heavenly sanctuary in which the ascended Christ is the High Priest. "Now the main point in what we are saying is this: we have such a high priest, one who is seated at the right hand of the throne of the Majesty in the heavens, a minister in the sanctuary and the true tent that the Lord, and not any mortal, has set up" (Heb. 8:1, 2).

Hebrews 9:1-7 describes the daily and Day of Atonement ministries conducted in the earthly sanctuary. Verse 8 explains that the way into the heavenly sanctuary was not available as long as the earthly sanctuary or temple was still functional. The services of the earthly sanctuary were a temporary symbol "until the time comes to set things right" (verses 9, 10). "But when Christ came as a high priest of the good things that have come, then through the greater and perfect tent (not made with hands, that is, not of this creation), he entered once for all into the Holy Place[7] [heavenly sanctuary], not with the blood of goats and calves, but with his own blood thus obtaining eternal redemption" (verses 11, 12). Hebrews 9:11-14 refers to two aspects of the earthly ministry that were abolished by Christ. First, the earthly animal sacrifices were replaced by the one sacrifice of Christ on the cross. Second, the priests' sprinkling of blood in the earthly sanctuary typified Christ's intercessory ministry for believers in the heavenly sanctuary. The result is that the conscience (or consciousness)[8] of the believer is purified "from dead works to worship the living God" (verse 14). The imperfect work of the earthly sanctuary or temple is now superseded by the perfect ministry of Jesus in the heavenly temple.

Not the moral law of Ten Commandments but the temporary ceremonial law was abolished when Jesus died on Calvary.

The "Law of Moses" May Mean the Ceremonial Law, or the Ten Commandments, or Both

This point is important because some interpreters of the Bible wish to argue that, since the Ten Commandments were part of the law of Moses, which the apostles said need not be kept any more (Acts 15), the Ten Commandments are not binding upon Christians. The simple answer is that, although the law of Moses included both the ceremonial law and the Ten Commandments because they were both given by God through Moses, in some passages in the Bible the law of Moses means specifically the ceremonial aspects of the law. If I say that I am flying to Australia tomorrow, you might ask, "What part of Australia?" I would answer, "Sydney." Australia is a large country. When I say that I am planning to visit Australia, I do not mean the whole country. I mean one city to which I am traveling. Just so, when the Bible writers speak of the law of Moses, they do not necessarily mean the whole complex of laws given through Moses. They sometimes mean ceremonial laws, sometimes the Ten Commandments, and sometimes both. Sometimes they mean the civil laws given by Moses. What is meant in Acts, chapter 15? First, let us look at some Bible passages that speak of the law of Moses.

The book of the law that Moses wrote undoubtedly included the Ten Commandments (Deut 30:10; 31:26; 33:4). The law contained in that book was to be written on the people's hearts (Deut. 30:11-14). Obedience to this law was to be the basis of their prosperity (verses 15, 16). Paul quotes Deuteronomy 30:11-14 (Rom. 10:6-10) and uses the passage as the basis of his definition of righteousness by faith in Christ. It is, therefore, inconceivable that the "book of the law" referred to in Deuteronomy 30:10 did not include the Ten Commandments.

Before he died, David instructed Solomon: "Be strong, be courageous, and keep the charge of the Lord your God, walking in his ways and keeping his statutes, his commandments, his ordinances, and his testimonies, as it is written in the law of Moses, so that you may prosper in all that you do and wherever you turn" (1 Kings 2:2, 3). Faithfulness to God's commandments written in the law of Moses was to result in prosperity for ancient Israel (verse 4). The very heart of God's will for Israel and the world was contained in the Ten Commandments. Without doubt the law of Moses included the Ten Commandments.

The book of Nehemiah identifies "the law of Moses " as "the law of God." (Compare Nehemiah 8:1-3 with verse 8.) This law that was read to the people included the ceremonial law (verse 14) as well as the Ten Commandments (Neh. 9:13, 14). The law given "through your servant Moses" (verse 14) included the Sabbath command, the fourth of the Ten Commandments.

Jesus said, "Did not Moses give you the law? Yet none of you keeps the law. Why are you looking for an opportunity to kill me?" (John 7:19). The law of Moses included the sixth commandment of the ten. It also included the command regarding circumcision (verses 22, 23). Thus the law of Moses included both the Ten Commandments and the ceremonial laws.

Hebrews 10:28, 29 warns of the danger of violating the law of Moses: "Anyone who has violated the law of Moses dies without mercy 'on the testimony of two or three witnesses.' How much worse punishment do you think will be deserved by those who have spurned the Son of God, profaned the blood of the covenant by which they were sanctified, and outraged the Spirit of grace?" In ancient Israel, the death penalty was to be meted out for rebellious violation of one of the Ten Commandments (Exod. 21:12, 15-17; 31:14, 15; Lev. 20:2, 9, 10, 13). The covenant referred to in Hebrews 10:29 is the everlasting covenant which involves the Ten Commandments written on believers' hearts (Heb. 10:16, 17). Violating the law of Moses was, and still is, tantamount to violating our covenant relationship with Christ.

The law of Moses spoken of in Scripture often includes the moral law of Ten Commandments. But it sometimes refers exclusively to the ceremonial law. Joseph and Mary obeyed the ceremonial requirements of the law of Moses by presenting baby Jesus at the temple. "When the time came for their purification according to the law of Moses, they brought him up to Jerusalem to present him to the Lord (as it is written in the law of the Lord, 'Every firstborn male shall be designated as holy to the Lord'), and they offered a sacrifice according to what is stated in the law of the Lord, 'a pair of turtledoves or two young pigeons'" (Luke 2:22-24). The law of Moses was the law of the Lord and, in this context, the reference is exclusively to its ceremonial stipulations.

Jesus instructed a leper whom He had healed to present himself to the priest "and, as Moses commanded, make an offering for your cleansing, for a testimony to them'" (Luke 5:14; compare John 7:23).

In Acts 15 the problem was not the Ten Commandments. The problem was that legalistic Jews were demanding that Gentiles who became Christians should be circumcised and observe the ceremonial aspects of the law of Moses (Acts 15:1, 5, 24). The apostles' answer to the problem proves that the Ten Commandments were not under discussion. "'For it has seemed good to the Holy Spirit and to us to impose on you no further burden than these essentials: that you abstain from what has been sacrificed to idols and from blood and from what is strangled and from fornication. If you keep yourselves from these, you will do well. Farewell.'" (Acts 15:28, 28). Are we, therefore, to assume that it was quite acceptable for these Gentile Christians to lie, to dishonor their parents, to steal, etc? Of course not! The

Ten Commandments were not the issue. The apostles were not instructing the new Gentile believers to ignore the Ten Commandments. They were telling them that they did not need to observe the ceremonial laws that had significance before the death of Christ. The apostles mentioned fornication because it was a special problem among the Gentiles. The law of Moses, as referred to in Acts 15, means specifically the ceremonial law, not the moral law of Ten Commandments.

It is not correct to contrast the law of Moses and the law of God, applying the former to the ceremonial law and the latter to the Ten Commandments. Nor is it true that the law of Moses, as spoken of in Scripture, always includes the Ten Commandments. Sometimes the law of Moses refers specifically to the ceremonial aspects of the laws given by God through Moses. This is the meaning of "the law of Moses" as it is used in Acts 15.

The Weekly Sabbath Is Part of God's Unchanging Moral Law

When the New Testament writers exalt the Ten Commandments as the standard of righteousness for Christians, they never exclude the Sabbath command. They never say that nine of these commandments must be kept, but not the Sabbath. In fact, we have very good evidence from the New Testament documents that the Sabbath, like the rest of the Ten Commandments, is to be observed by Christians.

The fourth commandment of the ten is just as binding upon Christians as the rest. Jesus said, "Therefore, whoever breaks one of the least of these commandments, and teaches others to do the same, will be called least in the kingdom of heaven; but whoever does them and teaches them will be called great in the kingdom of heaven" (Matt. 5:19). Yet there are millions of Christians who are breaking the fourth commandment, and many are telling people that it need not be kept. There is no Bible warrant for that. The spiritual and eternal danger to which these Christians are exposing themselves is very great indeed.

Jesus urged His disciples to pray that, when Jerusalem was about to be destroyed by enemy armies, they would not have to flee on the Sabbath day (Matt. 24:20). Why did Jesus urge this if He did not intend His followers to keep the Sabbath? Matthew 24:20 is not referring merely to the events just prior to the destruction of Jerusalem. Those events were types or examples of the events immediately preceding Jesus' second coming. In our era, just before Jesus returns, He commands us to keep holy His Sabbath day. His moral law of Ten Commandments, of which the Sabbath command is the very center, is still to be obeyed, because we love Him and He has saved us from sin (John 14:15; 15:10).

Years after the Cross, when Luke wrote concerning the Sabbath day, he gave no indication that it had been abolished or replaced by Sunday observance. The day of Jesus' crucifixion, the preparation day, was followed immediately by the Sabbath (Luke 23:54). "On the sabbath," the followers of Jesus, "rested according to the commandment" (verse 56). In other words, they kept the weekly seventh-day Sabbath in obedience to the fourth commandment of the decalogue. The next day, the first day of the week, later known as Sunday, was the day of Jesus' resurrection (Luke 24:1-5). Writing years after the crucifixion weekend, Luke made no comment to the effect that now the Sabbath command had been done away or that the weekly day of worship should now be Sunday. We can only assume that the Sabbath "according to the commandment" observed by Jesus' followers immediately after His death was the Sabbath honored by Luke and Jesus' apostles years later.

The disciples of Jesus consistently observed the weekly seventh-day Sabbath years after His death. They knew of no command abolishing the Sabbath or changing the day to Sunday. Paul and his fellow workers customarily worshiped and preached on the Sabbath day (Acts 13:14, 15, 42-44; 17:1, 2; 18:1, 4, 11). If the Sabbath command had been abrogated or changed, why didn't Luke say so when writing the book of Acts years after Jesus' death and resurrection?

Some interpreters argue that Paul went to the synagogue on the Sabbath day not because he wished to observe the Sabbath but because this was his best chance of reaching the Jews with the Christian Gospel. Of course he wished to win the Jews, but the evidence indicates that he kept the Sabbath even when he did not attend the synagogue. Acts 16 records that in Philippi Paul and his associates observed the Sabbath on the banks of a river. "On the sabbath day we went outside the gate by the river, where we supposed there was a place of prayer; and we sat down and spoke to the women who had gathered there" (verse 13). The result of that open-air Sabbath meeting was that Lydia was won to Christ and was baptized (verses 14, 15).

Jesus' followers consistently observed the seventh-day Sabbath after His death and resurrection, and we have the same privilege today. There is great blessing in obeying all of the commandments of God and great misery in refusing to obey. One of the main characteristics of the last-day church is that its members observe all of God's commandments. They "keep the commandments of God" (Rev. 12:17). "Here is a call for the endurance of the saints, those who keep the commandments of God and hold fast to the faith of Jesus" (Rev. 14:12).

A Few Passages Used by Opponents of the Ten Commandments

There is not space in this study to deal with all the arguments against the Ten Commandments used by antinomians. The evidence for the continual significance of the Ten Commandments for Christians as presented above is sufficient to prove the point. But we will take a brief look at a few passages misused by those who reject the Ten Commandments and the Sabbath.

Romans 10:4. The Revised Standard Version, like some other versions, paraphrases Romans 10:4: "For Christ is the end of the law, that every one who has faith may be justified." A literal translation of the Greek reads: "For Christ is the end of the Law unto (for) righteousness for all who believe."[9] The text is not teaching that Christ is the end of the law. It is teaching that Christ is the end of *the law as a means of righteousness* to those who believe. When they believe in Him, they accept His free gift of salvation and righteousness (Rom. 1:17; 3:22-24; 6:18; 8:9, 10). For them the attempt to earn salvation by their own efforts to obey the law apart from Christ has ceased.

Colossians 2:13-17. Colossians 2:13 indicates that our sins are forgiven because of Christ's death and our acceptance of Him. "And when you were dead in trespasses and the uncircumcision of your flesh, God made you alive together with him, when he forgave us all our trespasses." The next verse says that "the handwriting of ordinances" (KJV) was nailed to the cross. What is this handwriting of ordinances? Since the discussion is forgiveness of our sin (verse 13), we can conclude that our guilt was nailed to the cross. Jesus became sin for us (2 Cor. 5:21). "He himself bore our sins in his body on the cross, so that, free from sins, we might live for righteousness; by his wounds you have been healed" (1 Peter 2:24). The New Revised Standard Version translates Colossians 2:14: "erasing the record that stood against us with its legal demands. He set this aside, nailing it to the cross." There is no indication here that the Ten Commandments were nailed to the cross. Our guilt demanded that we die. Jesus died in our place. When He was nailed to the cross, so was our guilt.

What then is meant by Colossians 2:16 and 17? "Therefore do not let anyone condemn you in matters of food and drink or of observing festivals, new moons, or sabbaths. These are only a shadow of what is to come, but the substance belongs to Christ." The reference is to the ceremonial aspects of the law which were a shadow of the ministry that Jesus would perform for us. The phrase "feasts, new moon, sabbaths" in the Old Testament refers to those special occasions when ceremonial observances of various kinds were to be offered. (See 1 Chron. 23:31; 2 Chron. 2:4; 8:12, 13; 31:3; Neh. 10:33; Ezek. 45:17; Hosea 2:11.) As recorded in Numbers 28 and 29 the occasions on which special burnt offerings were to be offered included daily, weekly (Sabbath), monthly, and yearly occasions of worship and sacrifice. These sacrifices no longer need to be offered on these occasions because Christ has died, and no longer is His coming foreshadowed by the offering of animal sacrifices. The "food and drink" (Col. 2:16, RSV) evidently refer to the meal and drink offerings that were presented to God along with the burnt offerings. (See Num. 28:2, 5, 7, 9, 13, 14, etc.)

In addition to the weekly Sabbath there were seven annual ceremonial sabbaths observed by the Jews. These occurred on different days of the week each year. The seven annual ceremonial sabbath days were: (1) the first day of the Feast of Unleavened Bread (Lev. 23:7); (2) the last day of the Feast of Unleavened bread (Lev. 23:8); (3) the Feast of Weeks (First Fruits, or Harvest; later called Pentecost), fifty days after the feast of unleavened bread (Lev. 23:21; compare Exod. 23:16; 34:22;); (4) the Feast of Trumpets on the first day of the seventh month (Lev. 23:24, 25); (5) the Day of Atonement on the 10th day of the 7th month (Lev. 23:27-32); (6) the first day of the feast of tabernacles (Lev. 23:33-35); and (7) the last day of the feast of tabernacles (Lev. 23:36).

Paul's point in Colossians 2:16, 17 is that animal sacrifices now do not have to be offered on any of these occasions, whether daily, weekly, or yearly, because they were a shadow of Christ's sacrifice for us. Now type has met antitype, shadow has met reality, and the ceremonial law has been abolished. Two things were done away at the Cross: (1) our guilt; (2) the temporary ceremonial law.

The seven annual ceremonial sabbaths foreshadowed various aspects of Jesus' ministry. Hence, they do not have to be observed by Christians.

But the weekly Sabbath remains a perpetual memorial of Creation (Gen. 2:1-3; Exod. 20:8-11; Matt. 24:20; Heb. 4:9) and a sign of sanctification (Exod. 31:13). Therefore, Jesus requested His followers to observe the weekly Sabbath after His death and resurrection (Matt. 24:20). Sabbath observance remains a perpetual part of the everlasting covenant experience (Heb. 8:10-12).

Galatians 3:19-25 explains the correct function of the law prior to the Cross. "Why then the law? It was added because of transgressions, until the offspring would come to whom the promise had been made" (Gal. 3:19). The law existed from creation until Sinai (Rom. 5:13; 4:15), but not in the written form that was given there. In their slavery in Egypt, the Jews had largely forgotten God's law. At Sinai God proclaimed and wrote His Ten Commandment law "that the offense might abound" (Rom. 5:20, KJV); that is, so that the people could be made aware of the seriousness of sin (compare Rom. 7:13).

The law was given "till the seed should come" (Gal. 3:19, KJV). The Seed was Christ (verse 16). Paul was not telling the Galatians that the law was abolished at the Cross. He was explaining that Christ's perfect life is a greater demonstration of God's perfect standard of righteousness than is the law (1 Peter 2:21, 22; Phil. 2:5; 1 John 2:6). Nevertheless, the law still functions as the written standard of righteousness and a mirror of human sin (Rom. 7:7; James 2:23-25).

The word "till" in Galatians 3:19 does not limit the duration of the law; it does not mean that the law was abolished at the Cross. Paul wrote to Timothy, "Till I come, give attendance to reading, to exhortation, to doctrine" (1 Tim. 4:13, KJV). This did not mean that when Paul arrived Timothy was to stop studying and exhorting. Christ's perfect life points out our sin more effectively than does the written law, because He is the personification of the principles of His own law. But His coming did not abolish the law. He was the great light to whom the lesser light (the law) pointed.

The law was our "schoolmaster" (Gal. 3:24, KJV) or "disciplinarian" (NRSV) until the coming of Christ. The Greek word used in this verse is *paidagogos*. It means "*attendant (slave), custodian, guide* . . . the man, usually a slave . . . whose duty it was to conduct the boy or youth . . . to and from school and to superintend his conduct generally; he was not a 'teacher' (despite the present meaning of the derivative 'pedagogue. . . .)'"[10] When the boy came of age the paidagogos was no longer needed as his guide and protector.

We are no longer under the law in the sense that now Christ is a greater revelation of God to man than the law was before the Cross. Paul is not saying that the Ten Commandments were abolished by Christ. Before the Cross, law (moral, ceremonial, and civil) was the principal means by which the love and character of God were revealed to humans. When Jesus came, He provided a more perfect revelation of the character of God. Moreover, the law cannot justify us; Christ can because of His death and our repentance of sin. Now we are no longer under law as the supreme means by which God is revealed to us, nor are we dependent solely upon the law to point out our sin, nor are we under the condemnation of the law. Christ has superseded the law in all these respects. But as we have seen from many other Scriptures, the law still functions as the divine written standard of righteousness for Christians.

John 1:17. "The law indeed was given through Moses; grace and truth came through Jesus Christ." The law given by Moses included the moral law of Ten Commandments, the ceremonial law, and the civil laws. None of these laws were designed to save humans from sin. The Ten Commandments are a standard of righteousness, but they do not provide the means of salvation (Rom. 8:3). The ceremonial law pointed forward to Christ, but animal sacrifices could not save humanity (Heb. 10:1-4). Christ was "the Lamb slain from the foundation of the world" (Rev. 13:8). His grace was the only means of salvation for Old Testament people, as it is for us today (Hab. 2:4). Salvation has always been through Christ (Gen. 3:15), never by means of law. Christ's death atoned for the sins of Old Testament people just as it atoned for our sins (1 Cor. 15:17, 18; Heb. 9:15). God's law has always been the standard; Christ's grace has always been the means of reaching the standard.

As we near the end of human history, the Lord appeals to the entire world to come to Him and be saved. He has grace abundant to save the most sin-stained soul. And He has grace to enable us to obey His law. As we come to Jesus, He fills us with His Spirit, and we are empowered to obey His divine will as it is expressed in His law. Have you found Him as your Savior and Lord. Do you love Him sufficiently to keep His commandments?

Notes

1. "Scofield taught that the period during which man was subjected to the law ended at the cross. . . . Hence Dispensationalism, as expounded by one of its foremost systematizers, teaches two ways of salvation: that during the era of law, obedience to it was a condition of salvation, whereas during the age of grace, salvation comes simply through faith in Christ."— Daniel Payton Fuller, *The Hermeneutics of Dispensationalism* (Th.D. dissertation, Northern Baptist Theological Seminary, 1957), pp. 144, 145. See Fuller's lengthy discussion of the pros and cons of this dispensationalist teaching in his dissertation, chapter V, pp. 139-189. In his more recent work, *Gospel and Law: Contrast or Continuum? The Hermeneutics of Dispensationalism and Covenant Theology* (Grand Rapids, Michigan: William B. Eerdmans, 1980), pp. 18-46, Fuller points out that in more recent years dispensationalists have modified the earlier position on law and grace taken by Scofield and Chafer.

2. William E. Cox, *An Examination of Dispensationalism* (Philadelphia, Penn.: Presbyterian and Reformed Publishing Co., 1963), pp. 17-21.

3. "One of the Ten Commandments, that concerning the observance of the sabbath day, applied only to Israel as a distinctive feature of God's covenant with that nation: 'Wherefore the children of Israel shall keep the sabbath, to observe the sabbath throughout their generations, for a perpetual covenant. It is a sign between me and the children of Israel for ever' (Exodus 31:16, 17).

   "Thus the sabbath and the ceremonial laws related only to God's will for the nation of Israel and have no application to the Gentiles or to members of the Body of Christ in this dispensation."— Charles F Baker, *A Dispensational Theology* (Grand Rapids, Michigan: Grace Bible College Publications, 1971), p. 262. Baker elaborates his point of view: "In the majority of passages in the New Testament the word *law* refers to the Mosaic Covenant in whole or in part. The entire legal system consisted of three parts: the commandments (moral), the judgments (social), and the ordinances (religious). This law system was imposed upon Israel during the dispensation of Law, which was in force from Moses until the revelation given to Paul. Israel during that time was said to be under the law. Christ was born and lived under the law (Galatians 4:4). Believers in this present dispensation are specifically described as being '. . . not under the law, but under grace.' (Romans 6:14, 15)."— *Ibid.*, pp. 263, 264.

4. Charles F. Baker, *A Dispensationalist Theology*, p. 267.

5. *Ibid.*, p. 264.

6. My translation. The text does not read as in the Revised Standard Version: ". . . by abolishing in his flesh the law of commandments and ordinances." The Greek reads: *ton nomon ton entolon en dogmasin katargesas,* which translates literally "having abolished the law of commandments *in* ordinances." The word "ordinances" comes from the Greek *dogma* that is used five times in the New Testament: Luke 2:1; Acts 16:4; 17:7; Eph. 2:15; Col. 2:14. In Luke 2:1 the reference is to a decree of Caesar. Acts 16:4 speaks of the decrees of the Jerusalem Council. Acts 17:7 mentions decrees of Caesar. Colossians 2:14 refers to the death decrees against us because of our sin; that is, the decrees declaring us guilty and therefore worthy of eternal death, which were abolished when Jesus bore our guilt on the cross. Ephesians 2:15 could possibly be given the same meaning as Colossians 2:14. "The law of commandments in decrees" could refer to the guilt of both Jews and Gentiles that was handled at the cross. But since Paul is speaking of a particular "dividing wall" (verse 14) between Jews and Gentiles, it seems clear that he is referring to the ceremonial system involving circumcision, animal sacrifices, and the other services of the Israelite temple.

7. The Greek translated "Holy Place" is *ta hagia*, meaning 'holy places." The reference is to the heavenly sanctuary as a whole. In the Greek Old Testament, the Septuagint (LXX), the singular or plural of *hagios, ia, on* often refers to the sanctuary as a whole, including both the Holy and Most Holy apartments. For example, see in the Septuagint Exod. 36:1, 3, 4; Lev. 5:15; 10:4; 27:3; Num 3:31, 32; 4:12, 16; 7:9; 18:5.

8. The Greek word translated "conscience" (Heb. 9:14, KJV and NRSV) is *suneidesin*, accusative, singular, feminine of *suneidesis*, meaning "consciousness," "moral consciousness," "conscience."—Arndt and Gingrich.

9. My translation. The Greek reads: *telos gar nomou Christos eis dikaiosunen panti to pisteuonti.* Because the word for "end" (Greek *telos*) sometimes means "goal," "outcome," "object," some interpreters explain the text to mean that Christ is the goal or object to whom the law points. This idea is obviously a truth that is elsewhere taught in the New Testament, but it is not the real meaning of this passage. *Telos* often means "end" in the sense of "termination," "cessation." Because of the context of Romans 10:4, we can conclude its meaning to be that Christ is the end, finish, termination of the law for (as a means of attaining) righteousness. Christ does not abolish the Ten Commandments. Paul has already established that in Romans 3:31; 7:7, 12, 14; 8:3, 4. He is not contradicting himself here. Consistently with his discussion from Romans 9:30 through to 10:10, Paul is arguing that righteousness cannot be earned by lawkeeping. Righteousness is God's gift to us by the Holy Spirit (Rom. 8:9, 10). Having received that gift by faith, the law is established in

our hearts (Rom. 3:31). Christ brings to an end righteousness by works, when, because of our faith response, He is able to give us His righteousness. But the abolition of righteousness by works does not destroy the law. The law is to be kept by Christians as a result of their saving relationship with Christ.

10. William F. Arndt and F. Wilbur Gingrich, *A Greek-English Lexicon of the New Testament and Other Early Christian Literature*, 1957 ed., s.v. *paidagogos*.

Chapter 8

What Does Sabbath Observance
Have to Do with Salvation?

The Bible has much to say about Jesus' second coming. In fact, study of Bible prophecy leads to the conclusion that Jesus is coming again very soon. (For example, see Matt. 24.) The Bible also tells us how to prepare for this great event. Jesus instructed: "Keep awake therefore, for you do not know on what day your Lord is coming. . . . Therefore you also must be ready, for the Son of man is coming at an unexpected hour" (Matt. 24:42, 44). At every stage of history salvation is by God's grace, not by man's works (Eph. 2:8-10). Does this mean that we should just relax and do nothing, expecting God to do everything for us? Or is there something we can do to demonstrate our faith in Christ, the power of His presence in our lives, and our willingness to be spiritually ready to meet Him?

This chapter discusses three main questions. (1) What is God's last-day seal that is placed upon those whom He plans to take to heaven at His second advent? (2) What does Sabbath observance have to do with God's last-day seal? Is there some special relationship spelled out in Scripture between Sabbath keeping and reception of God's seal? (3) How do we identify the true Christian Sabbath day?

What Is God's Last-day Seal?

All genuinely believing Christians receive the gift of the Holy Spirit as the seal of God upon them. In his letter to the Corinthians, Paul explained that "it is God who establishes us with you in Christ and has anointed us, by putting his seal on us and giving us his Spirit in our hearts as a first installment" (2 Cor. 1:21, 22). To the Ephesian Christians, Paul wrote: "In him you also, when you had heard the word of truth, the gospel of your salvation, and had believed in him, were marked with the seal of the promised Holy Spirit; this is the pledge of our inheritance toward redemption as God's own people, to the praise of his glory" (Eph. 1:13, 14). When we accepted Jesus Christ as Savior and Lord, He fulfilled for us the promise He had given to His first disciples; He came to dwell in our hearts by the presence of the Holy Spirit. (See John 14–16.) This gift is the "pledge of our inheritance" (NRSV) or "the pledge that we shall enter into our heritage" (New English Bible).[1] The presence of the Spirit in the heart is what makes a person a Christian. "Anyone who does not have the Spirit of Christ does not belong to him" (Rom. 8:9; compare Eph. 3:16, 17). Unless the Holy Spirit dwells in our hearts we cannot be said to be Christians at all. We receive this first seal of the Holy Spirit when we first believe.

The *last-day* seal of God is given to those Christian believers who will not die but will be alive when Jesus comes. We can list the significant points in regard to the last-day seal of God as follows:

1. God gives this seal shortly before the close of probation. The close of probation, occurring a short time before the second coming of Jesus, is the point at which God declares that every human being has had an opportunity to make a decision for Christ. This is the point beyond which no one will be able to reverse his or her decision. How do we know that such an event will occur?

According to Revelation 7:1-3, the angels who are holding back the winds of strife in our world will let them go only when all true believers are sealed. The letting go of the winds of strife is the point beyond which no one else will be sealed. Unless people are sealed by then, they will be lost. Therefore, when the winds of strife and calamity are let loose by heaven's restraints being removed from our world, probation will close. Then it is that heaven's proclamation is made: "Let the evildoer still do evil, and the filthy still be filthy, and the righteous still do right, and the holy still be holy" (Rev. 22:11).

This is the point at which Jesus ceases interceding for our confessed sins in the heavenly sanctuary. Revelation 8:3, 4 symbolically depicts Jesus functioning as our High Priest in the heavenly sanctuary. He mediates for us. He mingles the merits of His intercession with our prayers, and our confessed sins are forgiven. But verse 5 depicts the end of this intercession. "Then the angel took the censer and filled it with fire from the altar and threw it on the earth; and there were peals of thunder, rumblings, flashes of lightning, and an earthquake." Then the judgment described in Daniel

7:9-14 will be complete. By then the heavenly court will have decided the future of every human being either for life or death (Dan. 12:1). Christ's faithful people will have received the end-time seal of God before this close of probation, and when universal trouble and calamity take over in our world, Christ's people will be filled with the Spirit and able to stand true to Him whatever the circumstances.

2. God's work of placing the end-time seal on believers (Rev. 7:1-8) is recorded after the story of the second coming of Jesus (Rev. 6:12-17). But the seal of God is not given after the second coming of Jesus. The reason for the arrangement of the material here in Revelation is simply that Revelation 6:17 asks an important question: "Who is able to stand?" The answer to that question is that those who have been sealed before the Advent will be able to stand without fear when Jesus comes. Revelation 7:1-8 answers the question of Revelation 6:17.

3. Revelation 6:9-11 describes how the people who died believing in Jesus are judged in the pre-advent, investigative judgment. White robes are given every one of them (Rev. 6:11). That is a symbolic way of saying that the faithful dead are judged worthy of eternal life. The next phrase speaks about the living. Despite the published English translations, the Greek reads very simply and is translated literally: ". . . and it was said to them [the dead saints] that they should rest yet a little time, until their fellow servants and their brethren who are about to be killed as they were, might be made complete [full, perfect]" (Rev. 6:11). The word "number" does not occur in the Greek text, nor is it, in most instances, germane to the verb that is used.[2] The passage is referring to the sealing of God's faithful living believers just before the close of probation. (Compare Rev. 6:11 with 7:1-8.) The heavenly judgment of the dead has taken place, and now the living believers are purified and made spiritually complete so that God can place His eternal seal upon them. Then the winds of strife are let loose. There will be a time of unprecedented trouble (Dan. 12:1; Matt. 24:21). But God's faithful sealed people will be sheltered. They will be spiritually ready to meet Jesus when He comes. They will not cry out for the rocks and the mountains to fall on them as others are doing (Rev. 6:15, 16). They will be able to stand confidently because they know the Lord is protecting them, and they will look up and welcome Jesus with great expressions of love and joy.

4. Revelation 7:4-8 refers to 144,000 sealed "out of every tribe of the people of Israel" (verse 4). The number 144,000 is not a literal number. It is

symbolic of the total number of those sealed around the world. How do we know? The book of Revelation is a highly symbolic book. It abounds in symbols. To know what these symbols mean we have to compare Scripture with Scripture. For example, in Revelation 7:1 the "four angels" obviously represent all the angelic hosts who are "ministering spirits, sent forth to minister for them who shall be heirs of salvation?" (Heb. 1:14, KJV). The use of the phrase "the four corners of the earth" (Rev. 7:1) does not mean to suggest that the world is square or flat as some medieval writers thought. In Scripture "four corners" are simply a symbol of universality. The phrase means "the whole earth."[3] "The four winds" are clearly a reference to the destruction and strife that will result when the angels cease holding earthly and demonic forces in check. In verse 2 the "east" (KJV) or "the rising of the sun" (NRSV) is a symbol of heaven from whence the sealing angel comes. The kings from the east (Rev. 16:12) are Christ and His angels who will come to destroy the wicked of earth (Rev. 17:14; 19:11-21).[4] The east represents heaven from whence they come. The seal in the foreheads of God's people (Rev. 7:4) is obviously not a literal mark that can be seen by examining people's foreheads. As we shall see, it symbolizes the spiritual preparedness of the people to whom it is given.

The point is that the passage we are examining (Rev. 7:1-8) is full of symbolism. Just so, the number 144,000 is a symbol of the holy character of the individuals who receive the seal of God. This number is made up of multiples of 12. It is 12 times 12,000. The number 12 in Scripture is sometimes used as a symbol of completeness and perfection. For example, the number 12 occurs often in the description of the Holy City, the New Jerusalem (Rev. 21:12-17). The point is that it will be a perfect city inhabited by perfect people. The 12 tribes of Israel mentioned in Revelation 7:4-8 do not exist today. Jews today do not know from which tribe they are descended. The tribes of Israel spoken of by John are a symbol of the true Israel of God, the faithful believers who make up the Christian Church around the world. (See Gal. 3:28; Rom. 9:6-8; 2:28, 29.) In the book of Revelation, Jews sometimes symbolize faithful Christians (Rev. 2:9). What a remarkable coincidence it would be if exactly 12,000 were saved from each of 12 literal tribes of Israel. Christ does not save in such an arbitrary way. He says, "Him that cometh to me I will in no wise cast out" (John 6:37, KJV). "And I, if I be lifted up from the earth, will draw all men unto me" (John 12:32, KJV). Jesus instructed His disciples to make disciples of all nations (Matt. 28:19). The sealing message of Revelation 7 is not only for Jews!

5. What is the last-day seal of God? The ancient Israelite High Priest wore a turban, on the front of which was a golden plate containing the inscription, "Holy to the Lord." (See Exod. 28:36-38; Lev. 8:9.) This is the Old Testament background to the imagery used in Revelation 7 and 14. God's last-day people are to wear the crown of spiritual victory (Rev. 3:11; 6:2). They wear the crown in two senses: (1) they have the gift of eternal life now (1 John 5:12-13); (2) they have victory over sin through the power of the indwelling Christ (1 John 5:4; Rom. 6:14; Titus 2:11-14).

The seal of God is "his name and his Father's name written on their foreheads" (Rev. 14:1). Those who overcome sin through the power of divine grace have Christ's name and the Father's name written upon them (Rev. 2:17; 3:12; 22:4). The Old Testament also predicted that God's people would be called by a new name (Isa. 62:2; 65:15). In the Old Testament, the Hebrew word for "name" (*shem*) is sometimes used to mean character (Isa. 57:15; Jer. 14:7, 21; Ps. 18:49). Many names in the Old Testament were intended to indicate the characters of those who had them. "Jacob" means "supplanter." "Israel" means "he prevails with God" (Gen. 32:28).

The seal of God in the forehead (Rev. 7:1-3), which is God's name in the forehead (Rev. 14:1), symbolizes the fact that His last-day people have received the gift of His character. Their minds have been made holy. They have received Christ's righteousness by the gift of the Holy Spirit (Rom. 8:9, 10). They are allowing Christ to live out His life through them (Gal. 2:20). And they are enjoying habitual victory over sin because they are depending upon the Lord and appropriating His power. They are enjoying the experience of true holiness spoken of in 2 Corinthians 7:1 and 1 Peter 1:15, 16. These sealed believers are the "wife" (KJV) or "bride" (NRSV) of Christ, to whom He has granted the white robes of His righteousness (Rev. 19:7, 8). They are spiritually "without fault" (KJV) or "blameless" (NRSV) before God (Rev. 14:5).[5] And they will be the righteous living on the earth when Jesus comes. This is what John meant when he wrote: "These were redeemed from among men" (Rev. 14:4, KJV). The saved of all ages are redeemed from a world of sin. Only the 144,000 are redeemed from among men, in the sense that they are taken to heaven without seeing death. They are redeemed as living believers from among living humanity.

Are you planning to be one of Christ's sealed believers in these last days? He longs to dwell within each of our hearts, and He wants to seal us finally and irrevocably so that we will be His for eternity. The decision to follow Jesus in everything must be ours. The work of sealing our decision is Christ's. After God's people receive this blessing they will still be tempted, and they will undoubtedly suffer persecution of one form or another. But they will be kept by divine power; they will be the righteous living on the earth when Jesus comes.

The Sabbath and the Seal of God

The Bible teaches that those who receive the gift of Christ's character will observe His Sabbath as a sign or seal of their spiritual experience. Thus the people who receive the last-day seal of God will be Sabbathkeepers.

Romans 4:11 proves that the words "sign" (*semeion*) and "seal" (*sphragida*) are sometimes used synonymously in Scripture. Abraham "received the *sign* of circumcision as *a seal* of the righteousness that he had by faith while he was still uncircumcised." (Italics supplied.) In Old Testament times literal circumcision was a sign or seal of the man's and the nation's covenant relationship with God. Circumcision in the flesh was a sign or seal of heart circumcision (Deut. 10:16; 30:6), the spiritual experience that God wanted all people to enjoy as a result of trust in Him, submission to His will, and constant fellowship with Him. When Jesus died on the cross, literal circumcision as a religious symbol was done away. Paul wrote: "Circumcision is nothing, and uncircumcision is nothing; but obeying the commandments of God is everything" (1 Cor. 7:19). "For in Christ Jesus neither circumcision nor uncircumcision counts for anything; the only thing that counts is faith working through love" (Gal. 5:6). Faith working through love is the means by which Christians are to obey God's commandments (1 John 5:1-5). So "he who is physically uncircumcised, if he keeps the law, will he not judge you who though having the letter of the law and circumcision are a transgressor of the law? (Rom. 2:27, NASB). Christians are true Jews who have experienced circumcision of the heart (verse 29), whether ethnically they are Jews or Gentiles.

Another sign or seal of believers' covenant relationships with God in both Old and New Testaments is observance of the seventh-day Sabbath. "'You shall keep my sabbaths, for this is a sign between me and you throughout your generations, given in order that you may know that I, the Lord, sanctify you'" (Exod. 31:13). "Moreover I gave them my sabbaths, as a sign between me and them, so that they might know that I the Lord sanctify them" (Ezek. 20:12). "And hallow my sabbaths that they may be a sign between me and you, so that you may know that I the Lord am your God" (Ezek. 20:20).

There is nothing in the New Testament indicating that the Sabbath sign or seal has been done away as has circumcision. In Old Testament times, the Sabbath was a sign of sanctification (holiness), the sign or seal of a covenant relationship with God. The Sabbath is still a sign of sanctification today and a sign of a Christian's covenant relationship with God. At every stage of history since creation, the Lord has asked mankind to keep holy His Sabbath day as a sign of His creatorship and of His gift of holiness for those who are seeking salvation. The Sabbath day originated at the end of creation week (Gen. 2:1-3). It was enshrined in the hearts and experiences of the patriarchs. God said, "Abraham obeyed my voice and kept my charge, my commandments, my statutes, and my laws" (Gen. 26:5). Undoubtedly those laws included the Sabbath law that was instituted by God at the end of creation week.

The Sabbath day was observed before Sinai (Exod. 16). Manna was given six days a week, but not on the Sabbath day. When the people disobeyed by looking for manna on Sabbath, the Lord rebuked them: "'How long will you refuse to keep my commandments and instructions? See! The Lord has given you the sabbath, therefore on the sixth day he gives you food for two days; each of you stay where you are; do not leave your place on the seventh day.' So the people rested on the seventh day" (Exod. 16:28-30). At Sinai, in giving the Ten Commandments, the Lord stated that the *reason* for keeping holy the seventh day is that "in six days the Lord made heaven and earth, the sea, and all that is in them, but rested the seventh day; therefore the Lord blessed the sabbath day and consecrated it" (Exod. 20:8-11). Thus the Sabbath commandment cites God's institution of the Sabbath at the end of creation week as the rationale for its existence and the reason why we should honor it.

The same "new covenant" is spoken of in the New Testament as in the Old. Under this covenant, into which Christians are to enter with God, His law is to be written on their hearts. Hebrews 8:10-12 quotes Jeremiah 31:33, 34: "This is the covenant that I will make with the house of Israel after those days, says the Lord: I will put my laws in their minds, and write them on their hearts, and I will be their God, and they shall be my people. And they shall not teach one another or say to each other, 'Know the Lord,' for they shall all know me, from the least of them to the greatest. For I will be merciful toward their iniquities, and I will remember their sins no more" (Heb. 8:10-12). The law written on the hearts of both Old and New Testament believers is the Ten Commandment law proclaimed by God from Mt. Sinai in the time of Moses. This is the law that Paul extols as established in our hearts by faith (Rom 3:31; 7:7, 12, 14; 8:3, 4). James agrees heartily, teaching that breaking one of the Ten Commandments makes a person guilty of breaking the whole ten (James 2:10-12). The result of breaking one or all is the same, eternal rejection and ruin. The fourth of the Ten Commandments is the Sabbath commandment. Hence, the Sabbath commandment, along with the other nine, is to be written on our hearts in the new covenant experience.

There is nothing in the New Testament to indicate that the Ten Commandments, including the Sabbath commandment, have been abolished as a standard of righteousness. Nor is there any indication that nine of the Ten Commandments are still valid, while the fourth has been done away.

The means of keeping God's Ten Commandment law is faith (1 John 5:1-4). But the law remains as the standard of righteousness. "Do we then overthrow the law by this faith? By no means! On the contrary, we uphold the law" (Rom. 3:31).

The Sabbath commandment (Exod. 20:8-11) contains the three facts about God, the Author, that were included in seals placed by ancient kings upon their documents. (See 1 Kings 21:8; Esther 3:10-12; 8:8, 10; Dan. 4:1-3; Ezra 1:1-4.) (1) His name is "Lord" (*Yahweh*). (2) His authority is that He is the Creator ("the Lord made"). (3) The extent of His dominion is the universe ("heaven and earth").

Those who will be sealed at the end of time are those who have received the gift of the character of Christ by the Holy Spirit. They are faithful Sabbath keepers who recognize God's day as the sign or seal of their covenant relationship with Him, their Creator and Redeemer.

The True Christian Sabbath

John tells us that when he was on the island of Patmos he received a vision from God "on the Lord's day" (Rev. 1:10). Many Bible commentators have assumed that the day was Sunday. They argue that, since the term

"Lord's day" meant Sunday in later Christian writings, therefore it meant Sunday for John. The question is, was John having a vision on the seventh-day Sabbath or Sunday?

Since he was one of Jesus' closest disciples, John was thoroughly familiar with Jesus' statement recorded in Mark 2:28: "Therefore the Son of man is Lord also of the sabbath" (KJV). Obviously Jesus was speaking of the seventh-day Sabbath, the only day for worship and rest that the Jews, to whom He was speaking, knew anything about. It is quite reasonable that, in writing Revelation, John would refer to the Sabbath as the Lord's day, because he had heard Jesus Christ claim it to be His own day.

The Greek phrase translated "on the Lord's day" in Revelation 1:10 is *en te kuriake hemera*. The word *kuriake* is a Greek adjective meaning "belonging to the Lord," "the Lord's."[6] In the later history of the early Christian Church, this word came to stand alone in Christian literature without the following word "day." Then from the second half of the second century on *kuriake* was the accepted word for Sunday, the day of Christ's resurrection.

A few important considerations must be kept in mind when discussing the phrase "Lord's day":

1. The first early Church father to use the term "Lord's day" to mean Sunday was Clement of Alexandria, writing about A.D. 190.[7] About A.D. 180 or 185 Bishop Irenaeus of Gaul spoke of Easter Sunday as the Lord's day.[8] Also the apocryphal *Gospel of Peter,* written about the middle of the second century, speaks of Easter Sunday as the Lord's day.[9]

2. The earlier so-called references to Sunday as the Lord's day in the writings of the Christian Church Fathers result from paraphrasing the Greek. They are not unequivocal references to Sunday. The *Didache* or *Teaching of the Twelve Apostles*, written somewhere between the late first century and the late second century, contains the statement, "On the Lord's of the Lord [or, "According to the Lord's of the Lord"] assemble, break bread, and hold Eucharist." The word "day" does not occur in the Greek text, even though most translators have inserted it. The text could mean, "According to the Lord's commandment. . . ."[10]

Ignatius, Bishop of Antioch, who was martyred in Rome about A.D. 115, wrote a letter to the Magnesians in which he said: ". . . no longer sabbatizing, but living according to the Lord's."[11] Manuscript evidence favors the reading: ". . . no longer sabbatizing, but living according to the

Lord's life." The word *zoen* (life) has been omitted by the editors of the Greek text.[12]

3. It is incorrect methodology to read back into the New Testament the late second century use of the word *kuriake* (Lord's day) to mean Sunday. The late second-century writers do not use the exact same phrase that John used in Revelation 1:10. They omit the word "day" (*hemera*). Moreover, since there is no evidence elsewhere in the New Testament of Sunday sacredness, we can assume that John's use of the phrase "Lord's day" is a reference to Jesus' statement as recorded in Mark 2:28. Words change meaning over time. By the end of the second century for some Christian writers "Lord's day" meant Sunday. But we have no evidence at all that it meant Sunday for John the Revelator or for anyone else living in the first century.

The Lord has a day (Revelation 1:10). That day is the Sabbath day (Mark 2:28). The Sabbath day is the seventh day (Gen. 2:1-3; Exod. 20:8-11). The seventh day Sabbath "according to the commandment," observed by Jesus' disciples after His death, was the day after the "preparation" day on which Jesus was crucified (Luke 23:54-56). We know that the preparation day was Friday because Jesus "rose again the third day" (1 Cor. 15:4, KJV; compare Luke 24:7), and he rose on "the first day of the week," Sunday (Luke 24:1). The word "preparation" used in Luke 23:54 is a translation of the word that in modern Greek means the sixth day, or Friday. Arndt and Gingrich's Greek lexicon says that the word for "preparation" means "Friday, on which day everything had to be prepared for the Sabbath, when no work was permitted. . . ."[13]

The next day after crucifixion Friday, Jesus' followers "rested the sabbath day according to the commandment" (Luke 23:56, KJV). Following that Jesus rose early on the first day of the week (Luke 24:1-3). Mark records: "Now after he rose early on the first day of the week. . . ." (Mark 16:9).

So the Sabbath day is the day after Friday and the day before Sunday. It was in Jesus' day and has been ever since. No calendar changes have ever changed the weekly cycle. Since Jesus' day, there has been one change in the calendar, from the Julian to the Gregorian calendar. The change was first made in Spain, Portugal, and Italy in 1582 in response to an edict of Pope Gregory XIII. Thus, our present-day calendar is known as the Gregorian calendar. In 1582, ten days were dropped out of the month of October. Thursday, the fourth of October, was followed immediately by Friday, the fifteenth. Although a number of days were removed from the month, the weekly cycle was left unchanged. Thursday was followed by Friday and Friday by Saturday, as had always been and has been ever since.

The seventh-day Sabbath in the twentieth century is the same day of the week as the seventh-day Sabbath in Jesus' day. Luke wrote his Gospel years after the death and resurrection of Jesus. If the Sabbath had been changed, why didn't Luke add a statement to that effect after he had written that the followers of Jesus rested on the Sabbath, the day after the sixth day on which Jesus was crucified? There is nothing anywhere in the New Testament to say that either Jesus or His apostles changed the Sabbath to the first day of the week or to any other day.

Since those who receive God's last-day seal are those who keep His Sabbath day holy, they will be following the instruction of Scripture that we observe the seventh-day (Saturday) as the day of rest and worship.

Did the Apostles Observe the Sabbath after Jesus' Ascension to Heaven?

There is not the slightest hint in the New Testament that the Sabbath was changed or abolished. The book of Acts records that the apostles kept the Sabbath very regularly.

The book of Acts records 84 Sabbath meetings held by Paul over a period of 10 years, from A.D. 45-55. On his first missionary journey, Paul with his companions arrived at Antioch in Pisidia. "And on the sabbath day they went into the synagogue and sat down" (Acts 13:14). At the invitation of the synagogue officials, Paul preached a sermon (verse 15 ff.). "The next sabbath almost the whole city gathered to hear the word of the Lord" spoken by Paul (verse 44).

On a subsequent missionary journey, "after Paul and Silas had passed through Amphipolis and Apollonia, they came to Thessalonica, where there was a synagogue of the Jews. And Paul went in, *as was his custom*, and on three sabbath days argued with them from the scriptures, explaining and proving that it was necessary for the Messiah to suffer and to rise from the dead" (Acts 17:1-3).

Later Paul visited Corinth (Acts 18:1). "Every sabbath he would argue in the synagogue and would try to convince Jews and Greeks" (verse 4). "He stayed there a year and six months, teaching the word of God among them" (verse 11). The obvious implication is that for 18 months Paul visited the synagogue every Sabbath day.

Sunday keepers often assert that Paul and his associate evangelists visited the synagogues on the Sabbath day because this was the most convenient way to meet with Jews for the purpose of leading them to Christ. But in Philippi, Paul and his associates observed the Sabbath in an open-air meeting. "On the sabbath day we went outside the gate by the river, where we supposed there was a place of prayer; and we sat down and spoke to the women who had gathered there" (Acts 16:13). As a result Lydia and her household, people from Thyatira, became baptized Christians. The apostles found a convenient place on the bank of the river for a Sabbath worship service and won to Christ those who paused to listen.

Why would Luke in writing the book of Acts record all these Sabbath meetings of the apostles and not say one word about any change of the Sabbath. If there were any inspired counsel to worship on another day or not to observe any day, why didn't Luke say so?

The Epistle to the Hebrews leaves no doubt that the Hebrews' Sabbath day is the correct day of worship for Christians. Referring to the Israelites who, on the way from Egypt to Canaan, rebelled against God and against Moses, the Christian author of Hebrews wrote: "And to whom did he swear that they would not enter his rest, if not to those who were disobedient? So we see that they were unable to enter because of unbelief" (Heb. 3:18, 19). But "while the promise of entering his rest is still open" (Heb. 4:1), none of us should fail to enter into it. Only true believers will enter God's rest (verse 3). This is why the ancient Israelites failed to enter God's rest. The author of the Epistle to the Hebrews reminds us of God's words in Psalm 95:11: "Therefore I swore in my anger that they should not enter my rest" (RSV; compare Heb. 4:3). Entering God's rest is identified as Sabbath observance: "For in one place it speaks about the seventh day as follows, 'And God rested on the seventh day from all his works'" (Heb. 4:4). But God's rest is still available to us: "So then, a sabbath rest still remains for the people of God; for those who enter God's rest also cease from their labors as God did from his. Let us therefore make every effort to enter that rest, so that no one may fall through such disobedience as theirs" (Heb. 4:9-11, NRSV). As God rested from His work of creation on the seventh day (verse 4), so we are invited to enter the spiritual rest of which the Sabbath rest is the sign and seal. Thus God's spiritual rest involves Sabbath observance.

The apostles, like Jesus, observed the seventh-day Sabbath as a holy day of worship and rest from secular labor. The Christian Church is "built upon the foundation of the apostles and prophets, with Christ Jesus himself as the cornerstone" (Eph. 2:20). That being so, Christian practice in regard to Sabbath observance should follow the example of Jesus and the apostles.

Is It Necessary for Every Believing Christian to Keep the Sabbath Day Holy?

While He was here on earth, Jesus consistently observed the seventh-day Sabbath. "When he came to Nazareth, where he had been brought up, he went to the synagogue on the sabbath day, *as was his custom*" (Luke 4:16). Throughout His ministry, not only did Jesus observe the Sabbath, He also tried to persuade the Jewish religious leaders that it is thoroughly consistent with God's law to relieve suffering and to supply spiritual and physical needs on the Sabbath day. When they complained because He healed the sick and permitted his disciples to pluck and eat grain on the Sabbath, Jesus defended His actions as consistent with good Sabbath keeping (Mark 2:23-28; Matt. 12:1-14). Jesus in no way condoned breaking the fourth commandment (Exod. 20:8-11) by engaging in secular work on the Sabbath day. After all, it was Jesus who had inspired Isaiah to describe Sabbath observance as "a delight," as "desisting from your own ways, from seeking your own pleasure, and speaking your own word" (Isa. 58:13, NASB). But Jesus pointed out that relieving human and animal suffering and supplying immediate spiritual and physical needs are activities that God regards as appropriate for the Sabbath day. Jesus simply stated the basic principle: "'The Sabbath was made for humankind, and not humankind for the sabbath; so the Son of Man is lord even of the Sabbath" (Mark 2:27, 28, NRSV). The legalistic, even fanatical regulations for Sabbath observance commanded by the ancient Pharisees were a denial of Jesus' principle that "the Sabbath was made for man." Jesus did not contravene the Sabbath command; He rejected the Pharisaic interpretation of it.

God's promises to the believer who observes the Sabbath as Jesus instructed are truly wonderful: "Then you will take delight in the Lord, and I will make you ride on the heights of the earth; and I will feed you with the heritage of Jacob your father, for the mouth of the Lord has spoken" (Isa. 58:14, NASB).

When Jesus was predicting both the fall of Jerusalem and His own second advent, He used the former as a type or example of the latter. He urged that those of His followers who would be living just prior to those events, should pray that they would not be obliged to flee from their enemies in the winter or on a Sabbath day. "Pray that your flight may not be in winter or on a sabbath" (Matt. 24:20, NRSV). The reason is obvious; fleeing from the enemy in the wintertime would be a cold and uncomfortable procedure. Fleeing from the enemy on the Sabbath day would make it impossible to rest and worship in peace as God wants His people to do.

Matthew 24:20 is speaking as much about circumstances immediately before Jesus' second advent as it is of conditions just before the destruction of Jerusalem. Matthew 24:15-20 records Jesus' statement: "So when you see the desolating sacrilege standing in the holy place, as was spoken of by the prophet Daniel . . . then those in Judea must flee to the mountains. . . . Pray that your flight may not be in winter or on a sabbath." The "desolating sacrilege" is a reference to the work of the "little horn" power of Daniel 8:9-13. In its initial fulfillment, this power was the Roman Empire which crucified Christ, destroyed the Jerusalem temple (A.D. 70), and persecuted God's people. But the little horn power in its later manifestation as the opponent of God's truth and people is to function until the second coming of Jesus. "He shall be broken, and not by human hands" (Dan. 8:25; cf. 2:34, 45). Therefore, Jesus' instruction to flee from the destructive work of the little horn power ("the desolating sacrilege," Matt 24:15) applies not only to those living just prior to the destruction of Jerusalem in A.D. 70, but also to those living at the end of time just prior to the time when Jesus will come to destroy the little horn power.

Hence, Matthew 24:20 is Jesus' command for end-time Christians to keep holy the seventh-day Sabbath. Not only were His followers to observe the Sabbath 40 years after His death at the time when Jerusalem was under attack from the Romans, but they are also to observe the Sabbath immediately before His second coming. Jesus spoke of the events surrounding the fall of Jerusalem as illustrative of the events just prior to and surrounding His second advent. So the instruction to observe the Sabbath applies as much to us as it did to His first disciples.

The First Angel's Message Includes the Sabbath Command

Revelation 14:1-5 describes the believers who are sealed before Jesus' second coming standing with Christ in the heavenly Jerusalem after His coming. They will be the blameless, righteous believers living on the earth when Jesus appears in the clouds of heaven. The second part of the chapter, Revelation 14:6-13 describes the messages to which these last-day sealed believers respond. "Then I saw another angel flying in midheaven, with an eternal gospel to proclaim to those who live on earth — to every nation and tribe and language and people. He said in a loud voice, 'Fear God and give him glory, for the hour of his judgment has come; and worship him who made heaven and earth, the sea and the springs of water'" (Rev. 14:6, 7). This angel or messenger symbolizes God's people who take the "eternal" (NRSV) or "everlasting" (KJV) gospel to the world just prior to the close of probation and the second coming of Jesus. The everlasting gospel is the good news of salvation by faith in Jesus Christ — salvation that results in obedience to all the commandments of God (Rom. 3:31; 7:7, 12, 14; 8:3, 4). It is a message of faith in Christ that results in the power to overcome sin and to reflect the loving character of Jesus Christ (1 John 5:1-5; Rev. 3:21).

This first angel's message that is to go to "every nation and tribe and language and people" includes the invitation to "worship him who *made heaven and earth, the sea and the springs of water*" (Rev. 14:6, 7; italics supplied). The language of the text is an obvious allusion to the fourth commandment. We are to keep the seventh day holy "for in six days the Lord *made heaven and earth, the sea, and all that is in them,* but rested the seventh day; therefore the Lord blessed the sabbath day and consecrated it" (Exod. 20:11). Revelation 14:7 is a call to honor our Creator by worshiping Him on His holy day. Of course, this act of Sabbath worship is simply a weekly high point of a life lived in a constant state of submission to the loving care and guidance of our Creator.

The end-time sealed believers who will eventually stand with Christ on "Mount Zion" (Rev. 14:1) are Sabbath keepers who have accepted the three angels' messages of Revelation 14:6-13. Because Christ is first in their lives, they delight to honor Him always, and especially on His holy day. In the kingdom of heaven and on the earth made new, God's faithful people who observed the Sabbath day here before the coming of Jesus will observe it throughout eternity. "From new moon to new moon, and from sabbath to sabbath, all flesh shall come to worship before me, says the Lord" (Isa. 66:23).

Christian believers always wish to follow Jesus' instruction. He instructed that we observe the seventh-day Sabbath right up until His second coming. And He said, "If you love me, you will keep my commandments" (John 14:15). How could anyone who claims to love Jesus refuse to keep His commandments? John writes: "For the love of God is this, that we obey his commandments. And his commandments are not burdensome" (1 John 5:3). We do not keep His commandments to be saved. We keep them because we are enjoying present salvation in Christ. We are saved by faith (Eph. 2:8-10), but saving faith is "faith working through love" (Gal. 5:6). True faith results in the law of God being established in our lives (Rom. 3:31). When we have true faith in Christ, we will not argue about whether it is convenient to keep holy His Sabbath day. We will do it because Jesus asks us to. Our Sabbath keeping will be the result and the evidence of our faith in Him. We will observe the Sabbath day as a memorial of creation and a sign of Christ's work of sanctification in our hearts. Sabbath keeping will be not only a sign of Christ's work for us, but also an observance that strengthens our relationship with Him. It will be a vital part of our Christian walk and a tremendous blessing to us as we prepare for the seal of God and an eternity with our Lord.

It was not convenient for Jesus to be born in a manger in Bethlehem; He did it because He loves us so much. It was not convenient for Him to live for 30 years in a degraded place like ancient Nazareth; He did it out of love for us. It was not convenient for Him to submit to the insults of the trial before the Jewish Sanhedrin, Herod, and Pilate; He did it because He wanted us to be saved. It was not convenient for Him to endure the infinite agony of the cross; He submitted to it so that He could bear the punishment for our sins.

Why should we talk of convenience when Jesus has done so much for us? He craves to save us from all sin, to fill us with His Holy Spirit and place His end-time seal upon us. Why not give Him that privilege? He loves you with an infinite love and will not stop pleading until you surrender all to Him and agree to follow Him all the way. That includes keeping His seventh-day Sabbath holy. Will you open your heart to Jesus just now and allow Him to transform your life?

Notes

1. The Greek word translated "pledge" or "deposit" is *arrabon*, which means *"first instalment, deposit, down payment, pledge,* that pays a part of the purchase price in advance, and so secures a legal claim to the article in question, or makes a contract valid . . . a payment which obligates the contracting party to make further payments."—William F. Arndt and F. Wilbur Gingrich, *A Greek-English Lexicon of the New Testament and Other Early Christian Literature* (Chicago: University of Chicago Press, 1957), s.v. *arrabon*.

2. The Greek verb *plerothosin* is the 3rd person, plural, aorist, subjunctive, passive of *pleroo*. This verb means "make full," "fill," "complete," "bring to completion," "fulfill," "bring to an end," The KJV, RSV, and NRSV translate this verb by "perfect" in Revelation 3:2. Revelation 6:11 is not saying that the righteous dead will sleep on until a certain number of martyrs is made up. It is saying that the dead are to rest until their living brethren are made complete or perfect in Christ. The text is parallel to Revelation 7:1-8. The living brethren who are made complete or perfect are the ones who are sealed with the end-time seal of God before the close of probation.

3. The Greek word *gonia* meaning "corner" is used in the Septuagint (LXX) as a symbol of completeness, entirety, or universality. For example, "Achaz . . . made to himself altars in every corner in Jerusalem" (2 Chron. 28:24, LXX). "Suddenly a great wind came on from the desert, and caught the four corners of the house, and the house fell upon thy children, and they are dead" (Job 1:19, LXX). Every corner of Jerusalem means throughout Jerusalem. The four corners of the house refer to the entire house. Just so, in Revelation 7:1, "the four corners of the earth" is a figure of speech meaning the entire earth, the universal world.

4. The Greek translated "east" (KJV) is *anatoles heliou*, meaning "*rising* of the sun, *east, orient*."—Arndt and Gingrich, s.v. *anatole*.

5. The Greek word *amomos* means "without fault," "unblemished," "blameless," "faultless."—Arndt and Gingrich. This same word is used in other passages in the New Testament to refer to the spiritual purity that is God's ideal for His people. (See Eph. 1:4; 5:27; Col. 1:22; Jude 24.)

6. Arndt and Gingrich, s.v. *kuriakos*.

7. Clement of Alexandria, *The Stromata, or Miscellanies*, v. 14; Alexander Roberts and James Donaldson (eds.), *The Ante-Nicene Fathers* (Grand Rapids, Michigan: Wm. B. Eerdmans, 1962), II, 469 (hereinafter referred to as *ANF*). See Kenneth A. Strand, "The 'Lord's Day' in the Second Century," in *The Sabbath in Scripture and History*, ed. Kenneth A. Strand (Washington, D.C.: Review and Herald, 1982), p. 346.

8. "Fragments from the Lost Writings of Irenaeus," 7; *ANF* 1:569, 570. See Strand (ed.), *The Sabbath in Scripture and History*, p. 346, 347.

9. *Gospel of Peter*, 9, 12; *ANF* 10:8. See Strand (ed.), *The Sabbath in Scripture and History*, p. 347.

10. *Didache*, 14:1. The Greek reads *kata kuriaken de kuriou sunachthentes. . . .*— Karl Bihlmeyer (ed.), *Die Apostolischen Vater* (Tubingen: J. C. B. Mohr, 1956), p. 8. See Strand (ed.) *The Sabbath in Scripture and History*, p. 348.

11. Ignatius, *Au de Magnesier, 9:1*, ". . . *meketi sabbatizontes, alla kata kuriaken zontes*." — Bihlmeyer, *Die Apostolischen Vater*, p. 91.

12. Kenneth A. Strand (ed.), *The Sabbath in Scripture and History*, pp. 348, 349.

13. Arndt and Gingrich, *A Greek-English Lexicon of the New Testament*, s.v. *paraskeue*.

Chapter 9
Whose Idea Was Sunday Observance?

Many Sunday observers argue that the change of the Sabbath from the seventh to the first day of the week dates back to Jesus and His apostles. They assert that Sunday observance replaced the seventh-day Sabbath for most Christians as early as the first century A.D. and became a fixed custom by the mid-second century. Therefore, they urge that all Christians today should regard the seventh-day Sabbath as a Jewish institution that should not be observed. Since Sunday was the first day of creation week (Gen. 1:5) and the day on which Christ rose from the dead (Matt. 28:1-10; Mark 16:1-9), it should be observed as a day of Christian worship and rejoicing in accordance with the custom of the early Christian fathers. In fact, Sunday keepers argue that observance of the seventh-day Sabbath is a highly legalistic custom that is thoroughly consistent with those Jewish ceremonial practices abolished when Jesus died on the cross.

This theory raises a whole series of questions in regard to the teaching of the New Testament and the testimony of history. Did Jesus change the day from the seventh to the first day of the week? Did the apostles urge that Sunday be observed as a memorial of the resurrection of Christ? Did they themselves observe Sunday as a special day of worship? Was first-day worship a substitute for Sabbath worship for most Christians as early as the second century A.D? Was the Sabbath regarded by early Christians as a purely Jewish institution with no significance for followers of Christ? What does history have to teach us regarding the reason for the change of the day from the seventh to the first day of the week?

These questions are vital for Christians today! If it happens to be unscriptural and unhistorical that Sunday observance was initiated by Christ and the apostles, those who argue so strenuously for it today are supporting a non-Christian practice. If Jesus and the apostles observed the seventh-day Sabbath, and Sunday keeping crept into the Christian Church over a period of centuries as pagan ideas and practices became more and more acceptable, those who reject the Sabbath today are spurning one of Christ's commandments and are, therefore, in grave danger of being rejected by God. To be a Christian is to believe and act as Jesus did (John 14:15; Rev. 3:21; 12:17; 14:12). To profess faith in Christ while rejecting aspects of His teaching and refusing to live and worship as He instructed is to be guilty of serious sin. "Whoever says, 'I have come to know him,' but does not obey his commandments, is a liar, and in such a person the truth does not exist; but whoever obeys his word, truly in this person the love of God has reached perfection. By this we may be sure that we are in him: whoever says, 'I abide in him,' ought to walk just as he walked" (1 John 2:4-6).

We will begin with the Scriptures and then turn to history for the answers to the questions we are asking. A much more complete discussion of the Sabbath-Sunday question can be found in the book edited by Kenneth A. Strand, *The Sabbath in Scripture and History* (Washington, DC: Review and Herald, 1982).

Did Jesus and the Apostles Change the Day of Worship from the Seventh to the First Day of the Week?

The word *Sunday* is not found in the Bible. In the New Testament the first day of the week is mentioned eight times. In none of the eight instances is the first day said to be a day of worship, never is it said to be the Christian substitute for the Old Testament Sabbath, and never do the texts suggest that the first day of the week should be regarded as a memorial of Christ's resurrection. Let us briefly consider each of the eight New Testament passages that mention the first day of the week.

Matthew 28:1, "After the sabbath, as the first day of the week was dawning, Mary Magdalene and the other Mary went to see the tomb. And suddenly there was a great earthquake. . . ." Jesus was crucified on Friday. He rested in the tomb over the Sabbath and rose early on Sunday morning. The verse indicates that the women disciples returned to the tomb at the very first opportunity after the death and burial of Jesus. Because the Sabbath came so soon after His burial, they could not approach the tomb again until after sundown on Sabbath evening. (The Sabbath began at sundown on the sixth day and ended at sundown on the seventh day; compare Lev. 23:32; Neh. 13:19; Mark 1:21, 32) Early Sunday morning was the most convenient time for them to visit the tomb.

Mark 16:1, 2, "When the sabbath was over, Mary Magdalene, and Mary the mother of James, and Salome bought spices, so that they might go and anoint him. And very early on the first day of the week, when the sun had risen, they went to the tomb." Mark records the same events as Matthew with the additional information that the women visited the tomb early on the Sunday morning for the express purpose of anointing Jesus' body with spices.

Mark 16:9, "Now after he rose early on the first day of the week, he appeared first to Mary Magdalene, from whom he had cast out seven demons." This verse simply records that, after His resurrection early on the Sunday morning, Jesus appeared to Mary Magdalene.

Luke 23:54 – 24:1, "It [the day of Jesus' death and burial] was the day of Preparation, and the sabbath was beginning. The women who had come with him from Galilee followed, and they saw the tomb and how his body was laid. Then they returned, and prepared spices and ointments. On the sabbath they rested according to the commandment. But on the first day of the week, at early dawn, they came to the tomb, taking the spices that they had prepared." The Sabbath came a few hours after Jesus' death on the cross. The women disciples "rested the sabbath day according to the commandment" (Luke 23:56, KJV). Then very early in the morning of the first day they visited the tomb to anoint the body of Jesus. The fact that they observed the Sabbath rest is sufficient indication that Jesus had never attempted to change the day or to suggest that after His death the first day would replace the Sabbath. Writing years after the event, Luke gave not the slightest hint that, even though the women disciples of Jesus observed the Sabbath, such a practice was no longer expected of Christians. He simply recorded that the Sabbath day "according to the commandment," which Jesus' followers were careful to observe, was the day after the crucifixion day (Friday), and before the resurrection day (Sunday).

John 20:1, "Early on the first day of the week, while it was still dark, Mary Magdalene came to the tomb and saw that the stone had been removed from the tomb." Mary Magdalene visited the tomb early the first day of the week. Nothing is said of Sunday as a day of worship or rest.

John 20:19, "When it was evening on that day, the first day of the week, and the doors of the house where the disciples had met were locked for fear of the Jews, Jesus came and stood among them and said, 'Peace be with you.'" On the evening of the first day of the week the disciples were assembled behind locked doors "for fear of the Jews." Jesus appeared to them at that time. The passage does not say that henceforth Sunday was to be the day for worship. Since it was the evening of the first day of the week that Jesus appeared to the disciples, it was after sundown. According to Jewish reckoning this was actually the beginning of the second day (Monday; compare Gen. 1:5, 8). A week later when Thomas happened to be present, Jesus met with the disciples again (John 20:26). But, writing years later, John records nothing regarding Sunday as a day of Christian worship. John's narrative gives no warrant for regarding Sunday as a substitute for the Sabbath or as a day to be distinguished by Christians above any other day of the week. And there is no indication in the passage that Sunday should henceforth be observed as a memorial of Christ's resurrection.

Acts 20:7, "On the first day of the week, when we met to break bread, Paul was holding a discussion with them; since he intended to leave the next day, he continued speaking until midnight." Since the meeting was held at night on the first day of the week, it may have been Saturday night. According to Jewish reckoning, the Sabbath ended and the first day of the week began at sundown of the seventh day. If it were Sunday evening, the event gives no suggestion that Sunday should be observed as a day of worship. The following verses record that Paul preached a sermon on Thursday. The next day after the meeting recorded in Acts 20:7 (Monday), Paul and his party set sail for Mitylene (Acts 20:13, 14). The following day (Tuesday) they arrived opposite Chios (verse 15). The next day (Wednesday) they passed Samos (verse 15), and the day after that (Thursday) they arrived at Miletus (verse 15). The elders of the church of Ephesus met Paul at Miletus, and he preached to them (Acts 20:16-36). Because a Christian service was held on Thursday, do we conclude that Thursday is a day for regular Christian worship replacing the observance of the seventh-day Sabbath? A religious service on Sunday, Thursday, or any other day certainly did not make that day a replacement for the seventh-day Sabbath or a day of regular Christian worship and rest. There is no special significance in the disciples breaking bread at this first-day meeting (Acts 20:7), for they broke bread "daily" (Acts 2:46). We are not told that it was a Lord's Supper celebration, nor are we told that henceforth Sunday should be the day for this service to be conducted. To read Sunday sacredness or Sunday observance into Acts 20:7 is to do violence to the text.

1 Corinthians 16:1, 2, "Now concerning the collection for the saints: you should follow the directions I gave the churches of Galatia. On the first day of every week, each of you is to put aside and save whatever extra you earn, so that collections need not be taken when I come. And when I arrive, I will send any whom you approve with letters to take your gift to Jerusalem." These verses may be literally translated from the Greek as follows: "And concerning the collection for the saints, as I instructed the churches of Galatia, so also you do. On the first day of the week let each of you place (or 'lay') *by himself*, storing up whatever he might be prospered, so that when I come there might be no collections." (Italics supplied.) The phrase "by himself" (*par' heauto*), followed by the participle "storing up" or "saving" (*thesaurizon*), rules out the possibility that this is a reference to an offering taken up in a worship service. The Christian believer was to check his accounts on Sunday and put by at home the money that he wished to give to Paul for the support of the church. When Paul arrived, then the offerings of each individual would be collected.

None of these eight New Testament references to the first day of the week (Sunday), provides any evidence that Jesus or His disciples changed the day of worship from the seventh to the first day. Nor is the first day of the week represented as a time to memorialize the resurrection of Christ. Whatever special significance was given to Sunday in the later history of the church, it had no basis in the teaching or practice of Jesus and His apostles.

As pointed out in the previous chapter, Jesus instructed His disciples to observe the Sabbath after His death (Matt. 24:20). Jesus' instruction was incorporated into His interpretation of Daniel 8 (compare Matthew 24:15 ff.). Daniel predicted that the work of the little horn power would continue until the setting up of God's kingdom (Dan. 8:25). Hence, Jesus' instruction to flee from the little horn power was not confined to Christians at the time of the destruction of Jerusalem (A.D. 70). Toward the end of time, during the great tribulation of Matthew 24:21, of which earlier tribulations were a type or preview, God's people will be obliged to flee again. Jesus' instruction that we pray that our flight will not be on the Sabbath day emphasizes His will that we engage in only those activities on the Sabbath that are consistent with worship and spiritual rest.

The record of the book of Acts (chapters 13, 16–18) establishes that the apostles consistently kept the Sabbath day as a time for worship and fellowship. This observance was not merely a means of meeting the Jews in the synagogue on their Sabbath day. In Philippi, Paul and his companions met for worship by the riverside. Luke says, "On the sabbath day we went outside the gate by the river, where we supposed [or "thought" or "assumed": Greek *nomizo*] there was a place of prayer. . . ." (Acts 16:13). The apostles selected a place by the river that they thought would be appropriate for their Sabbath worship service, and there they prayed and witnessed for their Lord.

Jesus and the apostles kept the seventh-day Sabbath and instructed others to do likewise.

Did the Apostle Paul Reject the Seventh-day Sabbath?

Despite the evidence that Jesus kept the Sabbath (Luke 4:16) and encouraged His followers to do the same (Matt. 24:20), and despite the evidence that Paul customarily observed the Sabbath (Acts 13, 16, 17, 18), some Bible students focus on certain passages in Paul's writings as supposed evidence that he sought to do away with the seventh-day Sabbath. The two passages that are usually presented are Romans 14:5, 6 and Colossians 2:13-17.

The Romans passage in context reads as follows:

"Welcome those who are weak in faith, but not for the purpose of quarreling over opinions. 2. Some believe in eating anything, while the weak eat only vegetables. 3. Those who eat must not despise those who abstain, and those who abstain must not pass judgment on those who eat; for God has welcomed them. 4. Who are you to pass judgment on servants of another? It is before their own lord that they stand or fall. And they will be upheld, for the Lord is able to make them stand. 5. Some judge one day to be better than another, while others judge all days to be alike. Let all be fully convinced in their own minds. 6. Those who observe the day, observe it in honor of the Lord. Also those who eat, eat in honor of the Lord, since they give thanks to God; while those who abstain, abstain in honor of the Lord and give thanks to God" (Rom. 14:1-6).

Referring to verses 5 and 6, R. C. H. Lenski incorrectly comments: "We see no reason for refusing to assume that the distinction here touched upon refers to the Jewish Sabbath. What other day would any Roman Christian judge to be above other days? That self-chosen days are referred to is scarcely to be assumed. It is not difficult to see that a few Jewish Christians, some of them who perhaps came from the old mother church in Jerusalem, still clung to the Sabbath much as the Christians did after Pentecost."[1]

If Lenski is correct, Paul was condoning those who were disregarding the seventh-day Sabbath? Other Sunday keeping scholars disagree with Lenski,[2] and he is most certainly in error. In his writings, Paul consistently accepted the authority of the Ten Commandments as the standard of righteousness. "Do we then overthrow the law by this faith? By no means! On the contrary, we uphold the law" (Rom. 3:31). Paul identified the law that faith upholds as the Ten Commandments. "What then should we say? That the law is sin? By no means! Yet, if it had not been for the law, I would not have known sin. I would not have known what it is to covet if the law had not said, 'You shall not covet.'. . . So the law is holy, and the commandment is holy and just and good. . . . For we know that the law is spiritual; but I am of the flesh, sold into slavery under sin" (Rom. 7:7, 12, 14). Christ died "so that the just requirement of the law might be fulfilled in us, who walk not according to the flesh but according to the Spirit" (Rom. 8:4).

It is inconceivable that one who had such a confirmed respect for the Ten Commandment law of God should summarily reject one of the commandments as no longer valid for Christians. Raoul Dederen pertinently comments: "It is to be noted, however, that the attempt to connect the Sabbath of the Decalogue with the 'days' mentioned in this passage is not convincing for everyone.[3] Who could have a divine commandment before him and say to others: 'You can treat that commandment as you please; it really makes no difference whether you keep it or not'? No apostle could conduct such an argument. And probably no man would be more surprised at that interpretation than Paul himself, who had utmost respect for the Decalogue, God's law, which is 'holy, and just, and good' (chap. 7:12). Christ, the norm of all Pauline teaching, was indisputably a Sabbathkeeper. And Paul himself, who evidently cannot be reckoned among the 'weak,' worshiped on the Sabbath 'as was his custom' (Acts 17:2, R.S.V.; cf. Luke 4:16).

"There is no conclusive evidence to the contrary. Paul was in no doubt as to the validity of the weekly Sabbath. Thus, to assume that when they were converted to Christianity by Paul, Gentiles or Jews would be anxious to give up the 'Jewish' Sabbath for their 'own day' is hardly likely. This could be expected only at some later time in the history of the Christian church, and for other reasons."[4]

A number of conclusions emerge from a careful consideration of the passage:

(1) Romans 14 is not speaking of moral issues on which we have a clear "Thus saith the Lord." Verses 1-4 clearly make the point that God accepts both the spiritually strong who eat any food as well as the weak who think they should eat only vegetables. Speaking of both groups verse 4 says, "And they will be upheld, for the Lord is able to make them stand."

(2) The stronger Christians who use any kind of food are not eating that which is physically harmful. For them to do so would be a contradiction of their Christian commitment. Earlier in the epistle Paul instructs: "I appeal to you therefore, brothers and sisters, by the mercies of God, to present your bodies as a living sacrifice, holy and acceptable to God, which is your spiritual worship" (Rom. 12:1). To deliberately appropriate as food that which God condemns as harmful (see Lev. 11; Isa. 65:3, 4; 66:15-17) cannot be said to be behavior that God can accept; nor is it an acceptable application of the Romans 12:1 counsel. In his first epistle to the Corinthians, Paul seriously warns against defiling the body temple. "Do you not know that you are God's temple and that God's Spirit dwells in you? If anyone destroys God's temple, God will destroy that person. For God's temple is holy, and you are that temple" (1 Cor. 3:16, 17). But in Romans 14, God accepted the diet of the non-vegetarians. The issue was not a matter of health. Since God accepted both parties, the dietary issue among the Roman Christians was a matter of indifference (*adiaphora*); it was not a question of right and wrong.

Paul says later in the chapter, "I know and am persuaded in the Lord Jesus that nothing is unclean in itself; but it is unclean for anyone who thinks it unclean. If your brother or sister is being injured by what you eat, you are no longer walking in love" (Rom. 14:14, 15). This parallels the remark in his epistle to Timothy: "For everything created by God is good, and nothing is to be rejected, provided it is received with thanksgiving" (1 Tim. 4:4) Are we therefore to assume that slugs and snails and the kinds of flesh condemned in the Old Testament as unfit for food can now be eaten because the Christian has been given unrestrained freedom in questions of diet? Obviously not! What Paul is saying is that everything that God created *as acceptable for food* may be partaken of. But Paul is not condoning the eating of that which would be harmful to health whether it is specifically mentioned in Scripture or not. Since our bodies are the temples of the Holy Spirit, imbibing that which is hurtful to health is a moral issue. The issue in Rome was not a question of health; it was a question of preference in matters that did not involve right and wrong in God's sight. But one party did not recognize that the specific dietary question was a nonissue. Vegetarians today who refrain from eating flesh for health reasons have a different motivation than did the vegetarians in the Roman church.

(3) In Romans 14:5, 6, Paul treats the controversy over days in a similar manner. The question was not a moral issue as it would have been if one of the Ten Commandments was being questioned. The Sabbath and worship are not even mentioned in the passage. The observance of the days in question, whatever days they were, was not a matter of right and wrong. The Lord accepted both parties, those who observed the days and those who did not. In the light of Matthew 24:20, the Lord could not have accepted anyone who did not honor His Sabbath day, as Jesus had honored it during his life on earth (Luke 4:16) and as Paul himself honored it (Acts 13, 16, 17, 18).

(4) Raoul Dederen has pointed out that there seems to have been a clear connection between the observance of days in Rome and the vegetarianism of the weaker Christians. Those who were abstaining from eating particular foods "in honor of the Lord" seem to have been those who were observing particular days in honor of the Lord (verse 6). Dederen's suggestion is that there was a party in the Roman church that chose to refrain from certain foods on certain days which they regarded as religious fast days. He writes: "Paul's statement in Romans 14:2, 'One believes he may eat anything, while the weak man eats only vegetables' (R.S.V.) is curiously analogous to his thought in verse 5, 'One man esteems one day as better than another, while another man esteems all days alike' (R.S.V.). He mentions the two cases together, and later in the chapter he declares that a man should not be judged by his eating (verses 10-13), which may imply that Paul is referring to fast days. It appears quite probable from the context that Paul here is correlating the eating with the observance of days.

Most likely—although it is impossible to ascertain this—the apostle is dealing with fast days in a context of either partial or total abstinence.

"Here again the Essenes may have caused the problem. It is certainly significant that besides abstaining from meat and wine—at least at times—they were also very specific in the matter of observing days. They sanctified certain days that were not observed by the general stream of Jews. . . .

"Some pertinent observations emerge now that could well tie in the matter of diet with that of esteeming certain days above others. The Essenes scrupulously abstained from meat and wine—at least at times. They added certain feast days to the regular Jewish calendar. The discussion over the point existed in Jewry prior to the advent of Christianity. Could it be that the controversy was carried over into the Christian church and finds itself reflected in Romans 14? In this case, the practice of the weak may be compared with the early Christian custom indicated in the *Didache* of fasting twice every week. Is it not significant, and relevant as well, that we have in this document too a matter of diet *and* days connected in a controversial issue?"[5]

The *Didache* or *Teaching* that Dederen cites is a late first- or early second-century document.[6] It reveals a controversy in the Christian church over fast days. The relevant statement reads: "Your fasts must not be identical with those of the hypocrites. They fast on Mondays and Thursdays; but you should fast on Wednesdays and Fridays."[7] The hypocrites are a reference to the Jews whose fast days were Mondays and Thursdays.[8] By contrast, Christians were to fast on Wednesdays and Fridays.

We know that in Jesus' day there was a controversy over fasting. (See Matt. 6:16-18; 9:14, 15; Mark 2:18; Luke 5:33-35.) In fact, in Jesus' parable of the Pharisee and the tax collector, the Pharisee prayed, "I fast twice a week" (Luke 18:12). It seems that it would not be unusual for the fasting controversy of Jesus' day to carry over into the early Christian church with lively discussion as to which days would be the most appropriate for fasting.

Some have suggested that the days referred to in Romans 14:5, 6 were the ceremonial feast days of the Jewish religious year. (See Lev. 23; Num. 28, 29.) Although this is a possibility, the suggestion seems to be ruled out by the fact that these days were feast days, not fast days. Paul's discussion of the controversy over days (Rom. 14) is associated with his discussion of abstinence from food. Hence it seems that Dederen's suggestion of the presence in the Roman church of an ascetic group like the Essenes who were insisting on abstinence from certain foods on certain days is the most likely explanation.

At all events, the passage gives no warrant for the conclusion that Paul rejected the seventh-day Sabbath.

A second passage that is often cited as evidence that Paul rejected the seventh-day Sabbath is Colossians 2:13-17. In the New American Standard Bible, the passage is translated as follows:

"13. And when you were dead in your transgressions and the uncircumcision of your flesh, He made you alive together with Him, having forgiven us all our transgressions, 14. having canceled out the certificate of debt consisting of decrees against us and which was hostile to us; and He has taken it out of the way, having nailed it to the cross. 15. When He had disarmed the rulers and authorities, He made a public display of them, having triumphed over them through Him. 16. Therefore let no one act as your judge in regard to food or drink or in respect to a festival or a new moon or a Sabbath day— 17. things which are a mere shadow of what is to come; but the substance belongs to Christ."

Verses 13 and 14 are speaking of God's forgiveness of the believer's sins made possible by Christ's death on the cross. Some would have us believe that the law was nailed to the cross. But this is not what the text is saying. It was our *indebtedness* in view of our having broken the law that was nailed to the cross. Verse 14 may be translated, "Blotting out the handwriting in decrees which was against us which was contrary to us, and he took it out of the way, nailing it to the cross." The "handwriting" (Greek: *cheirographon*) refers to a bond or certificate of debt.[9] The certificate of debt was "in decrees" (Greek: *tois dogmasin*). God had decreed that "the wages of sin is death, but the free gift of God is eternal life in Christ Jesus our Lord" (Rom. 6:23). Jesus took the death which was ours so that we can have the life which is His. (Compare Romans 5:15-21.) "He himself bore our sins in his body on the cross, so that, free from sins, we might live for righteousness; by his wounds you have been healed" (1 Peter 2:24). "The Lord has laid on him the iniquity of us all" (Isa. 53:6). "For our sake he made him to be sin who knew no sin, so that in him we might become the righteousness of God" (2 Cor. 5:21). It was our guilt borne by Jesus Christ that was nailed to the cross. As we have noted above, the law remains as the standard expression of God's righteousness. Christ died "so that the just requirement of the law might be fulfilled in us, who walk not according to the flesh but according to the Spirit" (Rom. 8:4).

Not only did Jesus suffer for our sins on the cross, he disarmed Satan and his cohorts and publicly displayed to the world and the universe the evil demons that they are. "He disarmed the rulers and authorities and made a public example of them, triumphing over them in it" (Col. 2:15).

Verse 16 adds the corollary: No one can now judge the believer in regard to ritualistic eating and drinking or in respect to the sacrificial observances involved in the practice of the ceremonial law. "These are only a shadow of what is to come, but the substance belongs to Christ" (verse 17).

The phrase "a festival [feast] or a new moon or a sabbath" (Col. 2:16, RSV) is an idiomatic or stylized reference to the ceremonial sacrifices offered in the ancient Israelite sanctuary or temple. The Old Testament background is in Numbers 28 and 29 and Leviticus 23, in which the burnt offerings daily, weekly, monthly, and yearly are listed. There were five yearly feasts, involving seven ceremonial sabbaths. The seven ceremonial sabbaths were:

(1) The first day of the feast of unleavened bread (Lev. 23:7).

(2) The last day of the feast of unleavened bread (Lev. 23:8).

(3) The feast of weeks, 50 days after the feast of unleavened bread (Lev. 23:21).

(4) The feast of trumpets on the first day of the seventh month (Lev. 23:24, 25).

(5) The day of atonement on the 10th day of the 7th month (Lev. 23:27-32).

(6) The first day of the feast of tabernacles (Lev. 23:35).

(7) The last day of the feast tabernacles (Lev. 23:36).

Seven Old Testament passages use some form of the phrase "feasts, new moons, sabbaths" (1 Chron. 23:31; 2 Chron. 2:4; 8:12, 13; 31:3; Neh. 10:33; Eze. 45:17; Hosea 2:11). Consistently these passages refer to the burnt offerings to be offered weekly, monthly, and yearly. Usually the feasts specify only the three pilgrimage feasts (Unleavened Bread, Weeks or Pentecost, and Tabernacles). The sabbaths must, therefore, include the ceremonial

163

sabbaths—otherwise Solomon, for example, would have failed to offer burnt offerings on the days of Trumpets and Atonement.

"Then Solomon offered up burnt offerings to the Lord on the altar of the Lord that he had built in front of the vestibule, as the duty of each day required, offering according to the commandment of Moses for the sabbaths, the new moons, and the three annual festivals—the festival of unleavened bread, the festival of weeks, and the festival of booths [tabernacles]" (2 Chron. 8:12, 13). If the "sabbaths" mentioned in the passage did not include ceremonial sabbaths, Solomon would have failed to offer the stipulated burnt offerings on the feast of Trumpets and the Day of Atonement, because the feasts as listed exclude these two ceremonial sabbaths.

The word *sabbath* (whether singular or plural) in the phrase "feast, new moon, sabbath" specifies the *burnt offerings* for weekly and annual (ceremonial) sabbaths. Colossians 2:16, 17 is simply teaching that *the sacrifices offered* weekly (sabbath), monthly, or yearly were a "shadow" pointing forward to Christ (see Heb. 8:5; 10:1), which lost their significance at the cross. Now no one has a right to judge those who reject these ceremonial observances which pointed forward to the sacrifice and heavenly ministry of Jesus Christ. The phrase "feast, new moon, sabbath" is simply a stylized way of referring to the temporary ceremonial observances that typified the work of our Savior.

Although the special animal sacrifices commanded for the weekly Sabbath (Num 28; Lev. 23) no longer have significance, the weekly Sabbath itself remains as a perpetual memorial of Creation (Gen. 2:1-3; Ex. 20:8-11; Matt. 24:20; Heb. 4:9) and a sign of sanctification (Ex. 31:13) and redemption (Heb. 4:9-11). The "food and drink" (Col. 2:16, RSV) may refer to the meal and drink offerings that were presented to God along with the burnt offerings (see Num. 28:2, 5, 7, 9, 13, 14, etc.). Or they may refer to ritualistic eating and drinking or abstaining from eating and drinking of the kind referred to in Romans 14:1-6. Or they may refer to eating or not eating food that had been offered to idols (1 Cor. 8).

The force of the passage (Col. 2:13-17) is that, since Christ has died for our sins, and we have now been forgiven, ceremonial, ritualistic observances that foreshadowed aspects of his sacrificial and mediatorial ministries have been done away, and no Christian should allow himself to be judged in respect to these ceremonial observances. Paul was not abolishing the weekly Sabbath which, according to the book of Acts, he consistently observed.

When and Where Did Sunday Observance Begin?

The history of the early Christian Church establishes that worship services on Sunday, associated with a progressive rejection of the seventh-day Sabbath, began in Rome during the second century A.D. While most Christians around the Mediterranean world were still observing the Sabbath, there grew up in Rome a veneration of Sunday. Gradually this practice spread from Rome to other places. By the early medieval period, Sunday observance of one sort or another was quite common in the eastern empire as well as in the west. There were three closely related reasons for this development beginning in Rome and spreading from there to other Christian centers:

1. **In the second century the Sabbath was made a fast day, while Sunday was a feast day.** Among the Jews the Sabbath was never a day of fasting, sadness and gloom. For them it was a festival occasion. In Leviticus 23 and Numbers 28, the Sabbath is included among the Jewish feast days. The apocryphal book of Judith says: "And she [Judith] fasted all the days of her widowhood, save the eves of the sabbaths, and the sabbaths, and the eves of the new moons, and the new moons, and the feasts and joyful days of the house of Israel."[10] The book of Jubilees issues a stern warning to the person who fasts on the Sabbath: "And every man who does any work thereon, or goes a journey, or tills (his) farm ... or whoever fasts or makes war on the Sabbaths: The man who does any of these things on the Sabbath shall die...."[11]

In the second-century Roman Christian church, the practices of Easter weekend were gradually transferred to every weekend of the year. Friday and Sabbath were fast days, while Sunday was a day of feasting and rejoicing in view of the resurrection of Christ. The result was that the Sabbath became a day of fasting and gloom by contrast with Sunday which was a day of joy and pleasantness.[12]

Early in the third century, Tertullian wrote of the Roman Christians: "Anyhow, you sometimes continue your Station [fast] even over the Sabbath, — a day never to be kept as a fast except at the Passover season, according to a reason elsewhere given."[13]

The evidence suggests that toward the end of the second century the Roman Church had begun to transfer the fasting practices of Easter weekend to every weekend of the year, by which Friday and the Sabbath were fast days, and Sunday a feast day. The gradual effect of this was to depreciate the Sabbath and exalt Sunday.

By the time of the Spanish Synod of Elvira (c. A.D. 306) weekly Sabbath fasting was the custom in the West: "We have decided that the error be corrected, so that we celebrate extensions of the fast every Sabbath day."[14]

In the early fourth century, while various places in the West were treating the Sabbath as a fast day, this was not the custom in the East. By the fifth century, the weekly Sabbath fast was a fixed custom in Rome. The reason is clearly brought out in the following statement of Pope Innocent I (402-417):

"A very clear reason shows why one should fast on the Sabbath. For if we celebrate the Diem Dominicum to show reverence for the resurrection of our Lord Jesus Christ not only on the day of Easter, but indeed also from one weekly cycle to another one, if we assemble together for the commemoration of that very day, and fast on the sixth holiday, we must not omit the Sabbath, which comes between the sadness and the joy of that period."[15]

Just as the Sabbath of Easter weekend was a fast day, so, it was reasoned, must be every Sabbath day of the year. The result was the denigration of the Sabbath to the level of a day of sorrow and mourning, by contrast with Sunday which was a day of Christian joy and rejoicing. The practical effect on Christians was to lead them to turn away from the Sabbath and to exalt Sunday as the special feast day memorializing Christ's resurrection.

Samuele Bacchiocchi writes: "That the Church of Rome was the champion of the Sabbath fast and anxious to impose it on other Christian communities is well attested by the historical references from Bishop Callistus (A.D. 217-222), Hippolytus (c. A.D. 170-236), Pope Sylvester (A.D. 314-335), Pope Innocent I (A.D. 401-417), Augustine (A.D. 354-430), and John Cassian (c. A.D. 360-435). The fast was designed not only to express sorrow for Christ's death but also, as Pope Sylvester emphatically states, to show 'contempt for the Jews' (*execratione Judaeorum*) and for their Sabbath 'feasting' (*destructiones ciborum*).[16]

2. Anti-Semitism. "Following the death of Nero, the Jews experienced a setback. Military, political, fiscal, and literary repressive measures were

taken against them on account of their resurgent nationalism, which exploded in violent uprisings in many places. Militarily, the statistics of bloodshed provided by contemporary historians, even allowing for possible exaggerations, are most impressive. Tacitus (c. A.D. 33-120), for instance, reports having heard that 600,000 Jews were besieged in the A.D. 70 war. Dio Cassius (c. A.D. 150-235), states that in the Barkokeba war of A.D. 132-135, some 580,000 Jews were killed in action besides the numberless who died of hunger and disease."[17]

Bacchiocchi points out that "under Vespasian (A.D. 69-79) both the Sanhedrin and the high priesthood were abolished; and under Hadrian . . . the practice of the Jewish religion and particularly Sabbathkeeping were outlawed."[18]

Bacchiocchi writes: "Literally, a new wave of anti-Semitic literature surged at that time, undoubtedly reflecting the Roman mood against the Jews. Writers such as Seneca (died A.D. 65), Persius (A.D. 34-62), Petronius (died c. A.D. 66), Quintilian (c. A.D. 35-100), Martial (c. A.D. 40-104), Plutarch (c. A.D. 46-after 119), Juvenal (died c. A.D. 125), and Tacitus (c. A.D. 55-120), who lived in Rome for most of their professional lives, reviled the Jews racially and culturally. Particularly were the Jewish customs of Sabbathkeeping and circumcision contemptuously derided as examples of degrading superstition."[19]

Christians were motivated to separate themselves from the Jews in the minds of the populace and rulers. They wrote against Jewish legalism and began to attack the Sabbath. Writing from Rome about the middle of the second century, Justin Martyr condemned Sabbath observance and provided the earliest account of Christian Sunday worship services:

"And on the day called Sunday, all who live in cities or in the country gather together to one place, and the memoirs of the apostles or the writings of the prophets are read, as long as time permits; then, when the reader has ceased, the president verbally instructs, and exhorts to the imitation of these good things. Then we all rise together and pray, and, as we before said, when our prayer is ended, bread and wine and water are brought, and the president in like manner offers prayers and thanksgivings, according to his ability, and the people assent, saying Amen. . . . But Sunday is the day on which we all hold our common assembly, because it is the first day on which God, having wrought a change in the darkness and matter, made the world; and Jesus Christ our Saviour on the same day rose from the dead.

For He was crucified on the day before that of Saturn (Saturday); and on the day after that of Saturn, which is the day of the Sun, having appeared to His apostles and disciples, He taught them these things, which we have submitted to you also for your consideration."[20]

Thus Sunday observance began in Rome in the middle of the second century A.D. Opposition to the religion of the Jews was a factor in the depreciation of their Sabbath and the gradual substitution of Sunday.

3. Pagan sun worship contributed to the development of Sunday veneration among Christians. Sun worship was one of the oldest practices in the Roman religion. From the early part of the second century A.D., the cult of Sol Invictus was very influential in Rome and other parts of the Empire. The emperor was regarded and worshiped as a Sun-god.

The planetary week was in common use in ancient Rome from the beginning of the Christian Era. The days of the week were named from the heavenly bodies as follows: Sun, Moon, Mars, Mercury, Jupiter, Venus, Saturn. The day of the sun began the series and was regarded as the most important day.

Christian converts from paganism tended to cling to their veneration of the Sun and, therefore, of Sunday. In early Christian art and literature the image of the Sun was often used to represent Christ, the true "Sun of righteousness." "In the earliest known Christian mosaic (dated c. A.D. 240), found below the altar of St. Peter in Rome, Christ is portrayed as the Sun (*helios*) ascending on the quadriga chariot with a nimbus behind His head from which irradiates seven rays in the form of a T (allusion to the cross?). Thousands of hours have been devoted to drawing the sun disk with an equal-armed cross behind the head of Christ and of other important persons."[21]

Bacchiocchi points out that early Christians ceased to pray facing Jerusalem. Instead they faced the sunrise (East). Christians adopted the pagan feast of the *dies natalis Solis Invicti* (the birthday of the Invincible Sun), December 25. Most scholars are convinced that the Church of Rome introduced and championed Sunday. Various Sun cults were present in Rome by the early second century. Their symbology was soon influencing Christian literature, art, and liturgy.[22]

The historical evidence establishes quite conclusively that, although the Sabbath was still kept by many Christians around the Roman world in the second century, the trend in Rome (and, as we shall see, also in Alexandria) was toward depreciation of the Sabbath and the exaltation of Sunday. The three main factors that led to this development were: (1) the Sabbath fast introduced in Rome in the second century; (2) anti-Semitism; (3) the influence of pagan religion on Christianity, since new converts tended to retain some of their old attachments to veneration of the Sun and the day of the Sun.

To What Extent Was the Sabbath Observed as a Sacred Day of Worship by Early Christians?

Kenneth A. Strand provides very convincing historical evidence that, although in Rome and Alexandria the trend was to replace weekly Sabbath worship with Sunday worship services, elsewhere in the Roman Empire the Sabbath was observed along with Sunday until the fifth century.

Strand writes: "The situation in Rome and Alexandria, however, was not typical of the rest of early Christianity. In these two cities there was an evident early attempt by Christians to terminate observance of the seventh-day Sabbath, but elsewhere throughout the Christian world Sunday observance simply arose *alongside* observance of Saturday."[23]

The evidence Strand presents is very impressive. Some of it is given here:

1. **Two fifth-century church historians, Socrates Scholasticus and Sozomen:**

"'For although almost all churches throughout the world celebrate the sacred mysteries [the Lord's Supper] on the sabbath [Saturday] of every week, yet the Christians of Alexandria and at Rome, on account of some ancient tradition, have ceased to do this. The Egyptians in the neighborhood of Alexandria, and the inhabitants of Thebais, hold their religious assemblies on the sabbath, but do not participate of the mysteries in the manner usual among Christians in general: for after having eaten and satisfied themselves with food of all kinds, in the evening making their offerings they partake of the mysteries.'"[24]

"'The people of Constantinople, and almost everywhere, assemble together on the Sabbath, as well as on the first day of the week, which custom is never observed at Rome or at Alexandria. There are several cities and villages in Egypt where, contrary to the usage established elsewhere, the people meet together on Sabbath evenings, and, although they have dined previously, partake of the mysteries.'"[25]

Strand comments: "Thus, even *as late as the fifth century* almost the entire Christian world observed *both Saturday and Sunday* for special religious services. Obviously, therefore, Sunday was not considered a substitute for the Sabbath."[26]

2. In the late second or early third century, Origen, the famous Alexandrian Church Father wrote of the proper kind of Sabbath observance: "'Forsaking therefore the Judaic Sabbath observance, let us see what kind of Sabbath observance is expected of the Christian. On the Sabbath day, nothing of worldly activity should be done. If therefore desisting from all worldly works and doing nothing mundane but being free for spiritual works, you come to the church, listen to divine readings and discussions and think of heavenly things, give heed to the future life, keep before your eyes the coming judgment, disregard present and visible things in favor of the invisible and future, this is the observance of the Christian Sabbath.'"[27]

3. The fourth-century compilation known as the Apostolic Constitutions, probably produced in Syria or elsewhere in the East, urged that both Sabbath and Sunday be observed.

"Have before thine eyes the fear of God, and always remember the ten commandments of God. . . . Thou shalt observe the Sabbath, on account of Him who ceased from His work of creation, but ceased not from His work of providence: it is a rest for meditation of the law, not for idleness of the hands."[28]

"But keep the sabbath, and the Lord's day festival [Sunday]; because the former is the memorial of the creation, and the latter of the resurrection."[29]

"Oh Lord Almighty, Thou hast created the world by Christ, and hast appointed the Sabbath in memory thereof, because that on that day Thou hast made us rest from our works, for the meditation upon Thy laws. . . . We solemnly assemble to celebrate the feast of the resurrection on the Lord's day, and rejoice on account of Him who has conquered death, and has brought life and immortality to light."[30]

"Let the slaves work five days; but on the Sabbath-day and the Lord's day let them have leisure to go to church for instruction in piety. We have said that the Sabbath is on account of the creation, and the Lord's day of the resurrection."[31]

4. Gregory of Nyssa and Asterius of Amasea: "Gregory of Nyssa in the late fourth century referred to the Sabbath and Sunday as 'sisters,' and about the same time Asterius of Amasea declared that it was beautiful for Christians that the 'team of these two days come together' — 'the Sabbath and the Lord's Day.' According to Asterius, each week brought the people together on these days with priests to instruct them."[32]

5. John Cassian: "In the fifth century John Cassian makes several references to church attendance on both Saturday and Sunday. In speaking of Egyptian monks, he states that 'except Vespers and Nocturns, there are no public services among them in the day except on Saturday and Sunday, when they meet together at the third hour [9:00 A.M.] for the purpose of Holy Communion."[33]

The historical evidence establishes that the Sabbath was kept by most Christians until at least the fifth century. Although Sunday was observed along with the Sabbath as a day for worship services, in most areas of the Roman Empire it did not replace the Sabbath. The trend in Rome and Alexandria, however, was for Sunday to replace the Sabbath. As we shall discover, in later centuries Sunday was treated as a day of rest, and Sabbath observance, although not discontinued by all Christians, was neglected by most.

When Did Sunday Observance Replace Sabbath Observance in the Practice of Most Christians?

Sunday gradually became a rest day. Although in the early Christian centuries Sunday worship services were held in Rome and Alexandria, and increasingly in other places, Sunday was not regarded as a day of rest required by the fourth commandment. The development toward regarding Sunday as the complete substitute for the seventh-day Sabbath was a gradual process from the fourth to the twelfth century.

1. Constantine made Sunday a civil rest day. His famous Sunday law of March 7, 321 reads as follows: "On the venerable Day of the Sun let the magistrates and people residing in cities rest, and let all workshops be closed. In the country, however, persons engaged in agriculture may freely and lawfully continue their pursuits; because it often happens that another day is not so suitable for grain-sowing or for vine-planting; lest by neglecting the proper moment for such operations the bounty of heaven should be lost."[34]

Kenneth Strand comments: "This was the first in a series of steps taken by Constantine and by later Roman emperors in regulating Sunday observance. It is obvious that this first Sunday law was not particularly Christian in orientation. We may note, for instance, the pagan designation 'venerable Day of the Sun.' Also, it is evident that Constantine did not base his Sunday regulations on the Decalogue, for he exempted agricultural work—a type of work strictly prohibited in the Sabbath commandment in Exodus 20:8-11."[35]

2. Theodosius I and Gratian Valentinian in A.D. 386 ruled that legal cases should not be heard on Sunday and that there should be no public or private payment of debt. Laws also forbad Sunday circus, theater, and horse racing.[36]

3. Ephraem Syrus (c. A.D. 306-373) wrote that the law requires rest for servants and animals on Sunday. The law is a reference to the Old Testament Sabbath commandment (Exod. 20:8-11).[37] Hence, by the second half of the fourth century some Christians were treating Sunday as a rest day in place of the seventh-day Sabbath, and they were justifying their practice by appealing to the fourth commandment.

4. The Council of Laodicea about A.D. 364. The council showed respect for the Sabbath as well as Sunday, but Canon 29 stipulated: "Christians shall not Judaize and be idle on Saturday but shall work on that day; but the Lord's day they shall especially honour, and, as being Christians, shall, if possible, do no work on that day. If, however, they are found Judaizing, they shall be shut out from Christ."[38]

While such fourth-century documents as the *Apostolic Constitutions* were urging that both Sabbath and Sunday be observed, the Council of Laodicea and certain influential church leaders were attempting to substitute Sunday for the Sabbath as the day of rest.

5. In medieval times the Sunday "Sabbath" displaced the Saturday Sabbath throughout Europe.[39]

i. Pope Gregory I (Pope from A.D. 590-604) demanded that all secular activities should cease on Sunday so that the people could devote their time to prayer.[40]

ii. The Arian rulers must have accepted Sunday as a day of rest and worship, for the Visigoths were defeated by the Romans in A.D. 543 because they refused to fight on Sunday.[41]

iii. Pepin III, known as "the Short" (714-68), the Frankish king, Charlemagne (c. 742-814), the first Emperor (from 800) of the 'Holy Roman Empire,' and their successors attempted to enforce rest on Sunday.[42]

iv. "By the twelfth century, Sunday had become quite fully the church substitute for the seventh day. The rest began at sunset and lasted until the next sunset. All secular work was strictly prohibited under stern ecclesiastical and civil penalties, for nothing except very stringent necessity was allowed to interfere with church attendance (though dispensations could be granted by ecclesiastical authority). This concept of Sundaykeeping was spelled out clearly by the great decretalists. In his collection of 1234, Gregory IX, for instance, collated a decree from the Synod of Mayence from the early part of the ninth century and a letter from Pope Alexander III to the Archbishop of Trondheim in Norway teaching how Sunday must be kept. Although those were local documents, they acquired a much greater authority when they were included in a major canonic collection."[43]

6. One notable exception to the above trend was the Christian Church of Ethiopia which observed both Sabbath and Sunday throughout the Middle Ages and has continued to do so until the present.[44]

7. In every Christian century, even during the Middle Ages, there have been faithful observers of the seventh-day Sabbath. Daniel Augsburger concludes his chapter, "The Sabbath and Lord's Day During the Middle Ages," by writing: "But also, all throughout that period there were groups of people who, either through the example of the Jews or because of their study of the Scriptures, attempted to keep the day that Jesus and the apostles had kept. For obvious reasons we know little about their number or their names, but their presence shows that in every age there were some who attempted to place the Word of God above the traditions of men."[45] He mentions, for example, the Passagini in the twelfth and thirteenth centuries. In 1420 a group of Sabbathkeepers in northern France were dealt with by the authorities. Also some of the Bohemian "Picards" were Sabbathkeepers. In the fifteenth century some of the English Lollards (followers of John Wycliffe) and certain Christians in the Scandinavian lands kept the Sabbath.[46]

The trend from the fourth century on was away from observance of the Sabbath by most Christians and the substitution of Sunday as the day of worship and rest. Even so, in every century there were those who resisted the trend by adhering faithfully to the seventh-day Sabbath of the Scriptures.

We now summarize this chapter by reiterating that Jesus and the apostles observed the seventh-day Sabbath. There is no evidence in the New Testament for Sunday as a day of rest and worship. The New Testament nowhere invites or instructs Christians to observe Sunday as a memorial of Christ's resurrection. The apostle Paul did not attempt to abolish the seventh-day Sabbath. He consistently observed it. The Sabbath was neglected and depreciated in second-century Rome and Alexandria. Sabbath observance was progressively replaced by Sunday observance in the centuries that followed. But time and tradition do not abolish the law of God. Jesus said, "Whoever breaks one of the least of these commandments, and teaches others to do the same, will be called least in the kingdom of heaven; but whoever does them and teaches them will be called great in the kingdom of heaven" (Matt. 5:19). John wrote, "Whoever says, 'I have come to know him,' but does not obey his commandments, is a liar, and in such person the truth does not exist; but whoever obeys his word, truly in this person the love of God has reached perfection. By this we may be sure that we are in him: whoever says, 'I abide in him,' ought to walk just as he walked" (1 John 2:4-6).

Dear Friend, do you love Jesus enough to walk as He walked? Do you love Him enough to keep His commandments? Jesus said, "If you love me, you will keep my commandments" (John 14:15). That includes the Sabbath commandment. Are you sure that your life is in His hands and that your name is written in the Lamb's book of life (Rev. 21:27)? Now is the time to make a decision for Him and for eternity. God is waiting longingly to take you into His arms of love and pour the Holy Spirit into your heart. Believe Him, accept Him, and follow His will in everything. Then you will have life and joy for eternity.

Notes
1. R. C. H. Lenski, *The Interpretation of St. Paul's Epistle to the Romans* (Columbus, Ohio: Wartburg Press, 1945), p. 821.
2. See Charles R. Erdman, *The Epistle of Paul to the Romans* (Grand Rapids, Michigan: Baker, 1983), p. 157; F. Godet, *Commentary on the Epistle to the Romans* (Grand Rapids, Michigan: Zondervan, 1883, 1956), pp. 456, 457; Howard Rhys, *The Epistle to the Romans* (New York: Macmillan, 1961), p. 172.
3. Dederen cites Joseph Parker, *Romans and Galatians, the People's Bible* (New York, 1901), 26:123-125; A Barnes, "Romans," *Notes on the New Testament* (London, 1832), 4:299, 300; Wilbur T. Dayton, *Romans and Galatians*, Wesleyan Bible Commentary (Grand Rapids, Mich., 1965), 5:85, 86.
4. Raoul Dederen, "On Esteeming One Day as Better Than Another—Romans 14:5, 6," in *The Sabbath in Scripture and History*, ed. Kenneth A. Strand (Washington D.C.: Review and Herald, 1982), pp. 335, 336.
5. *Ibid.*, pp. 336, 337.
6. Cyril C. Richardson, trans. and ed., *Early Christian Fathers* (Philadelphia: Westminster Press, 1953), pp. 161-163.
7. *Didache* 8:1, in Richardson, p. 174.

8. Speaking of the Jews, *The Interpreter's Dictionary of the Bible* (New York: Abingdon Press, 1962), vol. 2, p. 243 comments: "It was the custom of the pious to fast on the second and fifth days of the week (Ta'an. 12a; Luke 18:12; Did. 8:1), and the especially devout might fast even more (Jth. 8:6)."

9. See Randolph O. Yeager, *The Renaissance New Testament* (Gretna, Louisiana: Pelican, 1985), vol. 15, p. 64; William F. Arndt and F. Wilbur Gingrich, *A Greek-English Lexicon of the New Testament* (Chicago: University Press, 1957), s.v. *cheirographon.*

10. *Judith* 8:6; R. H. Charles (ed.), *The Apocrypha and Pseudepigrapha of the Old Testament* (Oxford: Clarendon Press, 1913), I:256; quoted in Erwin R. Gane, "The Significance of the Apostolic Constitutions and Its Sources for the History of the Early Christian Sabbath" (M.Th. dissertation: Andrews University, 1968), p. 141.

11. *Jubilees* 50:12, 13; Charles, *op. cit.*, II, 82; quoted in Erwin Roy Gane, *Ibid.*

12. See Kenneth A. Strand, *The Early Christian Sabbath* (Ann Arbor, Michigan: Ann Arbor Publishers, 1979), pp. 9-15.

13. Tertullian, *On Fasting 14;* Alexander Roberts and James Donaldson (eds.), *The Ante-Nicene Fathers* (Grand Rapids, Michigan: Wm. B. Eerdmans, 1965), IV:112.

14. C. J. Hefele, *A History of the Christian Councils* (Edinburgh: T. & T. Clark, 1894), I:146, 147; quoted in Erwin Roy Gane, "The Significance of the Apostolic Constitutions and Its Sources for the History of the Early Christian Sabbath" (M.Th. dissertation: Andews University, 1968), pp. 171, 172.

15. Innocent I, *Epistle* 25.4; J. Migne, *Patrologia latina* XX, col. 555; quoted in Erwin R. Gane, *Ibid.*, p. 179.

16. Samuele Bacchiocchi, "The Rise of Sunday Observance in Early Christianity," in *The Sabbath in Scripture and History*, ed. Kenneth A. Strand (Washington, D.C.: Review and Herald, 1982), p. 137; citing S. R. E. Humbert, *Adversus Graecorum calumnias 6 (PL* 143:937). See also Bacchiocchi, *From Sabbath to Sunday* (Rome: Pontifical Gregorian University Press, 1977), 185-198.

17. Bacchiocchi, "The Rise of Sunday Observance in Early Christianity," in *The Sabbath in Scripture and History*, ed. Kenneth A. Strand, p. 136. He cites Tacitus, *Historiae* 5, 13 and Dio Cassius, *Historiae* 69, 13.

18. Bacchiocchi, *Ibid.*

19. Bacchiocchi, *Ibid.*, p. 137.

20. Justin, *Apology* 1, 67; *The Ante-Nicene Fathers* I:186.

21. Bacchiocchi, *Ibid.*, p. 140.

22. Bacchiocchi, *Ibid.*, p. 141.

23. Kenneth A. Strand, "The Sabbath and Sunday from the Second Through Fifth Centuries," in *The Sabbath in Scripture and History*, p. 323.

24. Strand, *Ibid.*, pp. 323, 324, citing Socrates Scholasticus, *Ecclesiastical History 5, 22* in *Nicene and Post-Nicene Fathers/2 2:132.*

25. Strand, *Ibid.*, p. 324; citing Sozomen, *Ecclesiastical History* 7, 19 in *NPNF/2 2:390*

26. Strand, *Ibid.*

27. Strand. *Ibid.*, citing Origen, Homily 23, on Numbers, par. 4; J. Migne, ed. *Patrologia graeca* 12:749, 750.

28. *Apostolic Constitutions* 2.36; *ANF* 7:413.

29. *Apostolic Constitutions* 7.23; *ANF* 7:469.

30. *Apostolic Constitutions* 7.36; *ANF* 7:474.

31. *Apostolic Constitutions* 8.33; *ANF* 7:495.

32. Strand (ed.), *The Sabbath in Scripture and History*, p. 325, citing Gregory of Nyssa, *On Reproof (PG* 46:309, 310); Asterius of Amasea, *Homily 5, on Matthew* 19:3 (PG 40:225, 226).

33. Strand, *op. cit.*, citing John Cassian, *Institutes* 3.2; *NPNF/2* 11:213.

34. *Lex Constantini* a. 321 (*Codex Justinianus* 3.12.3), trans. in Philip Schaff, *History of the Christian Church*, 5th ed. (New York, 1902), 3:380, note 1.

35. Strand (ed.), *The Sabbath in Scripture and History*, p. 328.

36. Strand, *op. cit.* He cites the *Theodosian Code* 11.7.13 and 15.5.5, trans. by Clyde Pharr (Princeton, N.J., 1952), pp. 300, 433.

37. Strand, *Ibid.*, p. 329.

38. Strand, *op. cit.*, citing Charles J. Hefele, *A History of the Councils of the Church*, 2 (Edinburgh, 1876) 316.

39. See Daniel Augsburger, "The Sabbath and Lord's Day During the Middle Ages," in *The Sabbath in Scripture and History*, ed. Kenneth A. Strand (Washington D.C.: Review and Herald, 1982), pp. 190-214.

40. Augsburger, *Ibid.*, p. 193; citing Epist. 13:1, note (*PL* 77:1254, 1255).

41. Augsburger, *Ibid.*, p. 194.

42. Augsburger, *Ibid.*, p. 201.

43. Augsburger, *Ibid.*, p. 204.

44. See Werner K. Vyhmeister, "The Sabbath in Egypt and Ethiopia," in *The Sabbath in Scripture and History*, ed. Kenneth A. Strand (Washington D.C.: Review and Herald, 1982), pp. 169-189.
45. Augsburger, *Ibid.*, p. 210.
46. Augsburger, *Ibid.*, pp. 208-210.

Chapter 10
How, When, and Why
Does God Judge His people?

T he story is told of a businessman who was arrested for the murder of an accountant who worked in his office. He did all he could to convince the police that he was innocent, but all to no avail. They put him in prison, and the district attorney arranged for a murder trial. Now the fact is the man was innocent. He did not murder his employee. All those long weeks he was in prison he knew he was innocent, despite what people were saying about him, and despite the slanted stories that appeared in the news media. After weeks in prison, he was brought into court for the trial. It was a long hard ordeal lasting three weeks. Every day of that terrible trial the man was brought from prison to the court room. As he sat there before the judge and jury and listened to the lawyers' arguments for and against, he knew he was innocent.

Then came the final speeches for the prosecution and the defense. The innocent man listened while the prosecuting attorney depicted him in the worst possible colors. He was tempted to question his own sanity as he heard himself implicated in a murder plot that he had nothing to do with. His defense attorney did a good job of discounting the evidence. But what would the jury decide? With solemn faces the jurors left the courtroom, and everyone waited for two days for their final decision. The innocent man couldn't sleep or eat. He waited in agony of soul for a verdict that would either ruin him forever or make him a free man.

On the morning of the third day of the jury's seclusion, they filed back into the courtroom. The innocent man and his loved ones waited tensely for the verdict. They hardly dared to breathe. The sober looking jurors took their seats. The foreman stood to his feet. The judge asked, "What verdict do you bring?" The foreman calmly announced, "We find the accused innocent!"

Imagine the paroxysms of joy that overwhelmed the man's loved ones and friends! Imagine the enormous relief that swept over his soul!

But he was innocent all along; and he knew it! At the time of the arrest, during those long weeks in that miserable prison, and during the three agonizing weeks of the trial, he was innocent. Yet he was a captive. He couldn't go home to his dear ones, and he couldn't go to work. Not until the judge said, "You are free to go!" was he a free man. For weeks he had been an innocent man in bondage. Now he was both innocent and free!

This illustrates, at least in part, the investigative judgment that takes place in heaven before Jesus comes. The Bible says that believers in Jesus are innocent. Romans 8:1 says: "There is therefore now no condemnation for those who are in Christ Jesus." When our lives are surrendered to Christ, we are innocent, and God does not condemn us. But we have sinned, and the devil and his demons do condemn us and claim us as theirs, even though God has forgiven us. We are in this old prison house of a world, fallen human beings subject to suffering and death. We are innocent, but still in prison. Paul put it dramatically when he wrote that "we ourselves, who have the first fruits of the Spirit, groan inwardly while we wait for adoption, the redemption of our bodies" (Rom. 8:23). So we are innocent but bound in fallen natures in a fallen world.

The Bible teaches that only when the heavenly court hands down a verdict of eternal acquittal for those who are consistently believing in Jesus, only when the Judge of all the earth pronounces us irrevocably His for eternity, are we free to leave this old world of sin and go with Jesus to the heavenly Kingdom. Then we will be both innocent and ultimately free!

But why would there be any need for an end-time judgment? God knows everything. He knows everything about us. In fact, He knew it all ahead of time, because the Bible teaches that He sees the end from the beginning (Isa. 46:9,10). Then why does the Lord convene a court session in heaven to decide who should be saved and who lost? He knows already who will be saved and who will be lost.

It is important to realize that God is not concerned only with His own attitudes and reactions. If He had been content to satisfy only His own claims, Satan and his evil angels would have been destroyed as soon as they rebelled in heaven. That surely would have been just, and God had every right to do it. The reason that God did not do it but allowed these fallen demons to tempt and torture mankind for centuries was that He wanted the unfallen angels and the inhabitants of unfallen worlds, as well as the inhabitants of our world, to serve Him from love not from fear. The angels were created beings with limited insight. Many of them probably had some doubts about whether Satan's claims were totally false and evil. For God to destroy the devil immediately would have engendered the criticism that He was hasty and unjust.

Because God is concerned that sin should not rise up again after the wicked have been destroyed at the end of time, He wants all the inhabitants of the unfallen universe to be thoroughly convinced that the people He takes to heaven at the second coming of Jesus have a right to be there. And God wants the unfallen universe to understand without any doubt that every person whom He judges to be unworthy of heaven is justly condemned to eternal death.

The only way to convince the unfallen universe of His complete justice is to allow them to look into the records of people's lives, so that they can know for themselves who have genuinely believed in Jesus and who have not.

There is another point that is equally as important. As we shall see in a moment when we turn to the Scriptures, God wants His living people at the end of time to have victory over sin. He cannot take to heaven people who refuse to receive the Holy Spirit as the power to overcome sin. The heavenly judgment before Jesus comes is an ongoing scrutiny of people's lives, so that all heaven can know who is growing in Christ and who is refusing to grow. Our Lord promises to give us unlimited power to serve Him and overcome all evil. The judgment decides who at the end of time are availing themselves of that power and who are not. The life records of the dead are closed; it is easy for heaven to know where they stood in relation to Christ at the point of death. But it is not so easy to know what ultimate decisions the living are likely to make. God can foresee all this, but His unfallen created beings cannot. He gives every last-day living soul a chance to know Him sufficiently to be saved. He wants each one to make a final, unvarying decision to serve Him. When such a decision has been made by individuals, God will seal them, and the heavenly judgment will declare that their names should be kept in the book of life for eternity. Then they are taken to the heavenly Kingdom at the second advent of Jesus.

The pre-advent judgment is intended by God to be a great incentive to last-day people to turn to Christ and receive His Spirit into their hearts, so that their innocence in Christ will make it possible for the heavenly court to decide that their names should be kept in the book of life for eternity. The Lord wants to pronounce you eternally vindicated because you have accepted Jesus and are living consistently by faith in Him. God wants you to be one of those whom He will seal at the end of time (Rom. 7:1-3; 14:1-5), because, by His grace, you are consistently maintaining your born-again experience, and having victory over sin through the power of the indwelling Christ.

Now let us turn to the Scriptures and consider its solemn and exciting messages about the pre-advent judgment.

The Judgment Scene Described

Daniel, chapter 7 records that Daniel saw in vision four beasts rising up out of the sea: a lion, a bear, a leopard, and an nondescript beast. Those four beasts represented the four great empires that would dominate the eastern Mediterranean and subjugate the people of God for centuries. They were Neo-Babylonia, Medo-Persia, Greece, and Rome. On the head of the fourth beast Daniel saw ten horns. He was told that ten kings would arise out of the fourth empire (Dan. 7:7, 23). The Roman Empire was divided exactly as Daniel's prophecy predicted. In the 4th - 6th centuries A.D. the so-called "barbarian" tribes dismembered the Empire. Daniel had seen a little horn grow up on the head of the fourth beast (verse 8). This little horn pushed up three of the original ten horns, and it did terrible things against God and His people. Daniel 7:24, 25 enable us to identify this little horn power as the medieval Papacy. For 1,260 years ("a time, two times, and half a time") this little horn power (the Papacy) maintained ecclesiastical supremacy.[1] From A.D. 538 to 1798 it usurped the authority of Christ and opposed His truth and people. Daniel predicted that shortly after this period of Papal supremacy God would convene a judgment in heaven that would condemn the little horn power and vindicate His faithful people. After the Papacy had exercised ecclesiastical supremacy for centuries, then began the heavenly judgment. That is very clear from a comparison of Daniel 7:8, 9 with verses 21, 22, and verses 25, 26. The period of Papal supremacy ended in 1798 when the Pope was taken prisoner by Napoleon's general. This act simply marked the end of a process in the French Revolution during which the Papacy lost its iron grip on the governments of western Europe. We know that the heavenly judgment began shortly after this. In fact, as we shall see, the next chapter of Daniel actually gives the year when this heavenly judgment commenced.

What is the nature of this judgment? What kinds of decisions does it make?

First, we know that it is in heaven. Verse 9 says that God ("the Ancient of days," KJV; "the Ancient One," NRSV) took His place upon His throne, and assistant judges took their places upon thrones also. Throughout the Scriptures God's throne is depicted as in heaven.

Second, we are told that this judgment involves a court session in which books of record are examined (verse 10). That is why we call it an "investigative judgment." Books of record are investigated, and decisions are made on the basis of what is found in them. The phrase "investigative judgment" is not in the Bible, but it describes accurately the judgment that Daniel has depicted for us. The word "Trinity" is not in the Bible either, but it correctly refers to the three Persons who comprise our one God. Many terms that are not in the Scriptures are used by Bible students to describe truths that are thoroughly Scriptural. Hence, we use the term "investigative judgment" because it correctly describes what happens in heaven in the pre-advent judgment.

Third, we are told in Scripture that records of every human life are kept in heaven. It is on the basis of these records that the judgment can be conducted. There are three kinds of records mentioned in the Bible:

1. The book of life contains the names of all those who at any time have been born-again Christians (Luke 10:20; Phil. 4:3; Heb. 12:23; Rev. 20:12).

2. The sins of every human being are also recorded. They are recorded as forgiven for those who have accepted Christ's forgiveness (1 John 1:9). But they are recorded as unforgiven for those who have refused Christ and His forgiveness. (Compare Eccl. 12:14; Matt. 12:36, 37; Jer. 2:22; Rev. 22:12.)

3. A book of remembrance is kept in which God records the works of faith performed by His believing people (Mal. 3:16, 17).

Fourth, we are told that "one like the Son of man" is the defense Attorney in this judgment (Dan. 7:13, KJV). The title Son of man was Jesus' favorite name for Himself. (See Matt. 8:20; 11:19; 16:13; 18:11; 20:28; 24:27; etc.). Daniel 7:13 (KJV) says that the Son of man came "with the clouds of heaven, and came to the Ancient of days." Some Bible students have concluded that this must be a reference to the second advent of Jesus, because He will come with the clouds of heaven. (Compare Matthew 26:64). But here in Daniel 7:13 we are not told that the Son of man comes to this earth. He comes to the Ancient of days. Where is the Ancient of days? Verse 9 says that He is on the throne in the heavenly court. The coming here is Christ's coming to the heavenly court at the beginning of the pre-advent, investigative judgment. He functions as our Advocate or Attorney. The clouds of heaven surround the Son as He enters the heavenly court for the judgment. The Aramaic word for cloud used here is *'anan.* It is not only used in references to the second advent. It is often used in passages describing the Deity. Where God is, there is the cloud surrounding Him. (See for example Exod. 13:21; 24:15, 16; 33:9, 10; 40:33, 34; 1 Kings 8:10, 11; Psalm 97:1, 2.) It is very significant that Leviticus 16 records that Aaron was not to go into the Most Holy Apartment of the sanctuary every day, only on the Day of Atonement. The Lord added that this was "lest he die; for I will appear in the cloud upon the mercy seat" (Lev. 16:2, RSV). The only time the high priest, who represented Christ, saw that cloud was on the Day of Atonement.

Fifth, Daniel 7:14 says that in this judgment Christ receives His kingdom, that is, the names of those who are His for eternity. Revelation 7:1-3 indicates that in the last days the angels of heaven are instructed to hold back the winds of strife in our world, "till we have sealed the servants of our God in their foreheads" (verse 3, KJV) The servants of Christ are sealed because in the heavenly pre-advent judgment described by Daniel the decision is made that their names can be kept in the book of life (Dan. 12:1). At the end of the judgment Michael (Christ, the Son of Man) stands up. That means that He ceases His work of intercession and judgment. Then comes a time of terrible, unprecedented trouble in our world. But "at that time thy people shall be delivered, every one that shall be found written in the book" (Daniel 12:1, KJV). This is the only other place in Daniel, apart from 7:10, where books in heaven are referred to. The names of born-again Christians are always placed in the book of life in heaven (Luke 10:20; Phil. 4:3; Heb. 12:23). But in the pre-advent judgment the decision is made whose names can be kept there and whose names should be taken out. The names of those who have lost their born-again relationship with Jesus are removed from the book of life (Rev. 3:5). These are lost when the judgment ends, and they are put to death for eternity. But those who have their names retained in the book of life are sealed with God's seal, sheltered in the time of trouble following the close of probation (when Michael stands up), and taken to heaven with Jesus when He comes again. Since the pre-advent judgment decides who these people are, it is in this judgment that Christ receives "dominion, and glory, and a kingdom" (Dan. 7:14, KJV).

Sixth, the pre-advent judgment is not convened merely to condemn the little horn power. It also vindicates the faithful people of God who have been saved by grace and who are living victorious lives by faith in Christ. Daniel 7:22 says that when the Ancient of Days came to the heavenly court session, "judgment was rendered in favor of the holy ones of the Most High."[2] The Aramaic word translated "judgment" in Daniel 7:22 is *dina'*. It means "judgment," "justice," "vindication," "a court session."[3] (Compare Daniel 4:37) This word is used two other times in Daniel, chapter 7. In verses 10 and 26 it refers to the court session being convened, which, according to verse 22, has as it purpose the provision of justice for the maligned people of God.

Seventh, Revelation 3:5; 6:9-11; 19:7, 8; and 14:6, 7 throw additional light on what happens in this pre-advent judgment:

Revelation 3:5 says: "If you conquer, you will be clothed like them in white robes, and I will not blot your name out of the book of life; I will confess your name before my Father and before his angels." Only the names of those who are clothed in "white robes" will be retained in the book of life in the investigative judgment now going on in heaven. The white robes represent the righteousness of Christ bestowed upon believers by the Holy Spirit, resulting in behavior that is acceptable in the sight of God. (Compare Rev. 19:7, 8; 1 John 2:29; 3:7; Rom. 8:9, 10). Others who once knew Christ but who have lost their born-again relationship with Him will have their names removed from the book of life. Salvation depends on maintaining our relationship with Jesus. "The one who endures to the end will be saved" (Matt. 24:13).

Revelation 6:9-11: After centuries of martyrdom, the blood of the dead martyrs cries out symbolically from the ground, "Sovereign Lord, holy and true, how long will it be before you judge and avenge our blood on the inhabitants of the earth?" (verse 10). At the time of this cry, they are not yet eternally vindicated, and in a symbolic sense their blood is crying for justice. (Compare Gen. 4:10.) This proves that they were not judged at death, or at any time prior to this.

183

The record in the next verse is that the heavenly court vindicates them: "They were each given a white robe" (verse 11). That is the judgment of the dead. In view of their relationship with Christ at the time of death, they are eternally vindicated in the pre-advent judgment. We know this judgment of the dead is pre-advent because of the next phrase: ". . . and told to rest a little longer" (verse 11). After being judged and vindicated, the righteous dead are told to rest a little while until Jesus will come, raise them from the dead, and take them to the heavenly Kingdom.

After the vindication of the dead, something happens to their living brethren. The dead, who are asleep in their graves (1 Cor. 15:51; 1 Thess. 4:13), were told that they should rest a little longer, "until their fellow servants and their brethren, who are about to be killed as they were, might be made complete (might be made perfect)." That is an accurate, literal translation of the Greek.[4] The English translations all read much as does the Revised Standard Version: ". . . until the number of their fellow servants and their brethren should be complete, who were to be killed as they themselves had been." In fact, the word "number" does not occur in the Greek text, nor is it usually a part of the verb *pleroo,* as it is used throughout the Greek Scriptures. The text is not saying that the righteous dead are to remain in their graves until a certain number of their living brethren have been put to death. The message is that the dead are to rest on until their living brethren have been made complete in Christ. The Lord wants to give the living believers victory over sin through the power of the indwelling Holy Spirit (Rom. 8:9-10). Then He will call off the judgment, allow the time of trouble, and come to deliver both righteous dead and righteous living.

Revelation 19:7, 8: This chapter is written from the perspective of the end of the judgment. Now Christ's work of vindicating His people has been completed. Verse 2 indicates that God "has *judged* the great whore [Babylon; the little horn power] . . . and has *avenged* on her the blood of his servants." (Italics supplied.) In Revelation 6:10, the dead had cried out, "How long will it be before you *judge* and *avenge* our blood." In Revelation 19 we are told that it has now happened. God has judged and avenged. Then, looking back, John explains what happened to the faithful people of God during the pre-advent judgment. He calls it the "marriage of the Lamb" (Rev. 19:7). What John says can be literally translated from the Greek: ". . . for the marriage of the Lamb came, and his wife made herself ready. And it was given to her that she might be clothed with fine linen, bright and clean; for the fine linen is the righteous deeds of the saints" (verses 7, 8).

During the pre-advent, investigative judgment (the marriage ceremony of the Lamb), while the heavenly court session is in progress, God's living people are being prepared for the divine seal that will be given to them when they have received the righteousness of Christ into their hearts as the source of victory over sin. Righteous deeds (*dikaiomata*; Rev. 19:8) are possible only to born-again Christians. "If you know that He is righteous, you know that everyone also who practices righteousness is born of Him" (1 John 2:29, NASB). Only as we are filled with the righteousness of Christ by the Holy Spirit can we do anything that is righteous in God's sight. Then it is possible because Christ is living out His righteous life through us (Gal. 2:20). Righteousness within results in righteousness without. Righteous deeds are motivated and empowered by righteousness in the heart. Righteousness in the heart is Christ within by the presence of the Holy Spirit. (See John 14:18, 23; Rom. 8:9, 10.) This is the qualification for eternal vindication in the pre-advent judgment, and it is the qualification for the seal of God that is given to all those whose names are kept in the book of life by the heavenly court. (Compare Rev. 7:1-3 with 14:1-5.)

Revelation 14:6, 7 depict the "eternal" (NRSV) or "everlasting" (KJV) gospel being proclaimed worldwide before the second coming of Jesus. Part of that end-time gospel is the message, "the hour of his judgment has come" (verse 7). This judgment must be pre-advent, because it is part of the gospel proclaimed "to every nation and tribe and language and people," and because it is followed by two other messages (Rev. 14:8-12). The call is for all humanity to "fear God and give him glory, for the hour of his judgment has come" (verse 7). We fear God by respecting Him, trusting Him, and committing our lives to Him (Josh. 24:14; Eccl. 12:13; 1 Peter 1:17; 2:17). We give Him glory by partaking of the glory of His character (John 17:22) and allowing Him to live out His life through us (Gal. 2:20).

The message of the pre-advent, investigative judgment, described in Daniel 7:9-14, vitally concerns the salvation of each one of us. The crucial question we all must ask ourselves is, "Am I right with Christ? Am I living by faith in Him? Do I have the Holy Spirit continually dwelling in my heart? Am I allowing Christ to live out His life through me?" For people who can answer "Yes" to those questions, the heavenly pre-advent judgment is a wonderful blessing. This is the time when Satan's claims over our lives are finally and eternally denied. The Lord wants to seal each one of us as His chosen servants in whose hearts the power of evil has been broken.

Daniel 7 and 8 Are Parallel Prophecies

The prophecy of Daniel chapter 8 provided a preview of history from ancient times to the second coming of Jesus. It covers substantially the same extensive period of history that is covered in Daniel 7. The symbolism is somewhat different, and certain other events are emphasized. But the two prophecies are, for the most part, parallel.

The same investigative judgment is spoken of in both passages. Daniel 7 outlines the history of the world up to the pre-advent judgment. Daniel 8 does likewise. The two outlines can be placed side by side as follows:

DANIEL 7	DANIEL 8
The bear = Medo-Persia v. 5	*The ram = Medo-Persia* v. 3
The leopard = Greece v. 6	*The he-goat = Greece* vs. 5-8
The nondescript beast = Roman Empire v. 7	*The little horn = Roman Empire* vs. 9-12
The little horn = Papacy v. 8	*The little horn = Papacy* vs. 9-12
Judgment scene = pre-advent judgment vs. 9-14	*Sanctuary cleansing = pre-advent judgment* v. 14.

Because the two prophecies are parallel, it is apparent that the pre-advent judgment described in Daniel 7:9-14 is the same event as the cleansing of the sanctuary described in Daniel 8:14.

The Little Horn Power of Daniel 8

The little horn of Daniel 7 grew on the head of the fourth beast (verse 8). Since the fourth beast represents the power that succeeded Greece, we can conclude that the reference is to Rome, the Republic followed by the Empire. The power that inherited Roman territory and influence in the West after the dismemberment of the Empire was the medieval Papacy. Therefore we conclude that the little horn of Daniel 7 was the Papacy.

The little horn of Daniel 8:9-12 came to power at the end of the rule of the Hellenistic Kingdoms (verses 22, 23). The male goat of verse 8 represents Greece, the great horn that was broken symbolizes Alexander the Great, and the four prominent horns that grew in place of the broken great horn depict the four Hellenistic Kingdoms that succeeded Alexander. The four Hellenistic Kingdoms were Antigonid Macedonia that became a Roman province in 148 B.C.; Attalid Pergamum that became a Roman province in 133 B.C.; Seleucid Syria that became a Roman province in 63 B.C.; and Ptolemaic Egypt that became a Roman province in 30 B.C. The latter end of the rule of the Hellenistic Kingdoms was, therefore, 30 B.C. when Rome finally conquered the Mediterranean world.

The power that became exceedingly great at the end of the Hellenistic period was Rome. It was the western power described in Daniel 8:9. But the little horn power was predicted to continue till the "time of the end" (Dan. 8:17). It will function till "the last end of the indignation" (verse 19, KJV). Imperial Rome was followed by Papal Rome. Thus the little horn power of Daniel 8 represents both Rome pagan and Rome Papal. This little horn power is not to be destroyed until the second coming of Jesus. "He shall be broken, and not by human hands" (Daniel 8:25). The allusion is to the great image of Daniel 2 which is destroyed by a stone "cut from the mountain not by hands" (verse 45). The kingdom of God "shall crush all these kingdoms and bring them to an end" (Daniel 2:44). Preeminent among those end-time powers will be the little horn power of Daniel 8, the Papacy in its end-time manifestation.

Many scholars have argued that the little horn power of Daniel 8 represents Antiochus Epiphanes, the Syrian king from 175 to 163 B.C. But Antiochus Epiphanes did not reign "at the latter end" of the rule of the four Hellenistic Kingdoms. He was only the 8th monarch in the Seleucid dynasty of 26 kings. The little horn became "exceedingly great" (Dan. 8:9) and prosperous (verse 12), which Antiochus did not. Antiochus was driven out of Egypt by Rome. Antiochus' conquest of Palestine was a failure. By 165 B.C. the Maccabees had driven the Syrians out of Palestine and had rededicated the temple to Yahweh. Antiochus' conquest of Parthia and Bactria failed because he died in 163 B.C. before he had achieved his goal.

According to Daniel's prophecy, the little horn power would oppose God in three major ways: (1) It would persecute His faithful people (Dan. 8:10). (2) It would usurp the authority of the "prince of the host" (Dan.

8:11), a reference to the Messiah, the Christ (Dan. 8:25; 9:25; 10:21; 11:22; 12:1). (3) It would destroy Christ's sanctuary (Dan. 8:11) and its services (verses 11, 12).

The Roman Empire fulfilled these predictions. It crucified Christ, it persecuted His followers, and it destroyed the earthly sanctuary in A.D. 70. Papal Rome also fulfilled the prophecy. Throughout the medieval period it persecuted the people of God in the name of religion. It usurped the High Priestly ministry of Christ by the claims of the supreme pontiff and by the claims of its priests to forgive sins. Human mediation took the place of heavenly mediation. The "daily" (verses 11, 12; Hebrew: *tamid*), the mediatorial ministry of Christ that had been typified by the daily ministrations of priests in the earthly sanctuary, was usurped by the substitution of an earthly religion for the heavenly ministry of our Lord (see Hebrews 8, 9).

The Twenty-Three Hundred Days

The question in Daniel 8:13 is correctly translated: "*Until when* is the vision, [concerning] the daily (the regular sacrifice) and the desolating trespass, to give both the sanctuary and the host to be trampled?" Then comes the answer: "For twenty-three hundred evenings and mornings; then the sanctuary shall be cleansed" (verse 14, The New Jewish Publication Society Translation). The focus of both the question and the answer is on the event that will occur at the end of the 2,300 days. This event would bring the work of the little horn power to a close. The questions we must consider are: (1) What is symbolized by the 2,300 days? (2) What is the sanctuary, and what is involved in its cleansing? (3) How does the cleansing of this sanctuary answer the question of verse 13? How does this cleansing bring the work of the little horn power to a close?

First, we will consider the 2,300 days. The cleansing of the sanctuary (Dan. 8:14) was to begin after 2,300 days. We must notice some vital facts about this period of time:

1. *The phrase translated "days" means a 24 hour period.* The Hebrew phrase is *ereb boqer*. It means literally "evening-morning." Some form of this phrase is used 22 times in the Hebrew Old Testament. When a 24-hour period is intended the phrase is always "evening-morning," never "morning-evening." (See Gen. 1:5, 8, 13, 19, 23, 31; Exod. 27:20, 21 etc.). When the offering of the morning and evening sacrifice or the offering of incense is referred to, the phrase is always "morning-evening," never "evening-

morning." (See 1 Chron. 16:40; 2 Chron. 2:4 etc.). In Daniel 8:14 and 26 the phrase is evening-morning, a 24-hour period. The reference in Daniel 8:14 is not to the morning and evening sacrifices of the sanctuary. The reference is to 2,300 24-hour days which are used here as a prophetic symbol.[5]

2. *The 2,300 literal days of Daniel 8:14 are symbolic of 2,300 years.* The prophet was told that the work of the little horn power would continue till the end of time (Dan. 8:17, 19, 25, 26). Twenty-three hundred literal days would not reach to the end of time. The 2,300 days must refer to a period of centuries, not just to a period of 6 years 4 months.

3. *The relationship between Daniel 8 and 9 enables us to prove that the 2,300 days are years, and provides us the beginning date for the period.* The vision of Daniel 9 was given in 538 B.C., some years after the vision of Daniel 8. Daniel was having trouble reconciling his vision of chapter 8 with Jeremiah's predictions recorded in Jeremiah 25:11. He prayed for light (Dan. 9:1-19). Gabriel came to explain more fully the vision of chapter 8 (Dan. 9:21, 23). Gabriel told Daniel that "seventy week's (Hebrew "seventy sevens") were to be "cut off" (Hebrew: *chathak*) from the 2,300 days.[6] These "seventy sevens" must refer to 490 years, because they were to reach to the time of the Messiah (Christ). So 490 years were to be cut off from the beginning of the 2,300 days. You cannot have 490 years cut off from 2,300 literal days (6 years 4 months). Therefore, the 2,300 days of Daniel 8:14 must be a prophetic symbol of 2,300 years.

4. *What was the beginning date for the 2,300 years (Daniel 8:14) and the 490 years (Daniel 9:24)?* The answer is found in Daniel 9:25: "Know therefore and understand, that from the going forth of the commandment to restore and to build Jerusalem unto the Messiah the Prince shall be . . . ." (KJV). Both periods were to begin with the going forth of the commandment to restore and to build Jerusalem. When was that? Ezra 6:14 indicates that God's commandment for the rebuilding of Jerusalem, the restoration of the temple and its services, and the reestablishment of the Jewish state was put into effect by the decrees of three Persian monarchs. They were Cyrus, Darius, and Artaxerxes. Cyrus's decree for the return of the Jews was enacted probably in 537 B.C. That of Darius 1 was passed about 519 or 518 B.C. The decree of Artaxerxes I Longimanus was certainly put into operation in the autumn of 457 B.C. (See S. H. Horn and L. H. Wood, *The Chronology of Ezra 7* [Washington, D.C.: Review & Herald, 1953, 1970]).

Since God's command for the rebuilding of Jerusalem and the restoration of the state of ancient Israel was put into operation by three human decrees, we must use the third date, 457 B.C. Twenty-three hundred years from 457 B.C. bring us to 1844. Since the decree of Artaxerxes was put into effect in the autumn of 457 B.C., we can know that the cleansing of the sanctuary, the heavenly pre-advent judgment, began in the autumn of 1844.

2,300 YEARS

457 B.C.	1844 A.D.
Command to rebuild Jerusalem (Dan. 9:25; Ezra 6:14)	Beginning of pre-advent judgment (Dan. 7:9-14; 8:14)

Bible prophecy is delightfully specific in the way it identifies events to take place in the future. We can have confidence that such remarkable prophecies as this came from God. He alone is able to predict the future with such accuracy (Isa. 46:9, 10). We can be sure that we are living in the time of the heavenly pre-advent, investigative judgment. It began in 1844. Our Lord is waiting and working to bring people into such a close relationship with Himself that by the end of the judgment they will be sealed (Rev. 7:1-3), because the heavenly court will be able to keep their names in the book of life for eternity (Dan. 12:1). What did we discover to be the prerequisite for this? The continuing presence of Christ in our hearts by the Holy Spirit. The new birth is to be our uninterrupted experience, so that Christ's righteousness can be counted as ours in the heavenly judgment.

Why Is the Pre-Advent Judgment Called the Cleansing of the Sanctuary?

The cleansing of the ancient Israelite sanctuary (or temple) occurred on the Day of Atonement (the 10th day of the 7th month). The pre-advent judgment is the end-time antitype or fulfillment of that event.

According to Leviticus 16, two goats were taken by the High Priest on the Day of Atonement. One represented Christ and the other represented Satan. The one that represented Christ was slain, symbolizing Christ's death on the cross. Some of its blood was collected by the High Priest, and sprinkled on the mercy seat in the Most Holy Place, on the altar of incense in the Holy Place, and on the altar of burnt offering in the court. Thus every part of the sanctuary was symbolically cleansed of the record of pardoned sin. The sins of the people who had brought their sin offerings during the year had been forgiven already (Lev. 4:26, 31, 35). But by the sprinkling of blood in the daily service the pardoned record had been symbolically retained in the sanctuary. This record of pardoned sin defiled the sanctuary, so that it was necessary to cleanse it on the Day of Atonement.

While the High Priest was sprinkling the blood in the Most Holy Place in the presence of God Himself, the people were out in the court examining their hearts to be sure that all their sins had been confessed and put away. It was a time of self-examination, the putting away of sin from the life. (See Lev. 16:29; 23:29.) While a ministry was going on in the sanctuary, a divine work was taking place in the hearts of the people in the court. The Day of Atonement was an annual judgment day, on which both the sanctuary and the people were cleansed (Lev. 16:30, 33, 34).

What happened to those Israelites who refused to follow the Divine counsel of Leviticus 16:29? "And this shall be a statute for ever unto you: that in the seventh month, on the tenth day of the month, ye shall afflict your souls. . . ." (KJV; compare Lev. 23:27). Suppose an Israelite failed to "afflict" his soul on the Day of Atonement, what would happen to him? "For whatsoever soul it be that shall not be afflicted in that same day, he shall be cut off from among his people" (Lev. 23:29, KJV). In other words, the judgment of the Day of Atonement vindicated the faithful and condemned the unfaithful.

This once-a-year Day of Atonement was a symbol of the great work being done for the people of God from 1844 to the time when probation closes just prior to the second coming of Jesus. (See Rev. 8:5; 22:11.) The great end-time Day of Atonement is the cleansing of the heavenly sanctuary by the ministry of Christ our High Priest in the Most Holy Place of heaven. As Daniel 7 and other passages indicate, the books of record are being examined to determine who, as born-again Christians, have sought Christ's forgiveness for the past and, by His grace, have put away all sin from their lives. During Christ's judgment ministry in heaven, God's people on earth are coming ever nearer to Him, so that the born-again experience will be a daily, uninterrupted one. Through the power of Christ they are applying the counsel of 2 Corinthians 7:1: "Having therefore these promises, dearly beloved, let us cleanse ourselves from all filthiness of the flesh and spirit, perfecting holiness in the fear of God" (KJV). This has been God's wish for His people in every era of history. And in this time of judgment it is an especially vital work, because living believers, who are sealed with the seal of God, are to have victory over all sin, so that after the close of probation, when Christ's heavenly mediation has ceased, they will be filled the Holy Spirit and kept from sinning. (Compare Revelation 8:5; 22:11; 3:2, 5).

Because we are living in the last remnants of time, when Christ's Most Holy Apartment judgment ministry is in progress, we must seek the Lord with all our hearts, so that He can purify us, taking away our sin and giving us the wonderfully cleansing in-filling of His Holy Spirit.

The Linguistic Relationship Between Daniel 8:14 and Leviticus 16

Daniel 8:14 translates literally from the Hebrew text: "And he said to me, For two thousand three hundred evenings and mornings [days] then the sanctuary will be justified [nitsdaq]."[7] Competent Hebrew scholars have translated *tsadaq* by "cleansed." Jewish scholars translated the Hebrew Bible into Greek in the third and second centuries B.C., thus producing what we know as the Septuagint Version. They translated *nitsdaq* of Daniel 8:14 by *katharisthesetai*, which is the future, indicative, passive, third person, singular of the Greek verb *katharizo* that means "to make clean," "cleanse," "purify." They thus recognized the text as speaking of the cleansing of the sanctuary.

The King James Version translators rendered the latter part of Daniel 8:14, ". . . then shall the sanctuary be cleansed." The Douay Version translates the text, ". . . and the sanctuary shall be cleansed." The New Jewish Publication Society translation of the Hebrew Bible entitled *Tanakh: the Holy Scriptures* translates Daniel 8:14: "He answered me, 'For twenty-three hundred evenings and mornings; then the sanctuary shall be cleansed.'"

Since *tsadaq* means "to justify," why have so many competent scholars translated it by "cleansed" in Daniel 8:14? The answer is simply that, as it is used throughout the Old Testament, *tsadaq* has the connotation of cleansing as one of its meanings. In the Old Testament, as in the New, when God justifies a person, He declares that person righteous. It is a true to fact declaration. God never declares anyone righteous whom He has not made righteous because of their covenant fellowship with Him. Because Old Testament believers responded in faith to God's mercy and grace, He was able to declare them to be what He had made them, clean, pure, righteous people. (See Gen. 15:6 [compare Rom. 4:3-8, 19-25; Gal. 3:3-14]; 1 Kings 8:30-32; Exod. 23:7; Prov. 17:15; Isa. 53:11.)

In the Old Testament *tsadaq* is used synonymously with words meaning "to cleanse." For example, consider Job 4:17: "Shall mortal man be more just than God? shall a man be more pure than his maker." (KJV). In this verse, *tsadaq* is used synonymously with *taher,* which means "to cleanse," "to purify." The two statements in the text are parallel. In other words, to be justified is to be clean or pure.

Job 4:17 establishes the linguistic connection between Daniel 8:14 and Leviticus 16:19, 30. Leviticus 16 uses the verb *taher* ("to cleanse") in speaking of the cleansing of the sanctuary and the people on the Day of Atonement. Daniel 8 uses the verb *tsadaq* ("to justify") in speaking of God's work in the sanctuary. But according to Job 4:17, the verb *to justify* means *to cleanse, to purify.* In Job 4:17 *tsadaq* and *taher* are synonymous. It was, therefore, appropriate for Bible translators to render *tsadaq* by cleanse in Daniel 8:14.

Job 15:14 translates from the Hebrew text: "What is man, that he should be clean? and he which is born of a woman, that he should be righteous [justified]?" (KJV). The first verb in the Hebrew text is *zakah* that means "to be clear," "to be clean," "to be pure."[8] The second verb is the verb *to justify* (*tsadaq*). The two questions in the text are parallel. Thus to be clean is to be justified (or righteous). Again it is apparent that the verb *to justify* means "to cleanse," "to make clean." (Compare Job 25:4.)

Job 22:3 translates from the Hebrew: "Is it any pleasure to the Almighty, that thou art righteous [justified]? or is it gain to him, that thou makest thy ways perfect?" (KJV). Thus to be righteous or justified is to be perfect. The first verb in the text is *tsadaq*; the second is *tamam* that means "to finish," "to complete," "to perfect," "to destroy uncleanness."[9]

When believers are justified in the Old Testament, they are declared righteous because they are cleansed by God. The verb *to justify* includes the idea of cleansing. This is why the ancient rabbis who translated the Septuagint translated the verb *to justify* in Daniel 8:14 by the Greek verb *to cleanse.* And it is why so many other translators have done the same thing.

A second linguistic link between Daniel 8:14 and Leviticus 16 is the fact that the same Hebrew word for *sanctuary* is used in both passages. The Hebrew word for sanctuary used in Daniel 18:14 is *qodesh*. The same word is used seven times in Leviticus 16 (verses 2, 3, 16, 20, 23, 27, 33). In each instance of this word in Leviticus 16 the reference is to the Most Holy Place of the earthly sanctuary. In the same chapter, the Holy Place is spoken of as "the tabernacle of the congregation." Hence, the use of the word *qodesh* (sanctuary) has reference to the special judgment ministry carried on in the Most Holy Place by the high priest on the Day of Atonement, the 10th day of the seventh month of the Israelite religious year.

Considering Daniel 8:14 as referring to the heavenly *qodesh*, the sanctuary in heaven (Heb. 8:1, 2; 9:1-14), we can conclude that Daniel was referring to a heavenly judgment conducted in the Most Holy Place of the heavenly sanctuary. As there was a cleansing on earth, so there is a cleansing in heaven.

How Does Daniel 8:14 Relate to Its Context (Dan. 8:9-13)?

Daniel 8:14 is parallel with Daniel 7:9-14. The heavenly judgment on the basis of books of record described in Daniel 7 is the cleansing of the sanctuary described in Daniel 8:14. How does this heavenly pre-advent judgment answer the question of Daniel 8:13 and bring to an end the destructive work of the little horn power described in verses 9-12?

1. The pre-advent judgment, the cleansing of the heavenly sanctuary, vindicates the persecuted people of God. Daniel 7:22 emphasizes this point. The persecution of the saints (Dan. 7:21; cf. 8:10) continued "until the Ancient of Days came [to the heavenly pre-advent judgment; see verses 9, 10] and judgment was rendered in favor of the holy ones of the Most High." (Dan. 7:22, JPS). Hence, the pre-advent judgment of Daniel 7:9-14 and 8:14 vindicates God's persecuted people. The record of their forgiven sin is ultimately abolished, they are exonerated from the accusations and attacks of their spiritual and physical enemies, and they are prepared to meet their returning Lord.

2. The pre-advent judgment, the cleansing of the heavenly sanctuary, restores the place of Christ's sanctuary in the sense that at this time God directs His faithful people to look away from earthly, man-made religion and priestly mediation to the mediation and vindication of Jesus Christ in the heavenly sanctuary. The message of Hebrews 7–10 is now understood.

Christ is our High Priest. No earthly ministry can successfully usurp His Divine mediatorial and judgmental authority.

3. The adherents of a false, human system of religion (the little horn power) are judged and condemned as were those Israelites who on the Day of Atonement refused to enter into the spiritual experience that God had for them. The pre-advent judgment only vindicates Christ's *faithful* people (Dan. 12:1); the remainder are subject to condemnation and ultimate rejection.

Thus the cleansing of the heavenly sanctuary beginning in 1844, as predicted in Daniel 8:14, relates directly to the context (Dan. 8:9-13). The opposed and persecuted people of God are vindicated, the little horn power is condemned, Christ is exalted as the only true Mediator and Judge, and His work in the heavenly sanctuary is restored to its rightful place as the focus of the faith of His loyal followers.

Why Is the Pre-Advent Judgment Important to You?

In the pre-advent, investigative judgment believers are judged on the basis of their works (see Rev. 22:12; compare Ps. 62:12; Jer. 17:10; Matt. 16:27; 2 Cor. 5:10; 1 Peter 1:17; Rev. 20:12). Because they have accepted salvation by faith in Jesus Christ (Rom. 3:21-24; Eph. 2:8-10) and a continuous born-again relationship with Him, they are doing works that are acceptable in His sight (see 1 John 2:29). They are "righteous, just as He is righteous" (1 John 3:7) because He is living out His life through them (Gal. 2:20). "Their deeds have been done in God" (John 3:21). Their good works are the result of, and give evidence of their faith-grace fellowship with Christ (Rom. 3:31; 8:3, 4). Because they have accepted and applied Christ's promise that he is able to keep them from falling (Jude 24), they are eternally vindicated in the pre-advent judgment, and their names are retained in the book of life (Dan. 12:1). They have victory over sin, for "in their mouth no lie was found; they are blameless" (Rev. 14:5). These sealed, vindicated believers will be the righteous living on the earth when Jesus comes.

These are the faithful ones to whom Jesus referred in the parable of the wedding and the wedding banquet (Matt. 22:1-14). "But when the king came in to see the guests, he noticed a man there who was not wearing a wedding robe, and he said to him, 'Friend, how did you get in here without a wedding robe?' And he was speechless. Then the king said to the attendants, 'Bind him hand and foot, and throw him into the outer darkness, where there will be weeping and gnashing of teeth.' For many are called, but few are chosen'" (Matt. 22:11-14).

The many are called and the few chosen before the second coming of Jesus. No one is chosen, taken to heaven, and then put out of heaven because of not having on a wedding garment. The decision is made before the second coming of Jesus as to who belongs at the wedding and the wedding banquet. This decision is made in the same pre-advent judgment described in Daniel, chapters 7 and 8. Those wearing the robe of Christ's righteousness have their names retained in the book of life (Rev. 3:5). Those not clothed with Christ's righteousness have their names removed from the book of life. This decision is made *before* not *after* Jesus comes.

"Let us rejoice and exult and give him the glory, for the marriage of the Lamb has come, and his bride has made herself ready; to her it has been granted to be clothed with fine linen, bright and pure' — for the fine linen is the righteous deeds of the saints" (Rev. 19:7, 8). The bride, the church of Jesus Christ, is made ready for the Lord's coming and the heavenly banquet to follow (Rev. 19:9) by accepting the gift of Christ's righteousness (compare 1 John 2:29). Jesus used somewhat different imagery in His parable of the wedding feast. In His parable the guests are the ones made ready by being clothed with the heavenly garment of righteousness. But Jesus' meaning is the same as John's in the book of Revelation. God's people are made ready to meet their Lord by receiving the gift of Christ's righteousness. This is the only acceptable qualification for heaven. Those who refuse this gift are excluded from the kingdom of grace in the pre-advent judgment. Those who accept this gift are the sealed, vindicated believers who are the righteous living on the earth when Jesus comes. These are the ones who enjoy the magnificence of the heavenly banquet described in Matthew 22:11-14 and Revelation 19:9.

Since God "has fixed a day on which he will judge the world in righteousness" (Acts 17:31, RSV), since that day has arrived and the heavenly judgment is in progress, since we are judged by our works, and since our works are right in God's sight only as we are filled with the Holy Spirit (1 John 4:13-17), it is of first importance that at this very time we draw very near to Christ. To delay coming to the Lord could very well involve us in eternal ruin. Only as we enter into the fullest possible fellowship with Jesus will we be sheltered from the deceptions of the last days. Only as He is dwelling in our hearts by the Holy Spirit will we be kept from sinning and empowered to live as Jesus asks. The pre-advent judgment will decide every person's eternal destiny. Those who receive Christ's victory over sin will have their names kept in the book of life and will be sealed with the seal of the living God. Those who refuse Christ's victory will have their names taken out of the book of life, will receive the mark of the beast, and will be eternally lost. (See Rev. 14:6-12.)

Where do you stand, dear friend, at this solemn time of judgment?

"The judgment has set,
the books have been opened;
How shall we stand in that great day
when every thought, and word, and action,
God, the righteous Judge, shall weigh?

"O, how shall we stand that
moment of searching,
when all our sins those books reveal?
When from that court,
each case decided, shall be granted no appeal?"

– F. E. Belden[10]

The question is one that only you can answer. But we plead with you to give your life totally to Christ so that He can present His mercy and righteousness for you in the judgment.

Notes

1. The period during which the little horn power of Daniel 7 functions leads up to the pre-advent judgment (Dan. 7:25, 26). It would make no sense to interpret the "time, two times, and half a time" as three and one half literal years. This prophecy, like the time prophecies of Daniel 8 and 9, calls for the year-day principle, by which a day in symbolic Bible prophecy represents a year. (Compare Num 14:34; Ezek. 4:6.) A "time" in Bible prophecy means a year. (See Dan. 4:16 and 11:13.) A prophetic time or year is 360 days. Two times or years is 720 days. Half a time or year is 180 days. Therefore, three and one half times is 1260 days. Since a day in symbolic Bible prophecy represents a year, the 1260 days of Daniel 7:25 represents 1260 years. Further evidence for the 1260-year reign of the little horn power is found in six other Bible passages, all of which refer to the same period: Dan. 12:7; Rev. 11:2, 3; 12:6, 14; 13:5. Since a prophetic month had 30 days, 42 months comprise 1260 days.

   The 1260 years of Papal ecclesiastical supremacy began in A.D. 538 when Justinian's decree of 533, recognizing the Bishop of Rome as head of all the churches east and west, went into effect. The 1260 years ended in 1798 when Napoleon's general took the Pope prisoner. This was an event that symbolized the loss of Papal ecclesiastical supremacy in Western Europe at the time of the French Revolution.

2. *Tanakh: the Holy Scriptures. The New JPS Translation According to the Traditional Hebrew Text* (New York: Jewish Publication Society, 1985), s.v. Daniel 7:22.

3. Francis Brown, S. R. Driver, and Charles A. Briggs (eds.), *A Hebrew and English Lexicon of the Old Testament* (Oxford: Clarendon Press, 1951), s.v. *din.*

4. The subject of the verb in the Greek text is *hoi sundouloi auton kai hoi adelphoi;* "their fellow servants and their brethren." These are "about to be killed"; *hoi mellontes apoktennesthai.* The making up of a number is not necessarily germane to the meaning of the verb *pleroo,* and rarely in the Septuagint or the Greek NT does it have that connotation. *Pleroo* means "make full," "fill," "complete," "bring to completion," "finish," "fulfill," "bring to an end." In the KJV, the RSV, and the NRSV of Revelation 3:2, *pleroo* is translated by the English verb "to perfect." Revelation 6:11 is correctly translated, "And there was given to them each a white robe and it was said to them that they should rest yet a little time, until their fellow servants and their brethren, who are about to be killed as they were, might be made complete (perfect)."
5. Some scholars argue that the 2,300 days are either 2,300 literal days (6 years 4 months) in the reign of Antiochus Epiphanes or 1150 days (half 2,300 or 3 years 2 months) in the same reign. Those who argue for 1150 days regard the evenings-mornings as a reference to the morning and evening sacrifices. Twenty-three hundred such sacrifices would amount to 1150 days because the sacrifices were offered morning and evening. But the phrase *ereb boqer* (evening-morning) will not allow for such an interpretation. The phrase, as used throughout the Old Testament, refers to a twenty-four hour period. Thus the reference is to 2,300 days.
6. *Chathak* means "to cut," "cut off," "to decide." See Brown, Driver, and Briggs, *A Hebrew and English Lexicon of the Old Testament.*
7. *Nitsdaq* is the passive form of the verb *tsadaq* that means *to justify.*
8. Brown, Driver, and Briggs, *A Hebrew and English Lexicon of the Old Testament,* s.v. *zakah.*
9. *Ibid.,* s.v. *tamam.*
10. *The Seventh-day Adventist Hymnal* (Washington, D.C., Review and Herald Publishing Association, 1985), p. 416.

Chapter 11
Is Israel Still God's Chosen Nation?

Many Protestant Christians give a positive answer to this question. They regard the establishment of the nation Israel in 1948 as the beginning of the fulfillment of Old Testament prophecies dealing with the return of the Jews to their own land. They regard "the Six-day War, in June 1967, and its aftermath" as "an indication that history proceeds according to their understanding of God's plans for humanity. The history of the state of Israel provides them with encouragement and hope."[1] They believe that, during the millennium after the glorious appearing of Christ, the Old Testament promises to Israel as a nation will be completely fulfilled.

Most of those who hold this view are known as dispensationalists. Dispensationalism is a branch of evangelical Protestantism formulated in the nineteenth century by an Irish cleric, J. N. Darby (1800-1882), who became the leader of the Plymouth Brethren. Darby made numerous overseas lecture tours during which he succeeded in convincing leading and influential adherents of other denominations that his biblical interpretations were correct.[2]

The main lines of dispensational teaching systematized by Darby are as follows:[3]

1. *World history has been divided into "dispensations."* These are periods during which God has worked in different ways to save mankind. Some dispensationalists have identified seven such dispensations. For example, salvation between Sinai and the Cross was by law keeping; since the Cross salvation has been by grace alone.[4] In every dispensation man has failed to fulfill the divine will.

2. *The compartmentalization of Scripture.* Scripture is divided according to classes of people and dispensations. No single passage can have primary application to two dispensations at the same time. For example, it must be determined which are kingdom passages, referring to the Jewish kingdom on earth during the millennium, and which passages may be applied to Christians.[5]

3. *The literal interpretation of Scripture.* All conservative interpreters of the Bible believe that the Scriptures should be interpreted literally. But a literal interpretation of Scripture involves recognition of the symbolic nature of some passages. Apocalyptic prophecy makes a considerable use of symbolism. Dispensationalists insist on giving a literal interpretation to passages that are clearly intended to be symbolic or allegorical.

4. *The dichotomy between Israel and the church.* The Old Testament promises to Israel will be literally fulfilled at the end of time. They are not fulfilled for the Christian Church as spiritual Israel.[6]

One of the terms of the Abrahamic covenant was God's unconditional promise that Israel would have everlasting possession of the land of Palestine. Richard W. DeHaan wrote: "The descendants of Abraham were given the land of Canaan in a free, unconditional, and unchangeable grant from God."[7]

Dispensationalist Bible interpreters regard the Mosaic covenant as conditional, by contrast with the Abrahamic covenant which is unconditional.[8] The promise of the land through Moses was subject to the condition of obedience to God.[9] But the promise of the land to Abraham was unconditional. Irrespective of Israel's spiritual failure and rejection of the Messiah, at the end of time the land of Palestine will be fully restored to the Jews, and all the covenant promises to them as a chosen nation will be fulfilled.

John F. Walvoord, a recent leader of the premillennial dispensationalists, wrote: "All the major prophets and practically all the minor prophets have Messianic sections picturing the restoration and glory of Israel in this future kingdom."[10] The establishment of the nation Israel in 1948 is thought by the dispensationalists to have begun the fulfillment of the Old Testament prophecies in regard to the return of the Jews to their own land. Hal Lindsey wrote, "The one event which many Bible students in the past overlooked was this paramount prophetic sign: Israel had to be a nation again in the land of its forefathers."[11]

According to dispensationalists, when Jesus was on earth He offered the earthly kingdom to the Jews. Because they rejected it, the fulfillment of the Old Testament prophecies in regard to their rulership of Palestine and predominance over the nations could not be immediately put into effect. Of necessity there came a gap of centuries during which the Christian Church has played a separate and distinctive role designed by God. But this role is not a spiritual fulfillment of the Old Testament prophecies regarding Israel. The period of Christian Church history is a parenthesis, not foreseen by the Old Testament prophets and not designed to fulfill their forecasts. This period of the Church will come to an end when the Christian saints are secretly raptured seven years before the glorious appearing of Christ in the clouds of heaven.

5. *A Jewish concept of the kingdom.* The future kingdom is not the kingdom of Christ but a restoration of the Jewish kingdom which was not established in Christ's day because the Jews rejected it. Jesus preached the gospel of the kingdom. But the gospel of grace was not preached until the Christian Church was instituted. Then grace was revealed to Paul. The kingdom of God is the universal reign of God in human hearts. The kingdom of heaven, by contrast, is the earthly rule of God promised to the Jews. It will be established on this earth at the second advent of Christ.

6. *The pre-tribulation rapture.* The church is secretly raptured before a seven-year tribulation. Thus the church will not pass through the end-time tribulation. God's plan for Israel will be fulfilled after the church has been taken up to heaven. (We will consider the Bible teaching on the secret rapture in the next chapter.)

Clarence B. Bass rejects the view that the secret rapture doctrine is a legitimate aspect of premillennialism: "Unknowingly, many identify this as the only premillennial position, although in the entire history of prophetic interpretation this idea is unknown. Premillennialists have always believed that Christ would return personally, literally, and visibly to establish the millennial reign, but only with the advent of dispensationalism has the pre-tribulation concept emerged."[12]

7. *The purpose of the great tribulation.* The last seven years of this earth's history after the rapture of the Christian saints and before the glorious second coming of Christ are said to be the final week of Daniel's seventy-week prophecy (Dan. 9:24-27). During this seven-year period the great tribulation predicted by Daniel and Christ will occur.

The seven-year period is divided into two periods of three and one-half years each. During the first three and one-half years Israel enters into a covenant with the Antichrist. But at the end of this period the Antichrist breaks the covenant and begins a three and one-half year persecution of the Jews. This is all said to be in fulfillment of Daniel 9:27: "And he shall confirm the covenant with many for one week: and in the midst of the week he shall cause the sacrifice and the oblation to cease, and for the overspreading of abominations he shall make it desolate, even until the consummation, and that determined shall be poured upon the desolate" (KJV).

DeHaan explains: "He [the Antichrist] will make a seven-year pact with Israel. . . . The Jews, at least a representative group, will be in the land of Palestine, and they will feel secure in this agreement with the wicked prince, who is the Antichrist. He will honor this contract for about three and one-half years. During that time a temple will be built by the Jews, and they will set up some form of worship. Suddenly, however, this world dictator will turn against them, and on the very wing of their temple he will erect an image which he will insist they must worship."

DeHaan applies Daniel 9:27 and Matthew 24:15, 16 to this period and adds: "Other Scripture passages, including II Thessalonians 2:4 and Revelation 12:14-18, indicate that an image will be erected by the coming Antichrist, and that refusal to worship this idol will trigger a period of dreadful persecution, primarily for the Jews, but for all the other inhabitants of the earth as well."[13]

During the seven-year tribulation a literal 144,000 Jews, who have been genuinely converted to Christianity, will evangelize the world and win a multitude of converts to the faith. DeHann continues: "The great tribulation, which will follow the rapture of the Church, will be the means of Israel's conversion and this will precede the glorious second coming of the Lord Jesus Christ to this earth. During the tribulation, the world will experience its most grievous time in history. . . .

"The brighter side of the picture can be seen in chapter 7 of Revelation. God seals 144,000 Jews who apparently turn to Him in genuine faith early in the tribulation, and they become His witnesses. God supernaturally protects them, and they boldly proclaim His message. As a result of their ministry, a great multitude from every nation, kindred and tongue are saved (Revelation 7:9), many of whom will die in that day of trouble (Revelation 7:14). God, however, will preserve a remnant of saved Jews who will enter the millennium. The 144,000 who are sealed in Revelation 7 are still intact when we see them in Revelation 14. This is the nucleus of a godly remnant who will welcome our Lord when He comes to reign."[14]

8. *The nature of Christ's millennial reign.* The Jews and other peoples who refuse to accept Christ during the seven-year tribulation will be put to death, either during the tribulation or at the glorious appearing of Christ. They will not be raised to enjoy the millennium with Christ on this earth. During the millennium (1,000 years) Christ will reign from Jerusalem, and David will be His regent. The Old Testament prophecies regarding the full and complete restoration of Israel finally will be fulfilled. Israel as the chosen nation will be the center of the earth, and all other nations of the saved will give their allegiance to her.

"The temple is to be rebuilt and the sacrifices reinstituted. The relation of this sacrificial system to the death of Christ is 'commemorative,' not anticipatory. By temple ritual and a system of sacrifice Israel is to commemorate the wonders of the death of Christ, even as she unknowingly did by way of anticipation in the Old Testament."[15]

Some dispensationalists say that the Church will return to earth at the beginning of the millennium and have a place of honor along with Israel. Others say that during the 1,000 years the Church will dwell in the holy city hovering above the earth.

9. *The eternal state.* At the end of the millennium, the new Jerusalem of Revelation 21 and 22 will be the home of the Church, the redeemed of Israel, and the redeemed of all ages.

The whole scenario depends upon the idea of the unconditional promise of the land in the Abrahamic covenant and the unconditional promise of complete restoration of the Jews after the period of Babylonian captivity. The northern ten tribes were taken captive by Assyria in 722 B.C., and Judah was taken captive in three invasions of Nebuchadnezzar of Babylon (605, 597, 586 B.C.). Old Testament prophets predicted that, though God's chosen people would be punished for their sin, they would once more be restored to the promised land and would be given national greatness and glory. The dispensationalists regard these prophecies as unconditional. They are certain to be fulfilled literally, despite the Jews' rejection of Christ and the giving of the Gospel to the Gentiles.

In recent years "progressive" dispensationalists have considerably revised the classic formulation of the teaching provided by J. N. Darby, C. I.

Scofield, and Lewis Chafer. Although John F. Walvoord, Charles C. Ryrie and others provided some revisions of the theological system, recently more radical revisions have been provided by so-called progressive dispensationalists.[16] Even so, as pointed out by Darrell L. Bock, progressive dispensationalists still adhere to certain of the fundamental tenets taught by Darby.

Bock writes: "Despite these fresh emphases on continuity and circum-spection about prophetic detail, certain other positions within this approach are parallel to previous forms of dispensationalism. Progressive dispensationalism still believes in the future of Israel in a land involving an earthly millennium and making a distinction between Israel and the church. ... A pretribulational rapture (the belief that Jesus gathers the church be-fore embarking on his return to judge the world and set up the Millen-nium) is still held to by the vast majority."[17]

The questions raised by dispensationalism must be settled by a careful study of the Scriptures. What does the Bible say about the Abrahamic cov-enant? Was it the same as the covenant given through Moses? Was the prom-ise of the land conditional or unconditional? Did Jesus Christ offer the Jews an earthly kingdom or a heavenly one? What happened to their cho-sen nation status after they had rejected Christ? Were they still regarded by heaven as the chosen people for whom the Old Testament promises would be literally fulfilled? Or were they rejected as the chosen people? Is the pe-riod of Christian Church history an unforeseen parenthesis? Is it God's plan to restore Israel to national greatness, or are Jews in the Gospel age promised a part in the heavenly kingdom on exactly the same basis as other believers, an individual acceptance of Christ as Savior and Lord? These are the questions that we must address in this chapter.

The Promises of the Abrahamic Covenant Were Conditional

There is no Scriptural basis for the argument that the Abrahamic cov-enant promises were unconditional while those of the Mosaic covenant were conditional. The terms God offered Abraham were identical to those He offered Israel at Sinai. Therefore the blessings promised to Israel at Sinai on condition of their obedience to the covenant and the curses promised on condition of their disobedience all applied to the Abrahamic covenant just as surely as they did to the Mosaic covenant. The promise of the land to Abraham applied to his literal descendants only on condition that they remained true to God. The loss of the land resulted from their disobedience.

God's approach to Abraham as recorded in Genesis 17 indicates that there were conditions to His promises. The covenant could only be everlasting to Abraham and his descendants if they were loyal to these conditions. God said to Abraham, "'I am God Almighty; walk before me, and be blameless. And I will make my covenant between me and you, and will make you exceedingly numerous" (Gen. 17:1, 2). After giving the promise of the land for "a perpetual holding" (verse 8), the Lord added the condition: "God said to Abraham, 'As for you, *you shall keep my covenant*, you and your offspring after you throughout their generations" (verse 9, italics supplied).

Then the Lord gave the command that every male in Israel was to be circumcised (Gen. 17:10, 11). It is clear that circumcision was to be the outward sign of the heart relationship between Israelites and their God. God wanted them to be circumcised in heart (Deut. 10:16; 30:6). Circumcision of the heart is the same spiritual experience that is taught in the New Testament (Rom. 2:25-29). Abraham and his seed could not walk before God and be perfect merely by practicing outward circumcision. The Lord was looking for a heart relationship with His people, of which the practice of circumcision was to be the outward sign. Paul gives the real meaning of circumcision when he says: "He [Abraham] received the sign of circumcision as a seal of the righteousness that he had by faith while he was still uncircumcised. The purpose was to make him the ancestor of all who believe without being circumcised and who thus have righteousness reckoned to them, and likewise the ancestor of the circumcised who are not only circumcised but who also follow the example of the faith that our ancestor Abraham had before he was circumcised" (Rom. 4:11, 12).

Genesis 15 records: "And he [Abraham] believed the Lord; and the Lord reckoned it to him as righteousness" (Gen. 15:6). Then is recorded how God made the covenant with Abraham (verses 7-21). Suppose Abraham had not believed in the Lord and received the gift of his righteousness, would God have made the covenant with him, giving him the promise of the land? Of course not! And suppose Abraham had refused God's command that he should be obedient to His will (Gen. 17:1), would the Lord have restated His promises and given him the sign of circumcision? Since circumcision was the sign of a spiritual experience already enjoyed by Abraham, we can only conclude that, if he had not had that experience, the Lord would never have commanded him to practice the sign. And suppose Abraham or his seed had refused to keep the covenant that God had commanded (Gen. 17:9), would God's promises have been fulfilled for them? The indication in Genesis 17 is that everything depended on Abraham's and his descendants' faithfulness to God. The promise that the Israelites should inherit and continually possess the land of Palestine was conditional upon their faithfulness.

When Abraham had a son by Hagar, he spoiled God's plan of miraculously demonstrating that salvation is by faith not by human works. Paul refers to this as Abraham's lapse from the everlasting covenant relationship (Gal. 4:22-31). Only by breaking off the relationship with Hagar could Abraham renew his covenant standing with God and again become the heir to the divine promises.

The Lord offered Israel at Sinai the same covenant relationship that He had given Abraham. The Lord offered them "my covenant" (Exod. 19:5). This is the same "my covenant" spoken of nine times in Genesis 17. How appropriate that God should offer Israel at Sinai the same covenant terms that he had offered Abraham! After all, he had promised Abraham: "I will establish my covenant between me and you, *and your offspring after you throughout their generations*, for an everlasting covenant, to be God to you and to your offspring after you" (Gen. 17:7; italics supplied).

The New Testament teaches that the Abrahamic covenant applied to Israel at Sinai. Paul wrote to the Galatians: "My point is this: the law, which came four hundred thirty years later, does not annul a covenant previously ratified by God, so as to nullify the promise. For if the inheritance comes from the law, it no longer comes from the promise; but God granted it to Abraham through the promise" (Gal. 3:17, 18). So the giving of the law at Sinai did not change the terms of the covenant. God offered Israel the same covenant He had offered Abraham.

God commanded His covenant "for a thousand generations" (1 Chron. 16:15). This is "the covenant that he made with Abraham, his sworn promise to Isaac, which he confirmed to Jacob as a statute, to Israel as an everlasting covenant, saying, 'To you I will give the land of Canaan as your portion for an inheritance'" (verses 16-18).

Although God offered the Israelites the same righteousness by faith relationship that he gave Abraham, they did not make a genuine heart response. They said, "'Everything that the Lord has spoken we will do'" (Exod. 19:8; compare 24:3, 7). But their hearts were not in their words (Deut. 5:28, 29). They broke God's covenant by refusing the experience of Deuteronomy 6:4-6 and by turning to their man-made gods (Exod. 32; compare Jer. 31:32). God found fault with His chosen people (Heb. 8:8) "for they did not continue in my covenant" (verse 9). The faulty covenant of man's own works, by which he separates himself from a faith-grace union with God, is called the "first," or "old" covenant (Heb. 8:7, 13), because it was Israel's first experience at Sinai. By contrast, the "new" covenant (verse 8) is the Abrahamic or everlasting covenant of righteousness by faith which Israel accepted at Sinai after God had rebuked their sin (Exod. 34; 35). But throughout their history the Israelites tended to turn away from God, forgetting His covenant and lapsing into a self-made religion of works. (See Jeremiah 7.)

In the New Testament, the ceremonial law is sometimes included in the first or old covenant (compare Heb. 7:15-28; 8:1-7; 9:1, 11-15), not because it was to be the means by which Israelites earned salvation, but because it was necessary in view of the people's dismal failure to maintain faith in God. The people's old covenant failure necessitated a simple visual aid to faith, the ceremonial law. It provided an imperfect analogy of the future ministry of Jesus Christ. The sanctuary/temple ceremonies were to be performed by faith. But since these ceremonies were necessitated by the people's spiritual failure, and since they were an imperfect foreshadowing of the Messiah's work, they were regarded as part of the first or old covenant. As such, they were done away at the Cross.

The Lord told the Israelites who inherited the Abrahamic covenant promises (1 Chron. 16:14-18) that if they did not continue to maintain their covenant relationship with Him, they would be cursed physically and materially and expelled from the promised land. The message of Deuteronomy 29:9-13 is that "this covenant" (verse 9) given to Israel was the same one that "he swore to your ancestors, to Abraham, to Isaac, and to Jacob" (verse 13). Faithfulness to it would result in great blessings (Deut. 28:1-14), but unfaithfulness would bring terrible curses (verses 15-68). The Lord could not have been more explicit; rejection of His presence in the heart and of obedience to His commands would result in expulsion from the land of promise: "And just as the Lord took delight in making you prosperous and numerous, so the Lord will take delight in bringing you to ruin and destruction; you shall be plucked off the land that you are entering to possess. The Lord will scatter you among all peoples, from one end of the earth to the other; and there you shall serve other gods, of wood and stone, which neither you nor your ancestors have known" (Deut. 28:63, 64).

The promises of the Abrahamic covenant could have been fulfilled to Israel, and she could have become the predominant nation on earth, used of God to preserve His truth and to disseminate His love. But the original promises to Abraham, repeated through Moses, were conditional upon the continuing faithfulness of the people. Restoration after national calamity and captivity by other nations was dependent on repentance and submission to God's loving will. Bible history and prophetic forecasts underline that Israel as a nation has not and will not fulfill God's conditions. This is why there remains no divine purpose to fulfill the promises to Abraham regarding Israel's national superiority.

God's Promises to Restore the Land to Israel after the Captivity Were Conditional

Dispensationalists treat as unconditional the prophets' predictions regarding Israel's restoration after the Babylonian captivity. But the condition under which the Lord would return His people from the land of their captivity is stated quite simply: "When all these things have happened to you, the blessings and the curses that I have set before you, if you call them to mind among all the nations where the Lord your God has driven you, and return to the Lord your God, and you and your children obey him with all your heart and with all your soul, just as I am commanding you today, then the Lord your God will restore your fortunes and have compassion on you, gathering you again from all the peoples among whom the Lord your God has scattered you" (Deut. 30:1-3).

Having been restored to the promised land, Israel would be prospered if they would obey the commandments of the Lord (verse 9, 10). God visualized a faithful, obedient people who had learned the lessons of history so thoroughly that they would not wish to depart from His service again. They were to be cleansed from sin, filled with His Spirit, and were to live in conformity with the requirements of His law (Ezek. 36:24-33). "They shall never again defile themselves with their idols and their detestable things, or with any of their transgressions. I will save them from all the apostasies into which they have fallen, and will cleanse them. Then they shall be my people, and I will be their God" (Eze. 37:23). The Lord would make an "everlasting covenant" with them, dwelling perpetually among them and blessing them with spiritual and national superiority (verses 26-28).

Shortly after their restoration to Palestine, the Jews began breaking their covenant with God, failing to observe His Sabbath day, and living contrary to His will. Nehemiah expressed his concern that God's wrath would once again be brought upon Israel (Neh. 13:18), and he took very decided steps to insure that the people would reform their ways (verses 19-31).

The covenant that Jeremiah declared God would make with Israel after the captivity was a repetition of the everlasting covenant given to Abraham (Jer. 31:31-36). It contained both conditions and promises. God's law was to be written on the people's hearts; they were to know Him and to serve Him (verses 33, 34). This was the condition that would result in Israel never being rejected as the Lord's faithful people (verses 36, 37). But what if the people refused to allow the Lord to come into their hearts by His Spirit? What if they refused to obey His law and walk only in His ways? His promises could not then be fulfilled. Just as the curses of Deuteronomy 28 were fulfilled when Israel and Judah were taken captive by the Assyrians and Babylonians, so once again His unfaithful people would be rejected and scattered.

During the Babylonian captivity, Daniel actually predicted that, because of their rejection of the Messiah, probation would close for Israel as a nation, and it would be dismembered by its enemies (Daniel 9:24-27). There was no promise of restoration after Daniel's 490-year prophecy came to an end in A.D. 34.

The same conditions and promises are for us today as for ancient Israel. Even though in this life we may have suffering, sickness, and calamity, if we are willing to live for God, allowing His Spirit to abide in our hearts, He will preserve us for eternity. But if we reject Christ and live according to worldly ways and standards, we can only expect ultimate eternal loss.

Israel Failed to Fulfill the Conditions

The centuries after Israel's return from Babylonian captivity were notable for increased apostasy, deepening moral and spiritual decline, along with growing national pride and political corruption.

Malachi forcefully denounced the moral and spiritual corruption of restored Israel (Mal. 1:6; 2:1-17). In the centuries before the time of Jesus the nation descended to such depths of spiritual perversion that the Lord could not bless His chosen people. Jesus spoke of the arrogance, legalism, and hypocrisy of the Jewish religious leaders (Mark 7:6-9; Matt. 23). Man's laws had taken the place of God's laws, and religion had degenerated into a means of self-aggrandizement and money making.

Finally the nation rejected Jesus Christ as the Messiah, claiming, "We have no king but Caesar" (John 19:15, KJV). Little did the Jewish people realize that when they asserted, "His blood be on us and on our children" (Matt. 27:25), they were inviting heaven's final rejection of their nation as the chosen people and a repeated outpouring of the divine curses stipulated by Moses (Deut. 28). Jesus' predictions came true: "Therefore I tell you, the kingdom of God will be taken away from you and given to a people that produces the fruits of the kingdom" (Matt. 21:43). "See, your house is left to you, desolate" (Matt. 23:38). No assurance of reinstatement as God's chosen people was given to Israel after they had rejected Christ. Daniel's predicted period of probation finally came to an end with the stoning of Stephen (A.D. 34), and the Christian Church assumed its role as the international custodian of the oracles of the faith.

Jesus never offered Israel of His day an earthly kingdom, as the dispensationalists teach. Always He emphasized the spiritual nature of the kingdom. "The kingdom of God is within you" (Luke 17:21, KJV). "My kingdom is not of this world: if my kingdom were of this world, then would my servants fight" (John 18:36, KJV). The kingdom of grace in human hearts will merge at the end of history into the kingdom of glory (Luke 17:24; Matt. 25:34). When the people tried to take Jesus by force and make Him a king, He determinedly refused (John 6:15). Had the Jews accepted Him, undoubtedly they would have been retained as the chosen people to make known His salvation in the earth and to prepare the world for the eternal kingdom. But Jesus' purpose was not to establish an earthly kingdom at that time.

The dispensationalists' distinction between the "kingdom of heaven" as the earthly Israelite kingdom planned by God and the "kingdom of God" as the heavenly kingdom for all who believe is not supported by the biblical evidence. George E. Ladd comments: "It is to be noted at the outset that the two expressions seem to be quite interchangeable in the Gospels.... A few illustrations must suffice. In Matthew, Jesus begins his ministry with the announcement that the kingdom of heaven is near (Matt. 4:17), but in Mark he announces that the kingdom of God has come near and men are to repent and believe in the Gospel (Mark 1:15). In Matthew, the twelve offer the kingdom of heaven to Israel (Matt. 10:6-7), but in Luke they offer the kingdom of God (Luke 9:2). If in Matthew the Sermon on the Mount announced as the law of the kingdom of heaven is the law of the future earthly kingdom (Matt. 5:3), in Luke it is announced as something else, the law of the kingdom of God (Luke 6:20). According to Matthew the parables portray the mystery of the kingdom of heaven (Matt. 13:11), but in Mark (4:11) and in Luke (8:10) it is the kingdom of God. If in Matthew a Jewish remnant is to announce at the end of the age the good news that the earthly kingdom, the kingdom of heaven, is about to be set up (Matt. 24:14), then Mark says something quite different — that the *gospel* must be preached first to all the nations (Mark 13:10).

"Furthermore, if such a distinction is to be made, no adequate explanation has been suggested for the four times the expression 'kingdom of God' occurs in Matthew. One illustration will suffice. After the conversation with the rich young ruler, Jesus said to His disciples, 'Verily, I say unto you, it is hard for a rich man to enter into the kingdom of heaven. And again I say unto you, It is easier for a camel to go through the needle's eye, than for a rich man to enter into the kingdom of God' (Matt. 19:23-24). Here the two terms are clearly synonymous, and both are equivalent to salvation, eternal life. . . ."[18]

The Christian Church Is Spiritual Israel Which Has Replaced Literal Israel as God's Chosen People

Consider the teaching of the following Bible passages:

Galatians 3:9, 27-29: "For this reason, those who believe are blessed with Abraham who believed." "As many of you as were baptized into Christ have clothed yourselves with Christ. There is no longer Jew or Greek, there is no longer slave or free, there is no longer male and female; for all of you are one in Christ Jesus. And if you belong to Christ, then you are Abraham's offspring, heirs according to the promise."

Those who have Abraham's faith receive the blessings promised to him. Jews and non-Jews who have received Christ as Savior and Lord are counted as "Abraham's offspring, heirs according to the promise."

Romans 9:6-8, 23-26: "It is not as though the word of God had failed. For not all Israelites truly belong to Israel, and not all of Abraham's children are his true descendants: but 'It is through Isaac that descendants shall be named for you.' This means that it is not the children of the flesh who are the children of God, but the children of the promise are counted as descendants." "And what if he [God] has done so in order to make known the riches of his glory for the objects of mercy, which he has prepared beforehand for glory — including us whom he has called, not from the Jews only but also from the Gentiles? As indeed he says in Hosea, 'Those who were not my people I will call "my people," and her who was not beloved I will call "beloved,"' 'And in the very place where it was said to them "You are not my people," there they shall be called children of the living God.'"

The birth of Isaac was a miracle of God. This represented the fact that salvation is by faith, not by human effort. The true Israel of God are those who have faith in Christ, not those who are the natural children of Abraham. God has called all believers; "not from the Jews only but also from the Gentiles" (Rom. 9:24). Now Hosea 2:23 is fulfilled; Christian believers of all nations have now replaced literal Israel as God's chosen people.

Romans 2:27-29: "Then those who are physically uncircumcised but keep the law will condemn you that have the written code and circumcision but break the law. For a person is not a Jew who is one outwardly, nor is true circumcision something external and physical. Rather, a person is a Jew who is one inwardly, and real circumcision is a matter of the heart — it is spiritual and not literal. Such a person receives praise not from others but from God."

The "physically uncircumcised" are the Gentiles. If they obey God's law by faith in Christ, having His Spirit living in their hearts, they are counted as Jews and numbered among God's faithful ones. Only Jews who have the same spiritual experience are acceptable to God.

1 Corinthians 1:23, 24: "But we proclaim Christ crucified, a stumbling block to Jews and foolishness to Gentiles, but to those who are the called, both Jews and Greeks, Christ the power of God and the wisdom of God."

The message of "Christ crucified" is power and wisdom to both Jews and non-Jews who believe. The method of salvation is identical for both classes.

1 Peter 2:9, 10: "But you are a chosen race, a royal priesthood, a holy nation, God's own people, in order that you may proclaim the mighty acts of him who called you out of darkness into his marvelous light. Once you were not a people, but now you are God's people; once you had not received mercy, but now you have received mercy."

Peter was writing to faithful Christian believers in Gentile countries (1 Peter 1:1, 2). Christian believers of all nationalities are now God's chosen people, even though formerly this was not the case. Peter could not have been more specific in his terminology: "But you are a chosen race, a royal priesthood, a holy nation, God's own people."

Acts 10:34, 35: "Then Peter began to speak to them: 'I truly understand that God shows no partiality, but in every nation anyone who fears him and does what is right is acceptable to him.'"

Because of the vision he had received from God (Acts 10:9-16), dramatizing that the Lord receives believers of any nationality, and the manner in which the Lord led him to the household of Cornelius, Peter was convinced that God's chosen people are those from every nation who have submitted to the lordship of Christ.

The New Testament is thoroughly clear that the Christian Church, comprising all genuine believers in Jesus Christ, has replaced Israel as the chosen nation. Spiritual "Jews" are believers in Christ irrespective of their national heritage.

God's promise to Abraham, "in you all the families of the earth shall be blessed" (Gen. 12:3), has been remarkably fulfilled. Paul underlines the point. "And the scripture, foreseeing that God would justify the Gentiles by faith, declared the gospel beforehand to Abraham saying, 'All the Gentiles shall be blessed in you.' For this reason, those who believe are blessed with Abraham who believed" (Gal. 3:8, 9).

Jesus was a Jew. "Salvation is from the Jews" (John 4:22). Jesus' apostles who made enormous sacrifices to bring the Christian Gospel to the world were Jews. Paul, the great apostle to the Gentiles, was a Jew. Gentile Christians are deeply indebted to Jews for their cooperation with Jesus in launching and fostering the Christian Church and in disseminating the Judeo-Christian tradition.

The Promises of the Abrahamic Covenant Are Fulfilled to Christian Believers, Both Jews and Gentiles

The fact that all Christians are to live under the Abrahamic covenant is a prominent New Testament teaching. The heart of the covenant offered to all Christians is stated in Hebrews 8:10: "This is the covenant that I will make with the house of Israel after those days, says the Lord: I will put my laws in their minds, and write them on their hearts, and I will be their God, and they shall be my people." This is the same covenant promise that was given to Israel through Jeremiah (31:31-33). In fact, Hebrews 8:10 quotes Jeremiah 31:33. The covenant experience for Christian believers of having God's law written on their hearts was the very essence of the covenant between God and the Jews (Deut. 6:4-6). By faith Abraham obeyed God's law (Gen. 26:5), and this experience of righteousness by faith is the heart of the Abrahamic covenant (compare Gen. 17:10, 11 with Rom. 4:11, 23-25). Because Abraham believed God, righteousness was imputed to him. The righteousness of Christ was legally counted for him and bestowed upon him by the gift of the Holy Spirit (compare Rom. 4:1-5 with Gal. 3:5-14).

Paul's message is that, if we believe as Abraham did, we too will have righteousness imputed to us (Rom. 4:22-25). Christ's righteousness will be put to our account and also bestowed upon us by the gift of the Holy Spirit. The presence of the Spirit in our hearts is Christ's presence (John 14:18), and this divine indwelling is righteousness in our hearts (Rom. 8:9, 10).

Abraham's covenant experience is to be the experience of all those who submit to the loving lordship of Christ, whatever their nationality. The promise of Romans 10:10 is for all Christian believers around the world, Jews and Gentiles: "For with the heart one believes unto righteousness, and with the mouth one confesses unto salvation."[19] This identical experience is for Jews and non-Jews, for, in respect to salvation, "there is no distinction between Jew and Greek; the same Lord is Lord of all and is generous to all who call on him" (Rom. 10:12).

The logical conclusion is that, although Israel is no longer God's chosen nation because this status has been transferred to the Christian Church, individual Jews can be saved from sin and given eternal life on exactly the same basis as all Gentiles. By accepting Jesus Christ as Savior and Lord, they are included in the family of God.

This is the message of Romans, chapter 11. The attempt to make the chapter teach that the nation Israel is still God's chosen nation is quite futile. Note the following major points:

1. Some faithful Jews who believe in Christ are counted among the elect of God; the rest of the nation are blind (verses 5-8).

2. All but the believing remnant have been cast away (verses 5, 9, 10).

3. The majority of unbelieving Jews are likened to branches that have been broken off from a parent olive tree (verses 17-20; compare John 15:5). The parent stock is Christ.

4. The only way rejected Jews can be acceptable to God again is by believing in Christ (verse 23).

5. Believing Jews are grafted back into the parent stock again in the same way as believing Gentiles (verse 24).

6. "All Israel" that will be saved (verse 26) is not a reference to the literal nation Israel. Not even dispensationalists believe that the entire nation Israel will be saved. In the context of Romans 11, "all Israel" refers to those Jews who are elect "if they do not persist in unbelief" (verse 23) and those Gentiles who, because of belief in Christ, have been grafted into the parent olive tree. "The full number of the Gentiles" (verse 25) refers to the total number of Gentiles who will become believers in Christ before the end of time. These Gentiles plus the Christian Jews comprise "all Israel," in the New Testament sense of spiritual Israel which has inherited the promises to Abraham.

During the millennium the saved of all ages, including the faithful who lived before the Cross and believing Christians who have lived since then, are all in the heavenly kingdom. Revelation 7:15 speaks of them: "They are before the throne of God, and worship him day and night within his temple." The temple of God is in heaven, not on this earth (Rev. 11:19; 15:5). Not until the end of the millennium does the holy city, New Jerusalem, descend from heaven to this earth (compare Rev. 21:2 with 20:7-9). During the millennium the saved of all ages, including those who have passed through the end-time tribulation (see Dan. 12:1; Rev. 7:14), are occupying thrones in the heavenly temple judging lost human beings and angels (compare Rev. 20:4 with 1 Cor. 6:2, 3).

The idea that the literal nation Israel will be completely restored at the end of history, that during the millennium the Old Testament promises to Israel will be literally fulfilled is an unbiblical teaching. Because the Jews rejected Christ, they lost their chosen nation status, lost the promise that the land of Palestine would be theirs forever, and forfeited their national privilege of being the teachers of the Gospel to an unbelieving world. Our Lord bestowed upon His Church in all the world these covenant promises. The land will, indeed, belong to His people, but it will not be limited to Palestine. It will be first the heavenly Canaan during the millennium, followed by the earth made new at the end of the 1,000 years. Jesus said, "Blessed are the meek, for they will inherit the earth" (Matt. 5:5).

Whatever your national or racial heritage, salvation is for you, if you have accepted Christ as your Savior and Lord. You can trust Him to fulfill for you individually the eternal promises for true believers.

Notes

1. Yaakov Ariel, *On Behalf of Israel: American Fundamentalist Attitudes Toward Jews, Judaism, and Zionism, 1865-1945* (Brooklyn, New York: Carlson Publishing Inc., 1991), p. 121; see also p. 22.

2. *Ibid.*, pp. 25-54; see also Daniel Payton Fuller, "The Hermeneutics of Dispensationalism" (Th.D. dissertation, Northern Baptist Theological Seminary, 1957), pp. 65-137.

3. See Clarence B. Bass, *Backgrounds to Dispensationalism* (Grand Rapids, Michigan: Baker, 1960), pp. 13-47, on which my description of dispensationalism is largely based. See also Charles F. Baker, *Dispensational Theology* (Grand Rapids, Michigan: Grace Bible College Publications, 1971), pp. 583-616; Richard W. DeHaan, *Israel and the Nations in Prophecy* (Grand Rapids, Michigan: Zondervan, 1968), passim; L. E. Froom, *The Prophetic Faith of Our Fathers*, 4 vols. (Washington, D.C.: Review and Herald, 1954), IV:1220-1227; George E. Ladd, *The Blessed Hope* (Grand Rapids, Michigan: Eerdmans, 1956), pp. 5-14, 35-60; *Crucial Questions about the Kingdom of God* (Grand Rapids, Michigan: Eerdmans, 1952), pp. 101-117; Ernest R. Sandeen, *The Roots of Fundamentalism* (Grand Rapids, Michigan; Baker, 1970), pp. 59-80, 101, 136; C. I. Scofield, "The Course and End of the Age," *Bibliotheca Sacra* 108 (January-March, 1951), pp. 105-116; "The Last World Empire and Armageddon," *Ibid.*, 108 (July-September, 1951), pp. 355-362; "The Return of Christ in Relation to the Jew and the Earth," *Ibid.*, 108 (October-December, 1951), pp. 477-487; John F. Walvoord, *The Nations in Prophecy* (Grand Rapids, Michigan: Zondervan, 1967), pp. 41-52, 158-171; "Amillennial Eschatology," *Bibliotheca Sacra* 108 (January-March, 1951), pp. 7-14; "The Historical Context of Premillennialism," *Ibid.*, (April-June, 1951), pp. 153-166; "The Theological Context of Premillennialism," *Ibid.*, (July-September, 1951), pp. 270-281; "The Abrahamic Covenant and Premillennialism," *Ibid.*, (October-December, 1951), pp. 414-422.

4. See Bass, *Backgrounds to Dispensationalism*, pp. 33-36.

5. Daniel Payton Fuller, "The Hermeneutics of Dispensationalism," p. 6.

6. See H. K. LaRondelle, *The Israel of God in Prophecy. Principles of Prophetic Interpretation* (Berrien Springs, MI: Andrews University Press, 1983).

7. DeHaan, *Israel and the Nations in Prophecy*, p. 93.

8. Daniel Payton Fuller, "The Hermeneutics of Dispensationalism," p. 243.

9. Yaakov Ariel, *On Behalf of Israel*, p. 16.

10. John F. Walvoord, "The Historical Context of Premillennialism," *Bibliotheca Sacra* 108 (April-June, 1951), p. 154.

11. Hal Lindsey, *The Late Great Planet Earth* (Grand Rapids, Michigan: Zondervan, 1970), p. 43.

12. Bass, *Backgrounds to Dispensationalism*, p. 38; Daniel Payton Fuller, "The Hermeneutics of Dispensationalism," pp. 15, 18.

13. DeHaan, *Israel and the Nations in Prophecy*, pp. 88, 89.

14. *Ibid.*, p. 99.

15. Bass, *Backgrounds to Dispensationalism*, p. 44.

16. See Craig A. Blaising and Darrell L. Bock, eds. *Dispensationalism, Israel and the Church: The Search for Definition* (Grand Rapids, Mich.: Zondervan, 1992); Darrell L. Bock, "Charting Dispensationalism," *Christianity Today* (September 12, 1994), pp. 26-29; Stanley J. Grenz, *The Millennial Maze* (Downers Grove, Illinois: InterVarsity Press, 1992); Norman R. Gulley, "Dispensational Biblical Interpretation: Its Past and Present Hermeneutical Systems," *Journal of the Adventist Theological Society*, 4/1 (1993): pp. 65-93; "Progressive Dispensationalism: a Review of a Recent Publication," *Andrews University Seminary Studies* (Spring-Summer 1994, Vol. 32, No. 1), pp. 41-46; Robert L. Saucy, "A Rationale for the Future of Israel," *Journal of the Evangelical Theological Society* 28 (1985), pp. 433-442; "The Church as the Mystery of God," in *Israel and the Church: Essays in Contemporary Dispensational Thought*, edited by Craig A. Blaising and Darrell L. Bock (Grand Rapids, Mich.: Zondervan, 1992); *The Case for Progressive Dispensationalism: The Interface Between Dispensational and Non-Dispensational Theology* (Grand Rapids, Mich.: Zondervan, 1993).

Stanley J. Grenz writes: "In recent years, however, the success of dispensationalism has been paralleled by a growing questioning of the received dispensational orthodoxy. Adherents themselves have been tinkering with the system, modifying some of its more objectionable features. Others have abandoned it completely.

There are signs that the dominance of this viewpoint—at least in its classical expression—may be on the wane, just as was the fate of other eschatological systems in previous eras."—*The Millennial Maze*, p. 63. Despite the modifications in the theological system, "dispensationalists of all varieties adamantly reject the contention that the church is the New Israel."—*Ibid.*, p. 96.

Norman R. Gulley lists the changes accepted by progressive dispensationalists: "(1) Progressive fulfillment of Old Testament prophecies/ promises in the church age, and thus a rejection of traditional futurism. (2) Accepting the church as implicit in the Old Testament, and the moral law and the Sermon on the Mount as applicable in the church age rather than relegated to Israel in the millennium. (3) Accepting that Old Testament prophecy can have double fulfillments in the church age, such as Joel 2 at Pentecost (Acts 2) and in the future. (4) Progressive fulfillment of prophecy involving an acceptance of inaugurated eschatology and a rejection of the church age as a parenthesis between Israel in the Old Testament and Israel during the millennium. (5) Progressive fulfillment of prophecy involves rejection of a postponed kingdom and rule of Christ, and focuses on His present rule from heaven's throne over all on planet-earth. (6) Progressive fulfillment of prophecy rejects that there are two new covenants, one for Israel and the church, finding the one new covenant sequentially fulfilled—spiritually in the church age and physically to Israel in the millennium. (7) Progressive fulfillment of prophecy rejects the final difference between the earthly people of God (Israel) and the heavenly people of God (church), opting rather for a dwelling together in the new earth."— "Dispensational Biblical Interpretation," pp. 83, 84.

17. Darrell L. Bock, "Charting Dispensationalism," *Christianity Today* (September 12, 1994), p. 29.
18. George E. Ladd, *Crucial Questions About the Kingdom of God* (Grand Rapids, Michigan: Wm. B. Eerdmans, 1952), pp. 107, 108.
19. My translation. The Greek reads: *kardia gar pisteuetai eis dikaiosunen.* "With the heart one believes unto (for) righteousness." Note the translation of the RSV and the NIV. "Unto righteousness" is translated "and so is justified" (RSV) or "and are justified" (NIV) because the gift of Christ's righteousness is justification.

Chapter 12
Will the Rapture
Be Secret or Public?

Millions of Christians today believe that Christ will return secretly and take the church to heaven. Then, seven years later, He will come again in power and great glory. During the seven years between these two comings of Christ, the Antichrist is supposed to appear and cause the great tribulation. Thus, faithful Christians will escape the tribulation because they will be in heaven. All living believers and faithful Christians who have died since the day of Pentecost will be secretly taken to heaven in bodily form when the rapture occurs at the beginning of the seven-year period of tribulation.[1]

This teaching is based on a futuristic interpretation of Bible prophecy. In futurism, the Bible passages that speak of the Antichrist are not applied historically to the great medieval apostasy of Rome or to the false system of religion that the book of Revelation predicts will be instituted by the Papacy, apostate Protestantism, and spiritism near the end of time. This historical application of prophecy, which was largely accepted by the sixteenth-century Reformers, was rejected by Jesuit theologians in the counter-Reformation, the Roman Catholic reaction to the Protestant Reformation.

The first great futurist interpreter of Bible prophecy was Francisco Ribera (1537-1591), a Spanish Jesuit who taught at the University of Salamanca.[2] About 1590 he published a 500-page commentary on the book of Revelation, in which he denied the Protestant application of Antichrist to the Church of Rome. Ribera applied the first few chapters of Revelation to ancient Rome; the rest of the book, he said, would be fulfilled during a literal three and a half year period when an infidel Antichrist would persecute believers just before the second Advent of Christ. The Antichrist would be a single individual, who would conquer the world, claim to be God, rebuild the Jewish temple in Jerusalem, and abolish Christianity.

In his *Prophetic Faith of Our Fathers,* L. E. Froom comments: "Thus in Ribera's commentary was laid the foundation for that great structure of Futurism, built upon and enlarged by those who followed, until it became the common Catholic position. And then, wonder of wonders, in the nineteenth century this Jesuit scheme of interpretation came to be adopted by a growing number of Protestants, until today Futurism, amplified and adorned with the rapture theory, has become the generally accepted belief of the Fundamentalist wing of popular Protestantism."[3]

The futurist interpreter, George E. Ladd agrees: "The rediscovery of futurism is associated with the names of S. R. Maitland, James Todd, and William Burgh. [These were early nineteenth-century Protestant writers]. Before we turn to these men, we should note that a futurist interpretation of prophecy had earlier been recovered within the Roman Catholic Church. It will probably come as a shock to many modern futurists to be told that the first scholar in relatively modern times who returned to the patristic futuristic interpretation was a Spanish Jesuit named Ribera."[4]

Ladd points out that the revival of futurism among Protestants in the early nineteenth century did not at first include the doctrine of the pretribulation rapture[5] This doctrine was first taught by the Plymouth Brethren, a group joined by John Nelson Darby in 1827. He became the leader of this small denomination and, over a period of years, was able to popularize the secret rapture doctrine in England and America.[6] The secret rapture idea is, therefore, an outgrowth of the revival of futurism. Protestants have accepted a Roman Catholic kind of interpretation that is designed to protect the Papacy from being identified as the great beast power of Revelation 13 and 17. And multitudes have accepted the additional teachings of J. N. Darby and his supporters. These teachings, known as dispensationalism, include the doctrine of the secret rapture.

Since dispensationalist teaching comes from J. N. Darby, it is sometimes referred to as "Darbyism." The great American popularizer of Darby's teachings was C. I. Scofield, whose Scofield Reference Bible has been very influential since the early twentieth century. Other more recent study Bibles, such as the Ryrie Study Bible also present dispensationalist theology.

The main lines of dispensational teaching are given in the previous chapter. (See "Is Israel Still God's Chosen Nation?") The aspect of this teaching concerning us here is the idea that the church is secretly raptured before the seven-year tribulation. Dispensationalists think the secret rapture necessary so that God's plan for literal Israel can be fulfilled after the church has been taken up to heaven.

Clarence Bass comments: "Undoubtedly the point at which most people accept dispensationalism is in the doctrine of the rapture of the church before the great tribulation. Unknowingly, many identify this as the only premillennial position, although in the entire history of prophetic interpretation this idea is unknown. Premillennialists have always believed that Christ would return personally, literally, and visibly to establish the millennial reign, but only with the advent of dispensationalism has the pretribulation concept emerged."[7]

The seven-year period after the secret rapture and immediately before the glorious appearing of Christ is said to be divided into two periods of three-and-one-half years each. During the first three-and-one-half years Israel enters into a covenant with the Antichrist, who breaks the covenant at the end of that period. At the beginning of the second period of three-and-one-half years Satan overpowers the Antichrist and the world suffers the "time of Jacob's trouble." For the full seven years the gospel of the kingdom is preached [not the gospel of grace]. "An elect remnant of Israel, numbering 144,000, survives the tribulation to become the kingdom to which Christ returns after the seven years."[8] In His glorious, public appearing after the seven years, Christ brings the previously raptured saints from heaven with Him and establishes His millennial reign upon this earth.

Is this dispensationalist scenario for the end of human history taught in the Bible? Do the Scriptures predict a secret rapture followed by a seven-year tribulation prior to the glorious appearing Christ?

The Bible Words that Refer to the Second Coming of Christ

Some dispensationalist Bible interpreters think that a different Greek word is used in the New Testament for the coming of Christ to rapture the believers than that used for the later coming after the seven-year tribulation. They teach that Christ's coming to rapture the church secretly to heaven is referred to in the Greek New Testament as the *parousia*. His coming in power and great glory seven years later, they argue, is the "revelation," or, in Greek, the *apokalypsis*. If we could find such a distinction in the use of the Greek words, we might conclude that there is some point to their argument. In fact there is no such distinction.[9] The Greek New Testament uses three words in speaking of the second coming of Jesus: *parousia* which means "presence," "coming," "arrival," "advent"; *apokalypsis* which may be translated "revelation," "revealing," "disclosure," "appearing," "coming"; and *epiphaneia* which is translated "appearing," "appearance," "manifestation," "coming," (or, once in the King James Version, "brightness".[10]

The word *parousia* occurs 24 times in the Greek New Testament: The King James Version translates 22 of those instances by "coming": Matt. 24:3, 27, 37, 39; 1 Cor. 15:23; 16:17; 2 Cor. 7:6, 7; Phil. 1:26; 1 Thess. 2:19; 3:13; 4:15; 5:23; 2 Thess. 2:1, 8, 9; James 5:7, 8; 2 Peter 1:16; 3:4, 12; 1 John 2:28.

The King James Version translates two instances of *parousia* by "presence": 2 Cor. 10:10; Phil. 2:12.

The word *apokalypsis* occurs 18 times in the Greek New Testament. The meanings given to the word in the King James Version and the instances of those meanings are as follows:

"Revelation" (12 Times): Rom. 2:5; 16:25; 1 Cor. 14:6, 26; 2 Cor. 12:1, 7; Gal. 1:12; 2:2; Eph. 1:17; 3:3; 1 Peter 1:13; Rev. 1:1.

"Be revealed" (twice): 2 Thess. 1:7; 1 Peter 4:13.

"To lighten" (once): Luke 2:32.

"Manifestation" (once): Rom. 8:19.

"Coming" (once): 1 Cor. 1:7.

"Appearing" (once): 1 Peter 1:7.

The word *epiphaneia* occurs 6 times in the Greek New Testament: The King James Version translates it 5 times by "appearing": 1 Tim. 6:14; 2 Tim. 1:10; 4:1, 8; Titus 2:13.

Once in the King James Version *epiphaneia* is translated brightness: 2 Thess. 2:8.

A careful examination of the New Testament uses of the above Greek words reveals the following:

1. None of these texts speak of a secret coming of Christ. There is no such event to rapture the believers seven years before His grand public appearance in the clouds of heaven.

2. Each of the Greek words used in the Scriptures to refer to the second advent of Christ speaks of a public event that will be witnessed by humanity in general; including both righteous and wicked. What could be more public than the event described in 1 Thessalonians 4:15-17? (Verse 15 uses

parousia.) Or that portrayed in 2 Thessalonians 1:7-10? (Verse 7 uses *apokalypsis.*) Or that described in Titus 2:13 which uses *epiphaneia*? In each of these three passages a different Greek word for the second advent is used.

This New Testament truth that there is one second advent which will be seen by all is further emphasized in other passages of Scripture: "Look! He is coming with clouds; every eye will see him, even those who pierced him; and on his account all the tribes of the earth will wail" (Rev. 1:7; cf. 6:14-17). "This Jesus, who has been taken up from you into heaven, will come in the same way as you saw him go into heaven" (Acts 1:11).

3. Each of the three Greek words is applied to the coming in which, (i) believers are delivered from this earth; (ii) the wicked are destroyed. The two events occur simultaneously at the same coming of Christ. It is not true that *parousia* refers to a secret rapture of believers, while the *apokalypsis* is the public event seven years later. The *parousia* is the *apokalypsis*. The coming and the revelation of Christ are one and the same event. *Parousia* is used in 1 Thessalonians 4:15, which describes the deliverance of the righteous. The same word is used in 2 Thessalonians 2:8, which speaks of the wicked being destroyed. Likewise the apocalypse or revelation is the coming at which both righteous and wicked are dealt with; righteous translated and wicked destroyed. 2 Thessalonians 1:7-10 speaks of "rest" for the righteous "at the revealing [or revelation, or apocalypse] of the Lord Jesus from heaven with his powerful angels." But at this same revealing the Lord "in flaming fire" takes "vengeance on those who do not know God and on those who do not obey the gospel of our Lord Jesus Christ."

The epiphany (*epiphaneia*) is the "manifestation," "appearing" of Christ. Thus, according to the secret rapture teaching, it should refer not to the rapture of the church, but to the appearing of Christ at the end of the seven-year tribulation. In fact, it does refer to the appearing of Christ at which the wicked are destroyed. 2 Thessalonians 2:8 speaks of the "epiphany of his parousia," or "the manifestation [appearing] of his coming," at which the wicked are destroyed. Since, however, the "coming" here is the *parousia*, it is established that this is the same event as the epiphany. Moreover, 1 Timothy 6:14; 2 Timothy 4:8; and Titus 2:13 present the epiphany as the glorious event in which the righteous receive their redemption and reward. So, the epiphany is not just the manifestation of Christ to destroy the wicked.

It is the great public event at which the righteous are taken to be with their Lord.

Believers in the secret rapture use Matthew 24:37-42 as evidence for their interpretation. "But as the days of Noe were, so shall also the coming [*parousia*] of the Son of man be. . . . Then shall two be in the field; the one shall be taken, and the other left. Two women shall be grinding at the mill; the one shall be taken, and the other left. Watch therefore: for ye know not what hour your Lord doth come" (KJV). The taking of the one while the other remains is supposed to be a secret event at the beginning of the seven-year tribulation. But consider the context! The "coming" (*parousia*; vs. 37, 39) is likened to Noah's entry into the ark. What happened to those who were left out of the ark? Were they given a period of time to change their minds? Indeed no! They were destroyed in the waters of the flood. What happens to those who are left (verse 41) at the coming of Christ? Verses 50 and 51 answer: "The Lord of that servant shall come in a day when he looketh not for him, and in an hour that he is not aware of, and shall cut him asunder, and appoint him his portion with the hypocrites: there shall be weeping and gnashing of teeth" (KJV). That day is the day of the "coming" (*parousia*) spoken of in verses 37 and 39. The wicked who are left on this earth at the second coming of Jesus are immediately destroyed.

Luke's parallel emphasizes the point dramatically (Luke 17:33-37). After repeating Matthew's statement about the two women grinding together, Luke adds, "Two men shall be in the field; the one shall be taken, and the other left" (verse 36, KJV). The disciples asked, "Where, Lord?" (verse 37). They wanted to know where the ones not taken to be with Christ would be left. Jesus answered, "Wheresoever the body is, thither will the eagles be gathered together." The point is that the ones left behind will be immediately destroyed by the brightness of Jesus' coming (cf. 2 Thess. 1:7-9; Rev. 19:21).

It is important to understand that the "coming" (*parousia*) of Matthew 24:37 and 39 is the same coming described by Jesus in verse 27: "For as the lightning cometh out of the east, and shineth even unto the west; so shall also the coming [*parousia*] of the Son of man be" (KJV). Hence, the coming of Christ, at which he takes some from earth and destroys others, is a great cosmic, cataclysmic event. There is nothing secret about it. In fact, in the preceding verse, we have Jesus warning about any kind of secret coming: "Wherefore if they shall say unto you, Behold, he is in the desert; go not forth: behold, he is in the secret chambers; believe it not" (Matt. 24:26, KJV). Certainly, this is a different kind of secret coming to the one imagined by the secret rapture exponents; but Jesus' point was that His coming will not be secret in any sense. It will be a display of massive glory (verse 27), associated with the translation of the saved and the destruction of the wicked. [Notice the parallel between the next verse, Matthew 24:28, and Luke 17:37].

There is no distinction in Scripture between a secret rapture of the church and the revelation of Christ seven years later. The New Testament clearly teaches that Christ's second advent is one event, not two, and that this glorious coming is the time when believers are taken to heaven with Him and unbelievers are destroyed by the brightness of His divine presence. The parousia, the apocalypse, and the epiphany are one and the same event.

The Tribulation and the Resurrection of the Righteous Dead

Next we inquire, when does the great end-time tribulation occur? Is it before or after true believers are taken to be with their Lord? Related is the question, when does the resurrection of the righteous dead occur? Is it before or after the great end-time tribulation? Teachers of the secret rapture declare that only the resurrection of the righteous Christians who have died since the day of Pentecost occurs at the time of the rapture, and that this is before the seven-year period of tribulation. What does the Bible teach? We will answer these questions by referring to specific Bible passages.

1. According to Jesus, when will the tribulation occur, before or after the rapture of the elect? Jesus explained to His disciples: "Immediately after the suffering [*thlipsin = tribulation*] of those days the sun will be darkened, and the moon will not give its light; the stars will fall from heaven, and the powers of heaven will be shaken. 30 Then the sign of the Son of Man will appear in heaven, and then all the tribes of the earth will mourn, and they will see the Son of man coming on the clouds of heaven with power and great glory. 31. And he will send out his angels with a loud trumpet call, and they will gather his elect from the four winds, from one end of heaven to the other" (Matt. 24:29-31).

Jesus stated specifically that the rapture of His people (verse 31) will occur "after the tribulation of those days" (verse 29, KJV). The events of verses 29 and 30 occur just before and during the second advent of Jesus. Then His angels gather His elect from around the world (verse 31). The passage does not say that the elect come from heaven with Jesus. They are not gathered for ultimate salvation until the Son of Man comes "on the clouds of heaven with power and great glory" (verse 30).

2. According to Paul, when is the work of Antichrist performed, before or after the coming of Christ for believers? Paul clearly taught that the work of the Antichrist is performed before the coming of Christ for believers (2 Thess. 2:1-8). The apostasy and the appearing of the "man of sin" (verse 3, KJV) or "lawless one" (NRSV) occur before "the day of the Lord" (verses 2, 3). This "day of the Lord" (verse 2), for which the believers are to look, is the time at which the Antichrist is destroyed by the spirit of the Lord's mouth "annihilating him by the manifestation of his *coming*" (verse 8). The word *coming* in verse 8 translates *parousia*, the word which dispensationalists say applies to the secret rapture. But Paul applies the word to the coming at which the Antichrist is destroyed. This coming is the "day of the Lord" mentioned in verse 2, at which believers are gathered "together unto him" (verse 1, KJV). The work of Antichrist will be performed before Christ comes for believers.

3. According to the book of Revelation, do faithful Christian believers pass through the end-time tribulation? Jesus promises to keep His people "from the hour of trial that is coming on the whole world to test the inhabitants of the earth" (Rev. 3:10). This does not mean that He will take us out of the world, but that He will shelter us from the great tribulation that is coming. In fact, after the believers are in heaven, they are spoken of as "they who have come out of the great tribulation" (Rev. 7:14, RSV). The decrees passed by the end-time Antichrist against God's people would be meaningless if they were not still on earth (Rev. 13:15-17). Those who are faithful to the Lord will reject the image and mark of the beast. Some of them will be put to death, and none of them will be permitted to buy or sell. The ones who are saved are those who "had gotten the victory over the beast, and over his image, and over his mark" (Rev. 15:2, KJV). John was given a vision of these faithful ones in the heavenly Kingdom after they had, by God's grace, successfully resisted the demands of the end-time Antichrist. "And I saw thrones, and they sat upon them, and judgment was given unto them: and I saw the souls of them that were beheaded for the witness of Jesus, and for the word of God, and which had not worshipped the beast, neither his image, neither had received his mark upon their foreheads, or in their hands; and they lived and reigned with Christ a thousand years" (Rev. 20:4, KJV).

4. Does the first resurrection, the resurrection of the righteous, take place before or after the end-time tribulation? Revelation 20:4-6 answers the question: "4 Then I saw thrones, and those seated on them were given authority to judge. I also saw the souls of those who had been beheaded for their testimony to Jesus and for the word of God. They had not worshiped the beast or its image and had not received its mark on their foreheads or their hands. They came to life and reigned with Christ a thousand years. . . . 5 . . . This is the first resurrection. 6 Blessed and holy are those who share in the first resurrection. Over these the second death has no power, but they will be priests of God and of Christ, and they will reign with him a thousand years."

The first resurrection of Revelation 20:5, 6, the resurrection of the righteous dead, clearly comes after the great tribulation, because those who get the victory over the beast, his image, and his mark (verse 4) are included in this first resurrection.

5. Are the righteous raised secretly or when Christ appears publicly at His second advent? There is nothing secret about the advent of Jesus as spoken of in 1 Thessalonians 4:13-18 and 1 Corinthians 15:51-54. "The Lord himself shall descend from heaven with a shout, with the voice of the archangel, and with the trump of God" (1 Thess. 4:16, KJV). This is the same trumpet that is mentioned in 1 Corinthians 15:52, the sounding of which results in the resurrection of the righteous at the second coming of Jesus. It is a great public event. First Thessalonians 4:14 does not mean that God brings the righteous from heaven with Him when He comes. The text reads in the Revised Standard Version: "For since we believe that Jesus died and rose again, even so, through Jesus, God will bring with him those who have fallen asleep." This means that the Lord brings the righteous from the grave at the second coming of Jesus, as He brought Jesus from the grave after His crucifixion. The "dead in Christ" *rise* from the grave when the Lord descends "from heaven with a shout, with the voice of the archangel, and with the trump of God" (verse 16, KJV). The righteous dead do not come down with Christ in this great public coming. They *rise from the grave* to be with Him for eternity.

6. Who are the righteous raised at Christ's second advent? Do they include Old Testament believers? The righteous dead of all eras are raised in the same resurrection at the second coming of Jesus. There is absolutely no evidence that the Christian dead are raised in a secret resurrection before the rest of the righteous dead. First Corinthians 15:22, 23 contrasts death for all in Adam, with resurrection for all those "that are Christ's" at His second coming. The passage reads: "For as all die in Adam, so all will be made alive in Christ. But each in his own order: Christ the first fruits, then at his coming those who belong to Christ." This includes the faithful who died in Old Testament times. Those who are Christ's are those who died having Abraham's faith (Gal. 3:29). This includes multitudes of faithful ones who died before the time of Jesus. (Compare 1 Cor. 15:17-19.) Like Abraham, they died believing in the Messiah to come, and like Abraham, they will be raised in the first resurrection when the trumpet sounds at Christ's second coming (1 Cor. 15:51-54).

The first resurrection cannot be divided into two parts as the secret rapture teachers divide it. They say that the first part is the secret rapture of the Christians who died after Pentecost, and the second part is the resurrection of the Old Testament righteous at the second advent. The Bible has nothing to say about such a two-part first resurrection. It simply predicts that the righteous dead of all ages will be raised together at the second coming of Jesus. This will occur after the great tribulation in which God's people will be persecuted by the beast and his image (the end-time Antichrist).

Is There a Seven-year Tribulation?

There is no passage of Scripture that says there will be a seven-year period of tribulation before the second coming of Jesus. We have no idea from the Bible how long the end-time tribulation will last. The secret rapturists take a text in Daniel 9 completely out of context in an attempt to establish the idea of a seven-year tribulation.

Daniel predicted that a period of "seventy weeks" (or "seventy sevens") would be set aside by God as a period of probation for His chosen people, the Jews. "Seventy weeks are determined upon thy people and upon thy holy city, to finish the transgression, and to make end of sins, and to make reconciliation for iniquity, and to bring in everlasting righteousness, and to seal up the vision and prophecy, and to anoint the most Holy" (Dan. 9:24, KJV). Seventy times seven is 490.

Verses 25 and 26 read: "25 Know therefore and understand that from the going forth of the commandment to restore and to build Jerusalem unto the Messiah the Prince shall be seven weeks, and threescore and two weeks: the street shall be built again, and the wall, even in troublous times. 26 And after three score and two weeks shall Messiah be cut off. . . ."

Since the "seventy weeks" (verse 24) was to reach from the going forth of the commandment to restore Jerusalem to the time of the Messiah, the 490 must refer to years. 490 days or months would not reach so far. God's commandment to restore Jerusalem was put into effect by three Persian monarchs (Ezra 6:14): Cyrus, Darius I, and Artaxerxes I. Hence, God's commandment was not completely applied until the decree of Artaxerxes in the 457 B.C. This decree was put into operation in the autumn of that year.[11] 490 years from 457 B.C. brings us to A.D. 34.

Sixty-nine sevens (or weeks. 7 + 62 = 69), or 483 years, were to reach from 457 B.C. to the appearance of the Messiah (Daniel 9:25). Jesus Christ was baptized and His mission as the Messiah began in A.D. 27, just 483 years after 457 B.C. (Compare Luke 3:1, 21).

There remains one week of the 70 to be dealt with. The secret rapturists agree that the 69 weeks of this prophecy were fulfilled before the death of the Messiah. But they take the final week and apply it to the great tribulation just before the second coming of Jesus. They argue that a 2,000 year gap occurs between the end of the 69 weeks and the beginning of the 70th. There is not the slightest suggestion in Scripture that such an application of Daniel's 70th week is correct.

Quite the contrary! Jesus confirmed the covenant with the Jews for one week. "And he shall confirm the covenant with many for one week: and in the midst of the week he shall cause the sacrifice and the oblation to cease" (Dan. 9:27, KJV). Jesus confirmed the covenant to the Jews by: (1) His ministering personally to them for the 3 1/2 years, from His baptism to His death (from the autumn of A.D. 27 to the spring of A.D. 31); (2) His dying on the cross in the spring of A.D. 31; (3) His leading His disciples to minister only to the Jews for the next period of 3 1/2 years. (See Acts 1:8; 7:59–8:1; Heb. 2:3.) In A.D. 34, after the stoning of Stephen, the Gospel was taken to the Gentiles.

It was in the middle of that final week (AD. 27–34) that Christ's death caused "the sacrifice and the oblation to cease" (Dan. 9:27). The ceremonial system of the Jews came to an end as far as God was concerned, because the Old Testament sanctuary symbolism met its reality in the death of Jesus and His heavenly ministry to follow. Ceremonial animal sacrifices in the temple ceased to have significance. (See Matt. 27:51; Heb. 7:27; 9:11, 12.)

The final week of the seventy (the period from A.D. 27 to 34) was fulfilled right after the 69 weeks (the period from 457 B.C. to A.D. 27). To take that final prophetic week, or seven years, and separate it from the other 69 weeks (or 483 years) is to destroy the significance of the prophecy. Nowhere does the Bible say that the final week of Daniel's prophecy is fulfilled just before Jesus comes.

	483 yrs		3½ yrs	3½ yrs	
457 B.C.		27 A.D.		31 A.D.	34 A.D.

At the end of time there is no seven-year tribulation between a secret rapture and the public appearance of Christ. Before Jesus comes there will be a period of unprecedented tribulation that God's faithful believers will pass through. But the length of this period is not revealed in the Bible.

Will Christ Come Like a Thief?

As we have seen, the Bible speaks consistently of the second advent of Christ as a great public event. He comes like a thief only in the sense that He comes unexpectedly, not in the sense that he comes secretly.

Jesus likened His coming to that of a thief to those not watching and preparing. "Keep awake therefore, for you do not know on what day your Lord is coming. But understand this: if the owner of the house had known in what part of the night the thief was coming, he would have stayed awake and would not have let his house be broken into. Therefore you also must be ready, for the Son of Man is coming at an unexpected hour" (Matt. 24:42-44).

Those people who are not watching and ready for Jesus' coming will be destroyed when He comes unexpectedly like a thief. "The master of that slave will come on a day when he does not expect him and at an hour that he does not know. He will cut him in pieces and put him with the hypocrites, where there will be weeping and gnashing of teeth" (Matt. 24:50, 51). But the secret rapture people tell us that the wicked are not destroyed when Jesus comes as a thief. They think they are not destroyed until seven years later. Jesus was obviously speaking of the same coming in Matthew 24:43 as in verses 30, 31 and 50, 51. This is the coming that He likened to lightning shining from east to west (verse 27). It will not be a secret coming, but an unexpected one for those who are not watching prayerfully for Him. (See also Rev. 3:3; 16:15.)

Paul's use of the imagery of a thief's coming was very similar to that of Jesus. He will come like a thief to bring sudden destruction to the wicked (1 Thess. 5:2, 3). "But you, beloved, are not in darkness, for that day to surprise you like a thief; for you are all children of light and children of the day; we are not of the night or of darkness. So then let us not fall asleep as others do, but let us keep awake and be sober" (1 Thess. 5:4-6). For the righteous believers the coming of Jesus is not unexpected, like the coming of a thief. Clearly Paul was not using the metaphor of a thief to teach a secret rapture.

The statement of Peter is thoroughly conclusive. "But the day of the Lord will come like a thief, and then the heavens will pass away with a loud noise, and the elements will be dissolved with fire, and the earth and everything that is done on it will be disclosed" (2 Peter 3:10). Christ's coming like a thief will involve the heavens passing away with a great noise, and the elements melting with fervent heat; "the earth also and the works that are therein shall be burned up" (2 Peter 3:10, KJV). That is not a secret coming by any means. It is an event of massive cosmic proportions in which the wicked are destroyed and the faithful delivered.

The comparison of Christ's second coming to the coming of a thief in the night is not intended in Scripture to teach a secret rapture.

Are the Lost Given a Second Chance?

We will let the Bible answer for itself. "See, now is the acceptable time; see, now is the day of salvation!" (2 Cor. 6:2). There is not the slightest indication in Scripture that any lost person will have another chance after the second coming of Jesus. Just prior to Jesus' second coming, the proclamation goes forth: "Let the evildoer still do evil, and the filthy still be filthy, and the righteous still do right, and the holy still be holy" (Rev. 22:11). Characters are set unchangeably for eternity. Those who are righteous in

Christ then will be righteous for eternity, and those who are unrighteous will remain so just a little longer until they are destroyed at the advent. Jesus said that after that proclamation the next event is His second coming. "See, I am coming soon; my reward is with me, to repay according to everyone's work" (verse 12). The reward of the righteous is eternal life, but that of the wicked is eternal extinction (Matt. 25:46; Mal. 4:1-3; 2 Thess. 1:7-9).

This is the consistent message of Scripture, and it is emphasized dramatically in the visions that were given to John, recorded in the book of Revelation. Christ is depicted as coming with a great sickle to destroy the wicked (Rev. 14:17-20). He is portrayed as having a great sword proceeding from His mouth "that with it he should smite the nations" (Rev. 19:15, KJV). There is no suggestion that He is coming secretly for the righteous, after which the wicked will have another chance.

Where Will Christ Reign During the Millennium?

At His second advent, Jesus raises the righteous dead and translates them and the righteous living to heaven (1 Thess. 4:16-18; John 14:1-3). The dispensationalist distinction, that at the time of the secret rapture Christ hovers in the clouds while at His glorious coming He descends to the earth to establish His millennial reign, is not taught in Scripture. Jesus promised: "In my Father's house there are many dwelling places. If it were not so, would I have told you that I go to prepare a place for you? And if I go and prepare a place for you, I will come again and will take you to myself, *so that where I am, there you may be also*" (John 14:2, 3; italics supplied). Jesus is preparing a place for us in heaven. This is where He is, and this is the place to which He will transport the saved at His advent. Revelation 7:9-17 depicts the saved who have "come out of the great tribulation" (verse 14, RSV) "standing before the throne and before the Lamb" (verse 9). "For this reason they are before the throne of God, and worship him day and night within his temple" (verse 15, NRSV). God's throne and His temple are in heaven (Rev. 4:1, 2; 11:19). The holy city, the new Jerusalem does not descend to this earth until the end of the millennium (Rev. 20:7-9; 21:1, 2). There will be no temple in the new Jerusalem after it has descended to this earth: "And I saw no temple in the city for its temple is the Lord God the Almighty and the Lamb" (Rev. 21:22). The temple containing God's throne, before which the saved worship immediately after the second advent of Jesus (Rev. 7:15), is in heaven.

The saved live and reign with Christ in heaven for a thousand years (Rev. 20:1-4). "The rest of the dead [the lost of all ages and the wicked who were destroyed at Jesus' second coming] did not come to life until the thousand years were ended" (Rev. 20:5). The wicked remain dead until the end of the millennium. Then they will be raised. This is what the book of Revelation means when it says: "When the thousand years are ended, Satan will be released from his prison" (Rev. 20:7). Satan will be bound to this desolate earth for 1,000 years. Then the wicked are raised, and again Satan has an empire, a host of lost souls whom he can rule and organize to make a final assault on the saved people of God. At the end of the 1,000 years the "holy city, the new Jerusalem" comes down "out of heaven from God, prepared as a bride adorned for her husband" (Rev. 21:2). The saved of all ages are in the city, and Satan leads his hosts of lost people to attack the city. "They marched up over the breadth of the earth and surrounded the camp of the saints and the beloved city. And fire came down from heaven and consumed them" (Rev. 20:9). "This is the second death, the lake of fire; and anyone whose name was not found written in the book of life was thrown into the lake of fire" (Rev. 20:14, 15).

Then the earth is made new (Rev. 21:1), and God's redeemed people will live for eternity as perfect beings in a perfect universe, ruled over by a perfectly loving and just God (Rev. 21:3-7; Isa. 65:17-19; 66:22, 23).

Dear Bible student, have you made your peace with God by accepting Christ as your personal Savior from sin? He does not wish to destroy anyone (2 Peter 3:9), and His infinite love moves Him to plead with you to respond so that you can be among the saved in His Kingdom. Put away false man-made teachings and accept the clear and beautiful truths of the Word of God. Christ will come into your heart with great love and power, and you will have the inner assurance of eternal life with your Lord. Now is the day of salvation! Will you accept it?

Notes
1. The following are a few of the many sources that discuss this doctrine: Daniel P. Fuller, *Gospel and Law, Contrast Or Continuum? The Hermeneutics of Dispensationalism and Covenant Theology* (Grand Rapids, Michigan: William B. Eerdmans, 1980); Salem Kirban, *Special Kirban Report* (Huntingdon Valley, Pa.: Salem Kirban, Inc., 1980); Hal Lindsey, *The Late Great Planet Earth* (New York: Bantam Books, 1970, 1981); John F. Walvoord, *The Blessed Hope and the Tribulation* (Grand Rapids, Michigan: Zondervan, 1976); *The Rapture Question* (Grand Rapids, Michigan: Zondervan, 1979). For sources opposing the secret rapture

doctrine see: Clarence B. Bass, *Backgrounds to Dispensationalism* (Grand Rapids, Michigan: Baker, 1960, 1978); George E. Ladd, *The Blessed Hope* (Grand Rapids, Michigan: Wm. B. Eerdmans, 1956, 1960); Dave MacPherson, *The Late Great Pre-Trib Rapture* (Kansas City, Missouri: Heart of America Bible Society, 1974); *The Unbelievable Pre-Trib Origin* (Kansas City, Missouri: Heart of America Bible Society, 1973).

2. See Le Roy Edwin Froom, *The Prophetic Faith of Our Fathers* (Wash- ington, D.C.: Review and Herald, 1948), vol. 2, pp. 489-493.

3. *Ibid.*, p. 493.

4. George Eldon Ladd, *The Blessed Hope* (Grand Rapids, Michigan: Wm. B. Eerdmans, 1956), p. 37.

5. *Ibid.*, p. 39.

6. *Ibid.*, pp. 40-43.

7. Clarence B. Bass, *Backgrounds to Dispensationalism* (Grand Rapids, Michigan: Baker Book House, 1960), p. 38.

8. *Ibid.*, p. 42.

9. See John F. Walvoord, *The Rapture Question* (Grand Rapids, Michigan: Zondervan, 1979), pp. 172, 173. Walvoord, an ardent supporter of the pretribulation rapture, admits that the argument of pretribulationists based on the different Greek words used in the New Testament for the coming of Christ is incorrect. He writes: "Some pretribulationists have erred in claiming the word *parousia* as a technical word referring to the Rapture. That this is not correct is shown by its usage in passages referring to the coming of Christ after the Tribulation (Matt. 24:3, 27, 37, 39; 1 Thess. 3:13; 2 Thess. 2:8; 2 Peter 1:16). The word *apokalupsis*, translated "revelation," is likewise used of both events."— pp. 172, 173.

10. On the lexical meanings of these three Greek words see William F. Arndt and F. Wilbur Gingrich, *A Greek- English Lexicon of the New Testament* (Chicago: University of Chicago Press, 1957). For the meanings given to these words by the King James Version translators see J. B. Smith, *Greek-English Concordance to the New Testament* (Scottdale, Pennsylvania: Herald Press, 1965). See also George E. Ladd, "The Vocabulary of the Blessed Hope," in *The Blessed Hope* (Grand Rapids, Michigan: Wm. B. Eerdmans, 1956), pp. 61-70.

11. See Siegfried H. Horn and Lynn H. Wood, *The Chronology of Ezra 7* (Washington, D.C.: Review and Herald, 1953, 1970). This book establishes that Artaxerxes I's decree went into effect in the autumn of 457 B.C.